THE TIGERS OF BASTOGNE

THE **TIGERS** OF **BASTOGNE**

*Voices of the 10th Armored Division
in the Battle of the Bulge*

by Michael Collins & Martin King

CASEMATE
Philadelphia & Oxford

Published in the United States of America and Great Britain in 2013 by
CASEMATE PUBLISHERS
908 Darby Road, Havertown, PA 19083
and
10 Hythe Bridge Street, Oxford, OX1 2EW

Copyright 2013 © Michael Collins and Martin King

ISBN 978-1-61200-181-4
Digital Edition: ISBN 978-1-61200-182-1

Cataloging-in-publication data is available from the Library of Congress and
the British Library.

10 9 8 7 6 5 4 3 2 1

Printed and bound in the United States of America.

For a complete list of Casemate titles please contact:

CASEMATE PUBLISHERS (US)
Telephone (610) 853-9131, Fax (610) 853-9146
E-mail: casemate@casematepublishing.com

CASEMATE PUBLISHERS (UK)
Telephone (01865) 241249, Fax (01865) 794449
E-mail: casemate-uk@casematepublishing.co.uk

MIX
Paper from
responsible sources
FSC
www.fsc.org   FSC® C011935

CONTENTS

DEDICATION

This book is dedicated to all veterans of war, particularly those of the 10th Armored Division in World War II and notably John A. Collins Jr., who fought with Team Cherry as a member of Company F, 90th Cavalry Reconnaissance Squadron (Mechanized), in and around Bastogne during that bitter winter of 1944–45. He was author Michael Collins's grandfather and the inspiration for this book.

ACKNOWLEDGMENTS

Thank you to my co-author and friend Martin King and his family for their support during the writing of this book and for their hospitality during my trips over to Belgium. Thank you to my fiancée Lisa for her love, support, and understanding. Thank you to my parents, my brothers, sisters-in-law, nieces and nephew, and my immediate and extended family and friends for their love and support. My thanks to Howard Liddic, President of 10th Armored Division Western Chapter, for his help with photographs, General Orders, and other research, Phil Burge, Secretary/Treasurer of the chapter, and Craig Charlton, webmaster for the organization's internet site, for their help and support. Thanks to Klaus Feindler for his help with 20th Armored Infantry Battalion's history and contacts, Christian Pettinger for his help with photographs and other 10th Armored Division history, and Daniel Jordao and Marc Weber for keeping the 10th Armored Division history alive in Luxembourg. Thanks to Norman Faye for allowing use of his father's vast collection of photographs, Donald Naftulin for photographs and information about his father, Gail Ryerson Parsons for photographs of her father and other documents, and Jan Newsome for information and photograph of her uncle Barry Browne. Thanks to John Vallely of Siena College for his support, humor, and research help. And I feel a deep debt of gratitude to all the 10th Armored Division veterans who allowed us to tell their story, and to their family members for allowing us to keep their memory alive in this book. I also would like to remember those veterans that graciously supported our efforts who passed away before the publication of this book: Richard Barrett and Thaddeus Krasnoborski, both soldiers who served with the 420th Armored Field Artillery Battalion at Bastogne.

—MICHAEL COLLINS

Many thanks to my co-author and friend Michael Collins and his tremendous family for their continued enthusiasm and support for this work. Thank you most graciously to Steven Smith, Tara Lichterman, our editor Richard Kane, and the expert team at Casemate without whom none of this would be possible. Thanks also to my beloved clan: my wife Freya, my children Allycia and Ashley Rae, my brother Graham and my sisters Sandra and Debbie, my brother-in-law Marc, nephews Ben and Jake and my niece Rachel, my cousins Alan and Merle. Not forgetting clan Roberts: Julie, Marc, Samantha, and serving naval officer Jonathon. Posthumous thanks to my late Grandfather Private Joseph Henry Pumford who fought at Passchendaele in World War One and provided invaluable inspiration for all my early interest in Military History. He was promoted to corporal but then demoted for punching out a sergeant. He was unique in managing to terrify both sides in that conflict.

Special thanks to my dear friends Lt. Col. Jason Nulton and his wife Missy, Comdr. Jeffrey Barta, and Gen. Graham Hollands for their wonderful support and encouragement. Grateful thanks to our friend Mr. Roland Gaul at the National Military Museum in Diekirch for providing us with some excellent photographs for this volume. Top forensics expert Dr. Carlton Joyce provided invaluable information about the weaponry used in the siege. Thank you to the personnel at USAF Fort Dix and USAF Spangdahlem for their tremendous encouragement. Thank you also to Mrs. Carol Fish and the staff at the United States Military Academy at West Point for their ongoing support. Also, many thanks to the staff at the Pentagon. My thanks to Mrs Laura Passuello at Speciality Tours for her support and for helping to preserve history along with the Capital Area WWII Roundtable and the Hershey-Derry Township Historical Society Thank you also to the team at the Heintz Barracks "Nuts Cave" in Bastogne for allowing us unique access to everything we needed there.

Thank you to my friend and brother "Battle of the Bulge" veteran Mr. John R. Schaffner for his limitless wisdom and wicked sense of humor and Jeff Prior, who provided his father's diaries for the book. Thanks to the Battle of the Bulge Veterans Association for their excellent work and support. Not forgetting the Belgian connection, Dirk de Groof, Kristine, Rudy Aerts and Adeline who always kept our glasses filled and our appetites satiated.

Last but not least, a deep and heartfelt thank you to all the wonderful veterans who allowed us to interview and film them for this volume. They are the reason we do this. They are all national treasures and their stories *need* to be read.

They went with songs to the battle, they were young.
Straight of limb, true of eyes, steady and aglow.
They were staunch to the end against odds uncounted,
They fell with their faces to the foe.
They shall grow not old, as we that are left grow old.
Age shall not weary them, nor the years condemn.
At the going down of the sun and in the morning,
We will remember them.

(The "Ode of Remembrance" is an ode taken from Laurence Binyon's poem, "For the Fallen," which was first published in *The Times* in September 1914)

—MARTIN KING

PREFACE

It seems regrettable to me that Combat command B of the 10th Armored division didn't get the credit it deserved at the battle of Bastogne. All the newspaper and radio talk was about the paratroopers. Actually the 10th Armored division was in there a day before we were and had some very hard fighting before we ever got into it, and I sincerely believe that we would never have been able to get into Bastogne if it had not been for the defensive fighting of the three elements of the 10th Armored division who were first into Bastogne and protected the town from invasion by the Germans.— General Anthony McAuliffe, Acting Commander, 101st Airborne Division at Bastogne

Many people assume that the 101st Airborne Division was *solely* responsible for the defense of Bastogne and the surrounding area. Granted, the Screaming Eagles did supply the greatest number of soldiers and played the "starring role" in the drama that unfolded around this critical crossroads town, but the limelight enjoyed by the American paratroopers does detract from the attention that should be paid to the remarkable accomplishments of the tankers of the 10th Armored Division who preceded the 101st Airborne's arrival at Bastogne. "Terrify and Destroy" was the motto of the 10th Armored Division, which was also known as the "Tiger" division.

Although there have been many books written about the siege of Bastogne, it is our hope that this volume will fill in the blanks and tell the rest of the story, the other lesser-known side of the story of Bastogne. We believe that this book will pay long overdue homage to the men who fought and died with the 10th Armored Division. The full story of the Tigers of the 10th Armored at Bastogne has never before been told . . . until now.

Our previous book, *Voices of the Bulge*, covered the entire Battle of the

Bulge from the perspective of those who experienced it firsthand. More importantly it related stories from those who had never been heard. We knew from the onset that this would probably be the last chance to interview these veterans and record their experiences, so it became imperative for us to find as many survivors from the battle as possible. This was also the case when we started our research for this volume. Here, among other things, you will find veterans' accounts of what happened in Bastogne during those dark days retold by the unsung heroes who were there. The stories of these veterans have been compiled from a series of one-on-one interviews conducted over a three year period, augmented with the historical account of the battle primarily from the perspective of the 10th Armored Division and attached units. Hopefully this will give the reader a broader view of the struggle that occurred there and the conditions endured at the time.

There are always new theories to explore, new ideas to discuss and new characters to discover. We will introduce you to some of these characters in the chapters that follow.

Just outside Bastogne on the Rue de Clervaux there is a memorial plaque to the 10th Armored Division. It's strategically placed in front of a tank turret by the side of the road near the Mardasson memorial. This turret commemorates the route taken by Team Cherry as it moved out to Longvilly in that bitterly cold winter of 1944. The recently inaugurated plaque is a dedication to the 10th Armored Division and the attached units that struggled to defend Bastogne from Hitler's last serious offensive in the west. We were among many who campaigned to get the plaque placed there, albeit sixty-seven years after the fact, but such is the nature of Belgian administration: better late than never.

When we started this project we didn't have much to go on except a few names and a famous place. While Michael Collins visited the archives in Washington to find out more about the 10th Armored Division, I (Martin King) hit the road in Europe to see what I could uncover. The more we delved into this story, the more fascinating it became. It really did have all the elements and then some: conflict, humanity, inhumanity, and incredible courage amid the ruins of a city devastated by strife and conflict. That's the place we are going to visit in this book: Bastogne, December 1944–45.

———

When we toured around the east coast of the United States with our book *Voices of the Bulge* we gave small lectures about the remarkable characters that we had encountered during the process of writing it. Bringing the stories of the veterans we had interviewed to the public through that book and the ensuing promotion tour was a remarkable and fulfilling experience. There was just a great vibe about the entire situation. Most of the veterans' stories in our first book had never been heard, so relaying these previously unknown accounts gave us great satisfaction. We knew that by writing about these indomitable men and women we were helping to keep their stories alive, because that's what it's really all about; it's about keeping the stories of these heroes in public circulation and trying to ensure they and their deeds are not forgotten. All the research and years of work gave us a deeper and more profound understanding of veterans in general. Our admiration is based on respect and dedication. Respect for them and their dedication to duty and our collective dedication to ensuring they are never forgotten.

WALTER LEPINSKI, HEADQUARTERS COMPANY, 20TH ARMORED INFANTRY BATTALION

I entered the Army on November 4, 1942. I reported to the local board here in Winchester, New Hampshire and I was sent over to Fort Devens, Massachusetts. That was the place where we were sent to our destination where we would be assigned to our unit. We traveled by troop train and I was sent down to Ft. Benning, Georgia where the 10th Armored Division was training. I started with the 54th Armored Infantry and then later I was put into the 20th Armored Infantry Battalion. I was in Headquarters Company with the 20th Armored Infantry Battalion, and I drove halftracks and an M18 pack howitzer tank during basic training. I ended up in the motor pool, performing second echelon maintenance on the vehicles where I stayed in throughout the war.[1]

———

Both our grandfathers were war veterans who had served their respective countries in combat: my grandfather fought for the British army at Passchendaele in World War One and Mike's fought with the US army's 10th Armored division in the Battle of the Bulge in World War Two. We'd both grown up knowing about the fact that they had served their respective countries during times of war but not knowing precisely what they had done or achieved with their service. Mike's motivation for writing about this subject came from the fact that his grandfather never spoke about his experiences of fighting with Team Cherry at Longvilly near Bastogne. This instilled an overwhelming curiosity to discover precisely what he had done, and what it had been like to be in Bastogne during that terrible winter of 1944–45. My personal inspiration was augmented by touring the battlefields of Europe with World War II veterans and describing to the best of my ability what-happened-where to other like-minded enthusiasts. It isn't a morbid or mori-bund obsession to want to see the places where so many suffered. It's more of a quest to attempt to understand the mind-set and motivations of the in-dividuals who participated.

Recounting what the veterans experienced is like reciting from a sacred testament to human endurance, tenacity, and ultimately courage. Courage in the face of extreme adversity, courage despite the odds, courage displayed by ordinary men and women in extraordinary conditions. That's precisely our point here. They were, after all, just ordinary men and women. Regular Joe's and Joanne's from Anytown, U.S.A., or quiet country villages in Great Brit-ain, France, Germany, or anywhere you care to locate them because there aren't many nations or states that haven't been touched by conflict at some time or another during their history. The human race's voracious appetite for conflict is omnipresent even today, but *today* is not what this is about.

Between us, we have read countless volumes and spent innumerable hours sifting our way through dusty manuscripts in the bowels of remote ar-chives. Researching, checking, cross referencing, comparing notes, and draw-ing conclusions initially for our own satisfaction . . . to satiate our own appetite for information, the right information. No matter how many ac-counts one reads and no matter how many notes one makes, nothing, and I mean *nothing* compares to getting the information "firsthand" from someone who was actually there at the time, who saw the events unfolding, and par-ticipated in them: a veteran! These are the individuals who really get our un-divided attention.

Veterans remind us time and again that *time* is a delicate and deceptive thing in the minds of a soldier or someone who was there. "Years ago" and a "long time ago" can be meaningless to veterans. To some 'the events of years ago are fairly recent while to others "It's just like it happened yesterday" is a widely used catch phrase.

Many important people came to light during our research for this vol-ume. Their accounts are an integral part of relating the complete story be-cause in many cases they have information that we haven't heard before about Bastogne during those dark, bitterly cold days in the winter of 1944–45. Our intention is to draw you into their world. It's a place of great uncertainty, ex-treme violence, and abject terror where no one is safe and anyone can be killed at any time; a place where your best friend could be blown to pieces at any second, and your closest relative is the person beside you in the foxhole or sheltering in the same cellar. This was Bastogne in that grueling winter all those many years ago. No historian can ever know for certain exactly what was said at a particular time in history unless they were there in person and even then certain recollections can fade and alter with the passage of time. So unless the event was actually recorded all we can rely on is the testimony of those who experienced it firsthand. This is our only window into that other world of theirs.

INTRODUCTION

It's time to set the record straight and time to give credit where credit is due. The 10th Armored Division was different from the other U.S. armored divisions in many ways. The division enforced a strict disciplinary code that often exceeded written U.S. Army regulations. In combat the soldiers of the Tiger division often went above and beyond the call of duty and could ultimately be relied upon to perform their allocated tasks to the best of their ability. Captain John Drew Devereaux, a renowned Broadway actor and relative of Hollywood legend John Barrymore, said that 10th Armored Division soldiers were expected to button their tunics up to the neck where soldiers in other units were allowed to leave the top button undone. Initially Devereaux found this an unnecessary measure but eventually came to believe that it gave the 10th Armored Division a smarter appearance than others.

On 15 July 1942 the 10th Armored Division was activated at Fort Benning, Georgia. The 2nd Armored Division provided equipment and training areas for the new division. Officers from the 3rd and 11th Cavalry Regiments joined the original division cadre. Soon, men and equipment from across the United States arrived, and the new unit took shape. The transition from civilian to soldier went quickly. Major General Paul Newgarden, the 10th's commander, explained, "If we are to be successful, we must work like hell, play like hell, and fight like hell." The 10th did just that.

THOMAS HOLMES, INTELLIGENCE AND RECONNAISSANCE PLATOON, 54TH ARMORED INFANTRY BATTALION

I initially tried to get into the Air Corps in early 1942, I had two things against me, my eyesight was not what it should be, even though I was a catcher for a baseball team. I also had an arm that was not right, it was hurt when I was ten years old and I had operations on it. I had trouble with turning my hand upside down.

I got called for the Army and when I went down they were running people through pretty quickly, I didn't say anything and they didn't ask. I went down to the Battle Creek area in Michigan and then I was sent down to Columbus, Georgia where the 10th Armored Division was forming at the time in November, 1942.[2]

During the first year the soldiers were subjected to a rigorous and punishing training schedule at the "Tiger Camp." After grueling forced marches, endurance tests, night problems, dry runs, and firing problems the 10th radiated a special esprit de corps, among the ranks and, while participating in maneuvers in Tennessee, it demonstrated its prowess. Early in September 1943, the 10th relocated to Camp Gordon, Georgia. That fall, the 10th reorganized at the battalion level. The hard training continued, but at the same time, the Tiger special service office organized soldier shows, dances, concerts, and a full range of athletic events.

Early on the morning of 15 July 1944 the 10th was saddened by the death of the division commander, General Newgarden, in a plane crash. Major General William H. H. Morris Jr. assumed command and stressed continued excellence in battle training. Then, on 31 August 1944, the 10th entrained for Camp Shanks, New York, a port of embarkation just up the Hudson River from New York City. For two weeks, the Tigers made final preparation for overseas deployment.

On 13 September 1944 the division sailed from New York harbor in a convoy to an undisclosed destination. The journey had quite an ignominious start when the troop ship carrying most of the division's soldiers ran aground in the Brooklyn Narrows, within sight of the city's skyline. A squadron of hastily-assembled ferryboats spent a day transferring the men to the SS *Brazil*, a converted luxury. With a destroyer escort, the *Brazil* set out to catch up to the convoy. After avoiding a fall hurricane, the *Brazil* rejoined the convoy on 16 September. Two days later, U-boats attacked and torpedoed a tanker in the convoy. Despite this, the 10th arrived at Cherbourg, France, on 23 September 1944 and was the first American armored division to disembark on French soil having sailed directly from America.

Immediately, the 10th was assigned to Maj. Gen. Walton Walker's XX Corps, part of Lt. Gen. George Patton's Third Army. The Tigers spent a month receiving new equipment and training in the Normandy countryside. On 2 November 1944, the division received its baptism under fire at Mars La Tours. Later that month, the Tigers participated in the XX Corps capture of Metz. This action saw the construction of a 190-foot Bailey Bridge, the longest in the European Theatre of Operations. It was the first time in fifteen hundred years that the ancient fortress at Metz had fallen. After fierce fighting, the 10th pierced the vaunted "Siegfried Line" and led the Third Army into Germany on 19 November 1944.[3]

Earl Van Gorp of Company D, 3rd Tank Battalion, was enjoying a little respite from the heavy fighting that his unit had recently sustained as part of General Patton's Third Army: "We were in France and called on a Sunday afternoon, they didn't tell us where we were going. On the trip up we were with a group of tanks and we followed the leader."[4]

———

John "Jack" Prior, 20th Armored Infantry Battalion (AIB) was assigned as the chief medic with Team Desobry. He received various medals for serving in the U.S. Army during World War II with the 10th Armored Division in the European Theatre. His decorations include the Bronze Star, the Silver Star, the Legion of Merit, the Belgian Croix de Guerre, and the medals of the cities of Bastogne and Metz. He wrote, "I attempted to turn my litter bearers into bedside nursing personnel—they were assisted by the arrival at our station December 21st of two registered female civilian nurses. One of these nurses, Renee Lemaire, volunteered her services and the other girl [Augusta Chiwy] was black, a native of the Belgian Congo. They played different roles among the dying—Renee shrank away from the fresh, gory trauma, while the Congo girl was always in the thick of the splinting, dressing, and hemorrhage control."[5]

Nurse Augusta Chiwy volunteered to work with the 20th AIB at their aid station on the Rue Neufchateau. After it was bombed she continued working at the 101st headquarters at the former Belgian army barracks. On 24 June 2011 Augusta Chiwy was awarded the prestigious "Order of the Knight of the Crown." Later that same year the 101st Airborne honored her with the Civilian Humanitarian Award. When the Battle of the Bulge began she was working as a nurse at a general hospital under the auspices of the Augustine Congregation Sisters of Louvain. She went to Bastogne on 16 December at the invitation of her father. During a recently recorded interview she said, "I'll never forget the day that I met Doctor Prior. He had a kind face and you could tell that all the soldiers liked him very much. I was very nervous about working for the Americans because some of them didn't want a black nurse. Those were strange times indeed, very strange and very hard.

I had almost nothing to work with, neither did Renée. The smell inside the army hospital was terrible and if I close my eyes I can still smell it. I didn't smell that great either because I hadn't had a bath for four days."[6]

———

During their rest and recuperation period between the Battle of Metz and the Battle of the Bulge, the 10th Armored Division made history by test firing the U.S. Army's newest secret weapon. For most of World War II, precision in artillery fire pertaining to when a shell would explode, for example how far above the ground a round would go off, didn't exist. Artillerymen would set the time on the fuse by estimating how long the shell would be in flight. But in December 1944 the newly created proximity fuse was unveiled during a secret demonstration.

MAJOR WILLIS D. "CRIT" CRITTENBERGER, HEADQUARTERS BATTERY, 420TH ARMORED FIELD ARTILLERY BATTALION

After participating in the XX Corps' capture of Fortress Metz, the 10th Armored Division joined the Corps effort to break the Siegfried Switch in the Saar-Moselle Triangle. While in position near Perl, Germany, the 420th Armored Field Artillery Battalion was selected to organize and perform a demonstration of the new, then secret, VT [variable time] or POZIT fuze. All available Field Officers, particularly Artillerymen of XX Corps, were to attend.

On 6 December 1944 the Battalion Commanding Officer and an advance party strong in Survey, Fire Direction and Communications moved out to select a "Demonstration Area" suitable for this mission. The next day, 7 December, the Battalion followed, cutting across the Main Supply Routes of the three divisions in contact and covering the forty-three mile move in four hours. The nearest town on the maps was Marange, France on the southern edge of XX Corps. The Journal entry reads "Departed Perl, Germany at 1045 on mounted motor march to Marange, France, arriving at 1500. Distance travelled 43.6 miles. Weather cold and rainy. Morale good."

An "impact area" of rolling, varied terrain was picked. Shot-up vehicles and farm equipment were placed as identifiable targets in the valley, on the slope, and even on the crest, to best illustrate the standard height of burst of this new fuze. Survey and registration took place as others were laying communications for ourselves and to tie in to Corps lines should higher Headquarters need to reach any of the attendees. The usual "demonstration" services were set up; latrines, warming tents, parking areas, hot coffee, mess tents with a hot meal and yes, extra field glasses, a public address system and some folding chairs for the real VIPs.

The day of the "shoot," 11 December, dawned cold and rainy but happily not foggy. Our preparations for just such a day were both needed and appreciated. The Corps Commander Walton Walker led the list of attendees, dressed for the cold.

The firing went well. The targets had been placed to show that the new fuze would burst the shells uniformly above the target, whether it was on flat ground or on the slope, uphill or down. The hot meal and coffee were big hits too! Following the shoot, those interested talked to the Fire Direction and Survey crews and to the gun crews as well.

The remainder of the day was spent in "cleaning up the battlefield". The next day, 12 December our "vacation" was over and we marched back to the north boundary of XX Corps in the Merzig-Launstroff area to fire for Task Force Polk, the Corps' Mechanized Cavalry in an economy-of-force role holding a part of the "front". (Our Bastogne experience was but five days away).

This VT demonstration and hands-on experience stood us in good stead, for when the 4th Armored Division, Task Force Abrams broke the German ring around Bastogne our ammo train came with them, bringing in ammo with the new, now declassified, VT fuze and permission to shoot it. It worked beautifully "for real". Its use up and down the front had to be one of the big factors in winding up the Battle of the Bulge successfully for the Allies.[7]

WILLIAM SIMONOFF, B COMPANY, 3RD TANK BATTALION

I was drafted in high school when I was eighteen. During my senior year my principal called me down to register for the draft. Two weeks later I was called back down to the principal's office and I was drafted because they had accelerated me and he gave me my diploma. I reported to the induction station at San Pedro, California and the orders were that I would go to the Armored School at Fort Knox, Kentucky. Based on my test scores and IQ I was selected for special training at the armored school and after six months I was ordered to Fort Meade, Maryland and sent overseas as a replacement in November, 1944. I sailed on troop ship to Southampton, England, and witnessed depth charges being dropped on submarines while in the English Channel. I disembarked at La Havre and we marched 25 miles to a train station, we boarded box cars and we were sent to Thionville where we put in the motor pool and assigned to a crew. I was assigned to B Company, Third Tank Battalion.

We went up to the Ardennes almost immediately when I arrived but I had never had any training in snow driving. Fortunately I did not go off the road; the tank tracks were narrow on the road, and they kept slipping and sliding on the road. I watched what was ahead of me and I learned from what other tanks were doing wrong. We reached our unit as a whole as other units had driven off the road.[8]

———

During the Battle of the Bulge the 10th Armored Division and the Ardennes became forever linked due to a sequence of events that would become known in military history as the "Battle for Bastogne." Colonel William L. Roberts led Combat Command B (CCB) during the Battle for Bastogne. Roberts was born on 18 September 1890 and was a graduate of United States Military Academy at West Point, class of 1913. He rose up the officer ranks over the years and in 1940 was assigned as professor of military science and tactics at the Citadel in Charleston, South Carolina. Later he was assigned to the 20th Armored Division before joining the 10th Armored Division in 1943.

Colonel Roberts was given command of the division's Combat Command B—in World War II American armored divisions generally were organized for combat as two brigade-sized combat commands, A and B, with a Combat Command R (reserve), which was generally used for battalions that were resting, refitting, and retraining from previous actions, although on occasions armored divisions used their CCRs in an active combat role—when the 10th Armored Division landed in Europe and continued in this position until Brig. Gen. Edwin Piburn took over from 5 November 1944 until the Battle of the Bulge began on 16 December 1944, when Roberts temporarily reassumed command due to General Piburn being assigned to Combat Command A. Under the command of Colonel Roberts the names of Combat Command B's team leaders, such as young Major William R Desobry, Lt. Col. Henry T. Cherry, and Lt. Col. James "Smilin' Jim" O Hara, would become renowned as they defended the strategic crossroads city to the hilt.

Colonel William L. Roberts,
10th Armored Division, Silver Star Citation:
During the period 20–27 December 1944, Colonel Roberts and his commanders attached to the 101st Airborne Division during the siege of Bastogne, Belgium. The Capture of this point was essential to the successful expansion of the enemy breakthrough of 16 December 1944. The city was completely surrounded by enemy divisions who were attempting to destroy the defenders. With complete disregard for his personal safety, Colonel Roberts continuously exposed himself to the enemy bombing, strafing, armored and infantry

attacks in order to direct operations of his forces. His courage aggressiveness and gallant leadership contributed greatly to the successful defense of the city. His actions were in accordance with the highest standards of the military service. Entered service from West Virginia.[9]

The youngest of the three team leaders was Major William R. Desobry. Born in Manila, Philippines, on 11 September 1918 to Colonel and Mrs. E. C. Desobry, unlike many of his contemporaries Major Desobry was not a West Point graduate. In 1941 he graduated from Georgetown University School of Foreign Service where he received a commission into the U.S. Army through ROTC. Before joining the 10th Armored Division he initially served with the 29th Infantry Division. During the Battle of Metz he joined the 54th Armored Infantry Battalion, but was eventually assigned to the 20th Armored Infantry Battalion just before the Battle of the Bulge began on 16 December. Just twenty-six years old, "Des," as he was known to his friends, always put his men first and made an effort to communicate with them on virtually every level despite his often bureaucratic approach to the job. He was well respected and had already been through a few scrapes in his short military life.

Although Desobry was not as experienced as team leaders O'Hara and Cherry, nevertheless he displayed exceptional courage and fortitude when his team was assigned to defend the small village of Noville, just a few miles north of Bastogne, against overwhelming numbers. Today there's a street in Bastogne named after him.

Major William R. Desobry,
20th Armored Infantry, Silver Star citation:
On 19 December 1944, in the vicinity of Noville, Belgium, he was in command of an armored task force composed of tanks, infantry, tank destroyers, assault guns and mortars with the mission of holding the village at all cost. At daylight the first of a series of strong enemy attacks with armor and infantry was delivered and repulsed, as were all other attacks. After and during each attack, Major Desobry exhibited gallantry and good judgment in reorganizing and disposing his forces to meet attacks from any direction. His outstanding leadership and unerring sense of duty under heavy enemy fire encouraged the men serving under him to greater efforts in the performance of

an arduous duty. During an attack by the enemy he was seriously wounded and evacuated. The personal bravery, tenacity of purpose and fortitude displayed by Major Desobry were in accordance with the highest standards of the military service. Entered military service from New York.[10]

Lieutenant Colonel Henry T. Cherry had much in common with Gen. George Patton in that he liked to lead by the book. Born on 15 July 1911 in Macon, Georgia, Cherry was the oldest of CCB's three team leaders and a graduate of West Point, class of 1935. Cherry already had experienced heavy combat in November during the Battle of Metz where he received the Silver Star in November.

Lieutenant Colonel Henry T. Cherry Jr.,
3rd Tank Battalion, Silver Star citation:
For gallantry in action in France and in the vicinity of Merzig, Germany during the period 16 November 1944 to 27 November 1944. Lieutenant Colonel Cherry, with utter disregard for his own personal safety, led a rescue party over open ground to a hill occupied by the enemy one thousand yards distant where he assisted in the rescue of a wounded officer who was in immediate danger of being killed by enemy fire. The rescue was performed in daylight under continuous heavy observed enemy artillery and mortar fire, projectiles of which burst as close as ten to fifteen yards from the rescue party. The gallant act of Lieutenant Colonel Cherry reflects great credit upon himself and the military forces of the United States. Entered the military service from Georgia.

Despite having a reputation as a hard task master, a characteristic that did not particularly endear him to some of his soldiers, Cherry had a human side as well. William J. Brown, a company commander for B Company, 3rd Tank Battalion, wrote in the 10th Armored newsletter *Tiger Tales* about Colonel Cherry's role in his wedding:

In 1943, I had not had a furlough since joining the army 6 months earlier. I put in for a 10-day leave to get married. I had been engaged to my fiancée for one and a half years and we agreed that if I became an officer, we would get married. My C. O., Capt. William Kistler, approved the request but Col. Cherry rejected it, saying I was too young to be married. After a month my fiancée and I made arrangements through Capt. Shepherd, the Chaplain, to be married. When Col. Cherry found out he confronted me with the statement, "I thought I told you that you were too young." My reply surprised when I informed him that he could not dictate my private life. He asked if he was invited to the wedding, and as my bride's father could not be there, I told him that he not only was invited, but he could give the bride away, if he would. On April 29, 1943, Cherry arrived at the chapel early and spoke to my bride at the back of the chapel. He then came down the aisle and looked me in the eye and said, "Do you still want to get married?" After receiving an affirmative answer, he went back up the aisle and brought my bride down to me.[11]

Lieutenant Colonel James O'Hara, commanding officer of the 54th Armored Infantry Battalion, was known to his men for one simple physical attribute: his smile. Nicknamed "Smilin' Jim," no matter how serious the situation became he always sported a reassuring grin on his face while providing first-class leadership. Born at West Point, New York, on August 9, 1912, he was the son and grandson of West Point graduates. O'Hara completed his studies at West Point Military Academy in 1934. He married Elinore Harding in 1936. In 1942 Lieutenant Colonel O'Hara was appointed to command of the 54th Armored Infantry Battalion where he would remain throughout the rest of his service with the 10th Armored Division. Thanks to his almost constant smile his men often found it difficult to discern his moods or the gravity of the situation. His remarkably calm exterior under pressure earned him the loyalty and respect of his men. After his death in 1985 his former driver wrote a short poem about him:

"Smilin' Jim"
In the heat of the battle and the horrors of war
Smilin' Jim went on smiling but here's something more
He'd do any job for a private on up
Said many a solider, "there's a man that has guts!"
Like so many other he's gone from us now
And to their proud memory all of us bow
So to close this attempt to a tribute to him
Our own Colonel O'Hara was our Smilin' Jim[12]

Lieutenant Colonel James O'Hara,
54th Armored Infantry, Silver Star citation:
On December 23, 1944, in the vicinity of Marvie, Belgium, he was commanding an armored task force of infantry, tanks, supporting weapons and engineers, holding a sector of the perimeter defense of the city of Bastogne. A heavy enemy attack by infantry and armor was repelled. Doubtful that there was still contact with the unit on his right flank, he advanced under heavy small arms and artillery fire to assure himself that contact was being maintained. His gallantry, determination, and maintenance of morale among his men were directly responsible for repelling the second enemy attack later that night. Through his judgment, initiative, and foresight he gained the complete confidence and admiration of his men which was responsible for the perfection with which his force carried out its mission. His actions were in accordance with the highest standards of the military service. Enter military service from Minnesota.[13]

Lieutenant Colonel Barry D. Browne commanded the 420th Armored Field Artillery Battalion, which provided artillery support not only for Combat Command B but later on the 101st Airborne Division, as well. Born in Washington, D.C., Browne was the son of Maj. C. J. Browne, one of the early pioneers of the U.S. Army Air Corps. After his father's death in 1928, Barry and his family moved back to San Antonio, Texas, the hometown of his mother's family. Barry attended the United States Military Academy, graduated in 1938, and returned to Texas to serve with the 2nd Infantry Division's 15th Field Artillery. He continued with assignments with the 13th Armored Division and the 16th Armored Division before being assigned to the 10th Armored Division where he was given command the 420th Armored Field Artillery Battalion just prior to the division's deployment to France. At the time he was the youngest lieutenant colonel in the U.S. Army. He received a Silver Star for his conduct during the battle for Metz, France, and later was posthumously decorated with the Distinguished Service Cross for his leadership during the Siege of Bastogne. One of his officers, Stanley Resor, described Browne's leadership outside of Bastogne: "Barry did not visit his battalion fire direction center [normally the tactical, technical center of any artillery unit]. Instead, Barry was visiting and encouraging his deployed units and the infantry and armor he was supporting." Veteran of the 420th Frank Norris described Browne as "being in command of his Battalion and his war, with high morale and lots of 'can-do.' Barry also spoke glowingly about his marriage and his baby daughter. He was evidentially a man at peace with himself in the midst of a total war."

———

AUTHORS' NOTE: The chapters that follow begin with a weather report based on information from the London Meteorological Center and F7441 weather report forms that were kept in Claremorris Station, Connaught, until it closed in 1996. Apart from other things this book covers the time the 10th Armored division spent in and around Bastogne during the penultimate year of the World War II. It includes accounts of many of these unsung heroes who were witnesses to the siege. Those who were never sufficiently credited with their role in the defense of this city, those who fought, suffered, and defended Bastogne at a critical time during the largest land battle in U.S. military history. Here is the story of the 10th Armored Division based on first-hand veteran accounts of the raging storm on the front lines around Bastogne, retold by those who experienced the siege personally and lived to tell the tale.

CHAPTER ONE
FRIDAY 15 DECEMBER

Weather report for south Belgium, London
Meteorological Office, Friday 15 December, 1944:
*Low lying mist and fog, ground frost, mild north
easterly wind. Temperature: −5°C.*

Tanks and armored units played an integral part in defending Bastogne during that dark bitterly cold winter of 1944–45. The 10th Armored Division more than adequately lived up to its motto: Terrify and destroy. They executed all the basic mobility, action, shock, and surprise elements of armored combat to the limit. The surprise element was achieved by doing the unexpected: maneuvering and firing while maintaining concentration of firepower and speed. Successful armored intervention depended primarily on combined arms, coordination of teamwork, deliberate planning, and violent execution. Unfortunately due to the nature and urgency of the situation that began on the 16 December it wasn't always possible to do things by the book. Mistakes were indeed made and atoned for.

The city of Bastogne lay directly in the path of the rapidly advancing German Fifth Army. At the commencement of the German offensive it was the location of the headquarters of Maj. Gen. Troy Middleton's VIII Corps, which at the time was under the command the U.S. First Army. (On 20 December command of the corps was transferred to Patton's Third Army.) Bastogne was generally regarded as a vital communication center that gave access to numerous main roads and other smaller roads which converged on the city. As long as it was held by the Americans it presented a formidable obstacle to the progress of the German offensive

It was established early on at OKW (*Oberkommando der Wehrmacht*) that capturing the city would allow the German army free access to the road net-

work and facilitate easier supply lines out to its advancing forces. It was therefore generally accepted that Bastogne would have to be taken and its capture
would determine the success or eventual failure of the German offensive.

The initial problem facing the U.S. Army at was that VIII Corps only
had four divisions—the veteran 4th and 28th, and the untested 9th Armored
and 106th—covering around eighty miles of front that ran from Aachen in
the north, all the way through the Ardennes down to Luxembourg in the
south. Two of these divisions had never fired a shot in anger and the other
two were recovering from the hard fought battles they'd endured in the Hurtgen Forest.

The American army had proved on more than one occasion that it had
a remarkable capacity to adapt with the situation as it developed, but would
this be enough to stem the flow of German forces now pouring through the
Allied lines. This feature of the U.S. Army was the ultimate antitheses of the
German army, which rarely displayed the ability to improvise. Furthermore,
their inability to operate autonomously at anything below regimental level
would be become a defining factor in the Battle of the Bulge. It's surprising
in some respects how the Germans failed to use the terrain to their advantage.
It's surprising because they should have been able to rely on some familiarity
with the local geography because they had attacked through this area on quite
a few previous occasions. In this particular case familiarity did cause a certain
degree of contempt. In 1870 they attacked France through the Belgian Ardennes. In 1914 The Schlieffen Plan also incorporated using the Ardennes
as part of the invasion route as did the invasion of in May 1940 that opened
the war in the west. In contrast to this it was the Americans' first foray into
this region. The ETO (European Theater of Operations) high command had
somewhat erroneously concluded that the Ardennes region lacked any serious
strategic objectives making it unnecessary to place numerous divisions in this
area. Consequently, there were only four divisions placed there. Their situation was exacerbated by a lack of winter clothing because the ETO quartermaster had decided not to issue these provisions on the basis that they didn't
think the campaign would last until December 1944. "It will all be over by
Christmas" wasn't really an original idea, but in this case it would prove positively detrimental.

Unlike two of the four divisions holding in the line in the Ardennes, the
10th Armored Division had seen action. As part of Patton's Third Army they
had been committed to a hard fought battle around Metz. They had also had
the experience of coping with inclement weather conditions and the conse-

quences thereof. The division had arrived at Cherbourg in France directly from the United States, disembarking on 23 September. Its armored infantry had been thrown into the fray on 2 November in the Fort Driant area. This particular sector was relatively quiet at the time but during the course of 10 November they were engaged in fierce fighting as they supported the 90th Division in and around the Moselle-Saar triangle. They eventually crossed the Moselle River to the north in a wide encircling sweep and then attacked northeast and southeast in a two-pronged drive, which brought them into proximity of the Saar River. On 19 November the division crossed into Germany at Eft. The division had been making preparations for the Third Army drive to the Rhine and taking a small break from combat when it was ordered north. At the time the unit was commanded by Maj. Gen. W. H. H. Morris, a very experienced officer who had held his post since July 1944. General Morris, West Point class of 1911, was a World War I veteran who had seen action in the St. Mihiel and Meuse-Argonne regions of France. He had been wounded during these operations and had received a DSC for gallantry in action.

There had initially been a great difference in opinion among the Allied leaders on how to proceed following the breakout from Normandy. Various plans had been proposed and amended, but by early December 1944 Allied plans called for the northern and central groups of armies to move forward toward the lower reaches of the Rhine. It was generally believed that from these positions along the Rhine a final crushing blow could be delivered into the heart of Germany. A secondary line of advance would also be directed towards the Rhine from the southern group of armies. This secondary advance aimed to reduce the pressure on the primary northern attack by engaging as many German forces as possible in the south. To facilitate this plan, massed numbers of troops and armor were concentrated in the Aachen area to ensure rapid movement to the Rhine across the most favorable terrain.

Remaining forces were employed to sustain the Third U.S. Army in its planned offensive. Consequently, as a result of these concentrations some sectors of the line were lightly held. One such sector was that of VIII Corps in the Ardennes on the right flank of the U.S. First Army. The four divisions placed there were covering a front that was more than seventy-five miles long. Whereas a division could normally cover a front of five miles, some of the VIII Corps's divisions were covering almost thirty miles. Moreover two of the divisions were refitting after enduring a punishing battle east of Aachen in the Hurtgen Forest. The other two, the 106th and the 99th respectively were considered green and untested in combat. This situation was a calculated risk by Supreme Allied Commander Eisenhower.

From his headquarters in the picturesque Ardennes town of Spa, Lt. Gen. Omar Bradley had given his personal assurances that the Germans wouldn't attack during his tour of the area. For all intents and purposes he had no valid reason to suspect otherwise. Nevertheless, five days prior to the 16 December attack vague reports began coming through about a build-up of Nazi troops and armor along the border between Belgium, Luxembourg, and Germany. The Germans had successfully imposed radio silence ten days before the attack, but back in Bletchley Park the people who had cracked the Enigma code began intercepting reports of German units being transferred from the eastern front to the west.

On 15 December everything was quiet in Bastogne. Major General Troy Middleton had established the VIII Corps headquarters at the Heintz Barracks in the city and all was well. This over populated the former Belgian army barracks, which had been used by the Germans during the occupation, but since September 1944 had been taken over by the U.S. Army. There had been repeated requests made to strengthen the thin defensive line that ran from Aachen in the north all the way down to Luxembourg, but so far these requests had fallen on deaf ears. Information concerning German army activity had been acknowledged, but as it went up the chain of command its urgency dissipated resulting in a general "no cause for alarm" response by the time it reached the top.

Meanwhile Operation *Wacht am Rhein* (Watch on the Rhine), Hitler's ambitious plan to strike against the Allies and deliver a crushing defeat that would restore crumbling German morale, was poised to launch against the thin American line between Monschau, just to the south of Aachen, and Echternach on the eastern Luxembourg-German border. The intention was to destroy thirty Allied divisions in one fell swoop. Hitler designated four armies to execute his plan. Von Zangen and his Fifteenth Army had managed to escape from the Schelde estuary west of Antwerp relatively unscathed and were now designated to engage the First U.S. Army's left flank. Then there was the Sixth SS Panzer Army in the north commanded by a butcher's son and, by that stage of the war, chronic alcoholic Joseph "Sepp" Dietrich. This army consisted primarily of SS divisions, many of which had been requisitioned from the east to participate in this offensive. The center ground would be the responsibility of the German Fifth Army, commanded by General Hasso von Manteuffel; they were the most poorly provisioned, but the best

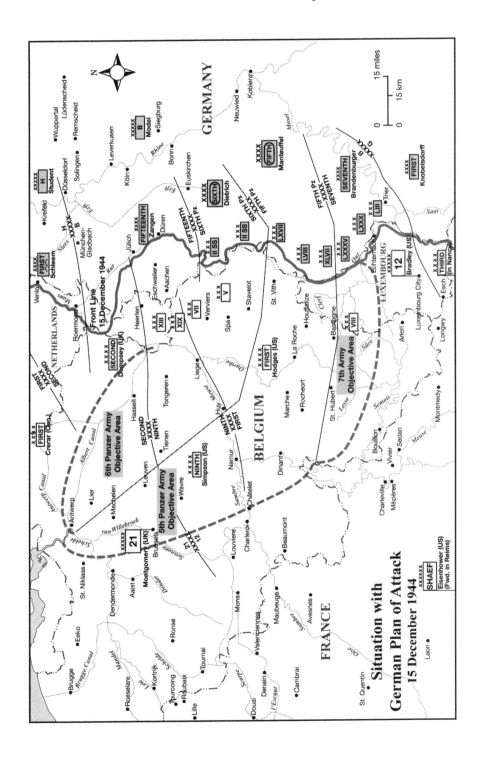

Situation with
German Plan of Attack
15 December 1944

lead of all three armies. In the south General Erich von Brandenburger was designated with the task of invading Luxembourg and stopping Patton in the event that he decided to head north to the Ardennes.

General Hasso von Manteuffel, commanding the Fifth Panzer Army, had given General Heinrich Freiherr von Lüttwitz's XLVII Panzer Corps the job of capturing Bastogne on the presumptive condition that he would have to succeed in this objective before crossing the river Meuse near Namur. General von Lüttwitz planned to attack along a seven-mile front with three divisions. General Kokott, commanding the 26th Volksgrenadier Division and the Second Panzer Division, commanded by Colonel Meinhard von Lauchert, would lead the assault with General Bayerlein's Panzer-Lehr Division following close behind them. The German commanders did not necessarily agree on the reasons for taking the city, but it was the primary objective en route to the Meuse.

Timing was going to be important. In fact timing was going to be everything. Bastogne had been a primary objective of the German forces in the May 1940 invasion of France. They fully understood the strategic importance of the place and although there was great disparity at OKW concerning the actual details of the offensive, all there agreed that Bastogne was the key to crossing the River Meuse, at least in the center. It was going to be vital if they wanted to maintain supply routes to Germany and keep the momentum. Each army was to have no fewer than four divisions each. The precise strength and composition of these divisions varied from army to army. Most of the respective commanders, however, believed that the plan for the offensive in the west was at best flawed and at worst forlorn.

———

All was quiet in and around Bastogne on 15 December. A few soldiers from the 28th Division were still hanging around town and entertaining the locals. The 28th was still in the process of replacing the casualties incurred during the terrible battle of the Hurtgen Forest, which had reduced the division's roles by four-fifths. A few miles south of Bastogne in Diekirch the division's 109th Infantry Regiment was enjoying a USO show that featured Marlene Dietrich at the top of the bill, wowing the troops with her husky, Teutonic, just-below-the-tone vocals, as well as her shapely legs. Soldiers of the 10th Armored Division were not so fortunate. Some of them had had to contend with yet another theatrical rendering by Capt. John Drew Devereaux, a renowned Broadway actor and relative of Hollywood legend John Barrymore;

the latter was a detail that he imparted at every opportunity. This did not detract from the fact that he was a fine soldier, sincerely admired, and respected by his subordinates and superiors alike.

TIMOTHY COLLINS, 54TH ARMORED INFANTRY BATTALION

When John [Devereaux] started out in the army, he was training to be a paratrooper, I heard that at the time he broke his leg. He was assigned to the armored infantry and he came in as a second lieutenant and a platoon leader. One day we had taken these pill boxes as we were coming into Germany and they kept attacking us on and off during the day and during the night. Lt. Devereaux came up and they sent a tank up to give us support, out in the open he jumped on top of that turret and started banging the top with his carbine to tell them to give us covering fire. In my book he was number one. The guys would do anything for him. I think his acting probably gave him the ability to mix with everybody and feel part of the whole group. I can't say that for all of the officers.[14]

> *First Lieutenant John D. Devereaux, 54th Armored Infantry Battalion, Bronze Star citation:*
> For heroic achievement in connection with military operations against an enemy of the United States, in the vicinity of Borg, Germany on 22 November 1944. While under heavy mortar, artillery, and small arms fire, Lieutenant Devereaux led his platoon in an attack through an open field on a fortified entrenched position held by the enemy. In reaching the objective it was necessary to go through dragon's teeth and barbed wire which were dominated by a large pill box. Leaving a group of men to fire into the apertures, Lieutenant Devereaux and two men attacked the pillbox from the flank. This action led to the capitulation of the pillbox and the immediate capture of 20 prisoners. Throughout the entire action, Lieutenant Devereaux's leadership, courage, and resourcefulness were a superior example to all his men and contributed immensely to the success of the operation. Entered the military service from New York.[15]

The 10th Armored Division's battles around Metz had introduced them to, among other things, the debilitating weather-related health problems that could arise from having to endure low temperatures and almost constant wet weather. Trench foot and hypothermia caused many casualties; after a rain soaked November in Alsace-Lorraine sickness in the army was rampant. One division reported over three thousand severe cases of trench foot. But this would prove to be only a taste of what was to come when they headed north to fight in the Battle of the Bulge.

WILLIAM RICHARD BARRETT, B BATTERY, 420TH ARMORED FIELD ARTILLERY BATTALION

I was born in Northeastern Iowa. Our family moved to a farm in Kansas before I started school. We lived on a small farm. I grew up and attended school in Solomon, Kansas. I answered the draft and was inducted the 23rd of September 1943. My first assignment was with the 16th Armored Division. I was there until spring of 1944. At that time a large group of the 16th trainees were shipped to the 10th. We finished basic training there and in Sept. we were headed overseas. On Sept. 23, 1944 we landed in Cherbourg, France. There we picked up our tanks (M-7), a 105 MM Howitzer that was mounted on a medium tank chassis. I remained in the same gun crew for the remaining time. The driver and I stayed on the same weapon.

Then it was an armored column across France to where we had seen action around Metz. I was living in the field and it was muddy. On Dec. 15th we received orders to move out the next morning. We had no idea where to, but we did know we were heading North.[16]

For the soldiers of the four divisions spread across VIII Corp's eighty-nine mile front the only enemy at the time was the bone chilling cold. They had heard rumblings a few miles to the east, but as far as their generals were concerned so far there was no hard intelligence to suggest that the Germans were planning a major offensive. Consequently neither the local population nor the Allies had any inkling that Germany was about to unleash a storm that would once again disrupt the tranquility of the centuries-old communities of the Ardennes.

PHIL BURGE, COMPANY C, 55TH ARMORED ENGINEER BATTALION

We did not know what was happening when we heard about the German offensive, we were in Metz resting and recuperating after the Battle of Metz, where one of my good friends stepped on landmine in [the city]. We had no idea what was going on, Maxwell Taylor was back in Washington, nothing was going to happen, this offensive just got everybody by surprise, it was just unthinkable that it was happening. We left Metz in the rain.[17]

CHAPTER TWO

SATURDAY 16 DECEMBER

Weather report for south Belgium, London
Meteorological Office, Saturday 16 December, 1944:
Mist and fog unlikely to clear in the course of the day.
Low cloud and ground frost. Temperature: −6°C.

Initially morale was high among the three Germans armies poised to unleash their fury on the sleepy Ardennes. Manteuffel's 5th Army in the center would be charged with the objective of taking Bastogne en route to the river Meuse. In those last few minutes before the cannons of the German field artillery opened up and *Nebelwerfers*—five-barreled mortars known to the Allied soldiers as Screamin' Meemies—began to splutter out shells on the American positions, German soldiers exchanged light banter about what they were going to do to the *Amies* (Americans) when they eventually met. Hans Herbst of the 116th *Windhund* (Greyhound) Division was looking forward to getting hold of some Lucky Strikes cigarettes and whatever other provisions he could purloin on the way. Georg Mussbach, radio operator on a Panther Mk IV tank crew, joked with his commander about how easy it was to take out a Sherman. All the commanders in the field agreed that timing was going to be of the essence on this occasion.

Why was Bastogne so important to the Germans? German high command had identified the strategic location of the city during the initial planning stages for the offensive. It had been generally agreed that the two key cities of Bastogne and St. Vith would have to be taken within the first forty-eight hours if they were to achieve their intended objective of reaching Antwerp and dividing the Allied forces.

Most of the German senior commanders agreed with this plan but there were those who had serious reservations about Operation *Wacht am Rhein*.

Field Marshal Otto Moritz Walter Model for one disagreed with the whole plan and was the only general at the time who dared to openly oppose Adolf Hitler. During this time Hitler's temperament was at best unpredictable and at worst paranoid. Undoubtedly this was in part a result of an attempt on his life in July 1944 instigated by General Von Stauffenberg and other high ranking military officers. It was while recuperating from the injuries he sustained in the assassination attempt that he ruminated on the possibilities of going on the offensive in the west. General Hasso-Eccard Freiherr Von Manteuffel, Fifth Army commander, also harbored serious reservations about the planned offensive in the west that he voiced to Von Rundstedt, who concurred, but neither had the nerve to openly state their dissenting opinions.

LIEUTENANT CARL W. MOOT JR., HEADQUARTERS, 420TH ARMORED FIELD ARTILLERY BATTALION

No battle action in immediate area. The 420th AFA Bn. was bivouacked in the small town of Wehingen, between the Saar and Moselle Rivers. The line between the German and American armies was the Saar River. The three forward observers were taking turns each night, watching across the Saar from a prominent hilltop. Our mission was to report any gun positions, German movements, etc., that we could see and to direct the artillery on any worthy targets that we could observe. I was assigned as the all night Observer on this night and preceded to the hilltop shortly after dark. Nothing unusual happened all night, just the normal gunfire sounds and muzzle flashes. I recall hearing German vehicle engines running as if trucks, tanks or other vehicles might be moving across the river, however those noises were common and had been heard for several days, no significance was attached to them.[18]

––––––––

The city of Bastogne rests on an elevated plateau in the province of Belgian province of Luxembourg, a few miles from the country of Luxembourg's border to the south and about twenty-two miles west of Germany. It was regarded as one of the most important towns in the Ardennes and had been for centuries. Seven roads meet there making it a popular market town. It is surrounded by gentle rolling hills, prime agricultural land, and a few planted forests that were used mainly for logging. Bastogne was the heart of a farming community.

At precisely 0530 on 16 December 1944 the men of the 106th Division were suddenly hit with the full force of an all-out Nazi offensive. The German advance through the Ardennes had begun in earnest as three German armies simultaneously launched their attacks along an eighty-nine mile front against a thinly held American line. The attack came as a complete surprise; U.S. forces were caught napping. To the north, just west of the Belgian-German border at the village of Losheim, the German Sixth Army, primarily made up of SS divisions, poured through a gap screened by the 14th Cavalry Group at the V and VIII corps boundary between the 99th and 106th divisions. Farther south General Hasso von Manteuffel led his Fifth Army west towards Bastogne. Erich Brandenburger completed the southern end of the triple-play of destruction crossing the German border into Luxembourg with his Seventh Army and hammering into the 4th Division, which like the 28th Division was also recovering from combat in the Hurtgen Forest.

WALTER LEPINSKI, HEADQUARTERS COMPANY, 20TH ARMORED INFANTRY BATTALION

We had over 60 days of combat and we were brought back to Reméling, France for some rest and recuperation before our next assignment. When I got there, the engineers had set up showers and we were taken to them by the truckload. I took a shower, got some new clothes, and encamped. It felt so good to be away from combat, especially the artillery and I was looking forward to getting our vehicles back in tip top shape and get[ting] some ammunition. The minute I got back from my shower I was told that the Captain wanted to see me at the CP. I wondered what the hell was going on, it was really hectic at that time. He had all the noncoms there at the CP, telling them where to go and what their orders were, and he told me to get my men and vehicles ready to roll at a moment's notice. I did not get a chance to ask him what was going on, so I went back to my men and told them what they needed to do and got them ready to roll. It was not that long after that we got on the road and joined up with a convoy and we headed north. I did not know a thing, where we were going or what was going on, I was unaware at the time.

The 10th Armored Division's Combat Command B was to play a prominent role along with the gallant 101st Airborne Division in holding Bastogne while the U.S. Third Army wheeled north to reinforce their position. Nevertheless, due to their excellent mobility the 10th Armored was the first division to arrive on the scene and deploy to the assigned areas.

JOHN FLETCHER, 54TH ARMORED INFANTRY BATTALION

When the Germans attacked in the Ardennes December 16, 1944, the 10th was fighting in France with General Patton's 3rd Army. CCB was not committed so we went north into Bastogne, split into 3 teams, and hit the German army about 5 miles beyond Bastogne. Being greatly out-numbered, we were forced back into Bastogne and then we were joined by the 101st Airborne.

We first hit the Germans outside of Wiltz. After very heavy fighting, my unit was forced back into the small town of Marvie, which is on the perimeter of Bastogne. We were attached to the 327th Glider Infantry, and the night before Christmas we retreated to the city of Bastogne. Marvie is in a depressed area, which helped us because the German artillery was going over our heads.[19]

During the opening days of *Wacht am Rhein* the Tiger Division's Combat Command B played a key role in defending Bastogne from the German on-slaught, filling the holes left by the overwhelmed elements of the 9th Armored Division's CCR (combat command reserve). CCR had faced the initial attack courageously, but outnumbered and outgunned it began to falter and retreat in disarray, adding to the need to bring in fresh troops as quickly as possible. When the German attack commenced in earnest CCR found itself committed to fighting desperate delaying actions against long odds.

When then the German attack started, the 9th Armored Division had been in VIII Corps reserve, backing up the three infantry divisions on the line; now it was committed to fighting hopeless delaying actions as the American forces fell back. The 10th Armored Division's CCB moved into this fluid, vague situation without any intelligence on the situation.

On that crucial 16th day of December, Combat Command B, 10th Armored Division, was bivouacked in the vicinity of Reméling, France, undergoing a rehabilitation period from the hard combat around Metz. As yet unsubstantiated rumors originating in the north repeated the vague story of a German attack on the U.S. First Army's front. Events developed rapidly. Early on the morning of 17 December CCB received orders to move out.

MAJOR WILLIAM R. DESOBRY, 20TH ARMORED INFANTRY BATTALION

One night I got an order that we were going to move north the next morning at dawn and this was, let's see, the night of 16th of December. We were going to go into the First Army reserve. Well, that broke our hearts because, you know, First Army—hell, we were in Third Army and the First Army, as great as it was, you know, young guys, we were first string and they are not, which is not true but that's the way we felt. And so we didn't think much of this. But, anyway, we got to that border at night, and whenever we marched in this advance guard main body formation, we moved tactically. We were set up that way and so we just put the orders out that the IP would be at a certain place at whatever time it was in the morning. So we all went back to sleep.[20]

At VIII Corps headquarters in Bastogne Major Malcolm Wilkey, a G-2 intelligence officer, openly voiced his concerns about the state of the corps's frontline defenses, which he had observed the previous day while visiting his friend Major Rudolph Sherrick, 109th Infantry Regiment, 28th Division, in Diekirch, Luxembourg. Normally a U.S. Army division front during World War II was five miles, but in some cases in VIII Corps green divisions, such as the 106th, covered more than twenty-five. ETO hadn't initially regarded this as a serious problem. Despite being far too thinly spread out there hadn't been any noticeable activity in their sector and the front was relatively quiet. Some as yet unconfirmed reports had remarked on an increase in German army activity, but back at Lt. Gen. Omar Bradley's 12th Army Group headquarters in Spa no one had acted on this information. In fact when Bradley had remarked, "The Germans are probably building their defenses in preparation for our attack in February," most generals had agreed with him.

He couldn't have been more wrong. Well-liked by his soldiers and regarded as an excellent administrator, General Bradley was widely regarded among fellow generals as a fastidious and down-to-earth man who didn't suffer fools lightly. He'd studied at West Point with his longtime friend and former classmate Dwight D. Eisenhower. In December 1943 President Roosevelt had decided that Eisenhower should be appointed the top commander for the western Allies. In January 1944 Ike was officially designated as the Supreme Allied Commander Allied Expeditionary Force (SHAEF). This was a favorable arrangement for Bradley who wasn't above calling on his old friend for favors when the occasion demanded it.

ALLAN P. ATWELL, 28TH DIVISION

I was assigned to a rifle company of the 28th Infantry Division on December 16th. The hospital was emptied of all who could walk. I was headed toward Bastogne as a rifleman replacement when asked if I would be interested in becoming a military policeman. I made a quick decision and became one on the spot. Our biggest concern as MPs was to look for Germans dressed up as American soldiers.

If a jeep had black canvas covering the lights, that would give us cause for further investigation. Passwords at roadblocks were a big thing. As I remember, there would not be a particular password but they would ask for a word only an American would normally know. Like players on baseball teams, or what states certain cities were in, or possibly where a river might flow and in what direction. It was a little scary. I, myself, never confronted a German soldier under these conditions . . . that I was aware of, anyway. I saluted General Patton one day as he rode by in his sheepskin jacket and pearl pistols.[21]

(Those were ivory-handled pistols, not pearl. General Patton once seriously berated a GI for remarking that he liked the pearl-handled pistols. "Only a pimp from a cheap New Orleans whorehouse would carry a pearl-handled pistol" retorted Patton in his time honored bullish fashion.[22])

At the time Lt. Gen. George S. Patton was in command of the U.S. Third Army. When the 10th Armored Division joined this army Patton gathered them together and delivered his legendary pep talk. He would have addressed them in a manner that gave the impression that they were the sole recipients of these renditions, when in fact he would have given almost exactly the same speech to all the other divisions in the Third Army. That was the man's talent. General Patton understood the power of rhetoric and knew full well how to present himself.

Third Army's dash across France after the Normandy campaign was already something of a legend despite the fact that the speed of the advance had become a logistical nightmare. A division in the field needed seven tons of supplies every day and keeping pace with demand was almost over-extending the Red Ball Express. Patton wanted glory so bad he could almost taste it. He was so eager to throw his army into the fray and get after the German's that it occasionally clouded his judgment. Nevertheless his time was approaching and in the race to Bastogne history would record him as being the right man, in the right place at the right time.

MAJOR WILLIS D. CRITTENBERGER, HEADQUARTERS BATTERY, 420TH ARMORED FIELD ARTILLERY BATTALION

We were north of Metz when the Bulge began, in the small town of Launstraff, France, right on the German border, when we were ordered up to Bastogne, Belgium. We heard about the Bulge because we always tuned our half-track radios to the BBC. They overlapped, and around 0200 we got a warning order from Division Headquarters saying they were getting ready to go north. Then around 0800 we got our orders to be part of CCB and go to Bastogne. On the 17th we drove about sixty miles up to Luxembourg and stayed overnight.[23]

CLAIR BENNETT, F COMPANY, 90TH CAVALRY
RECONNAISSANCE SQUADRON (MECHANIZED)

I was in a chateau in Sierck, France, I was told by a runner to return to HQ, I did not pay attention to him but the second time he told me I did. I had heard that tale before but this time it was real. Then as we were moving out, we found out that the Germans were attacking Belgium.[24]

Since mid-November the 10th Armored Division had been on the offensive. The Tiger division had braved incessant autumnal rains and crossed the Moselle River at Malling, then driven over to the Saar River, north of Metz. The men of the 10th were currently taking a short break prior to preparing for the Third Army drive to the Rhine, when it was interrupted by the German offensive. Although back at SHAEF they were unaware of magnitude of the German attack on the 16th they issued orders directing the 10th Armored Division to be temporarily attached to First Army's VIII Corps to counter what appeared to be a serious German attempt at a breakthrough along the Belgian-Luxembourg border with Germany.

———

In Bastogne there was a lot of shouting of orders and shouting in general as men from the 28th Division rallied. Information had reached Corps Commander Middleton that the Germans were breaking through all along the front. Now he was faced with the arduous task of formulating a plan to preserve and maintain his thin defenses against this growing onslaught. His primary concerns were the two towns of Bastogne and St. Vith. The city of Bastogne rested on an elevated plateau giving it a commanding view of the surrounding area, and being centrally located it was regarded as a key strategic objective by both sides. Middleton decided to deploy the bulk of his reserve along the road net east of Bastogne where the 28th Division was now heavily engaged against vastly superior numbers. The ominous task of defending the approach roads to the east fell to CCR of the 9th Armored Division.

———

Team Cherry after action report:
>   December 16, 1944
>   Team Cherry received a warning order at 1830 hours from CCB, alerting team for movement to vicinity of Luxembourg.[25]

CHAPTER THREE

SUNDAY 17 DECEMBER

Weather report for south Belgium, London
Meteorological Office, Sunday 17 December, 1944:
*Dense fog. Overcast, ground frost, snow on the high
ground, mild north easterly wind. Temperature: −7°C.*

As dawn broke 17 December at the 10th armored division camp
in Reméling, France, disheveled GIs emerged from their tents
into the brisk morning air. Raucous coughing, swearing, and spitting accompanied their current arduous revival to form as they surveyed the various
forms of transport preparing to move north. Engines were filling the air with
heavy exhaust fumes as they shuddered and lethargically groaned to life. M3
halftracks, M4A1 Sherman tanks, M10 and M18 tank destroyers all turned
over the frozen earth like ploughs as they maneuvered their way into the column that was preparing to move out.

———

420th Armored Field Artillery Battalion after action report:
Dec 17
Battalion moved to Cessingen, Luxembourg, marching 40.4 miles.
B/796 AAA attached to battalion.[26]

By 1320 on December 17, in compliance with the recently received order,
Combat Command B, 10th Armored Division, was taking its first steps toward Bastogne. Initially it moved to the vicinity of Merl in Luxembourg.
After a forced march of seventy-five miles in eighteen hours, Combat Command A had struggled through the most unremitting winter weather to reach
their destination. They headed north and then directly east toward Echter-

nach to support the badly mauled 4th Division who had found themselves directly in the path of the German 7th army. Like the 28th Division a few miles north of them, the 4th "Ivy" Division had suffered greatly in the Hurtgen Forest debacle. Combat Command A reached their destination on time and ensured that the Germans were not going to get any farther west of the 4th Division's position for the duration of the battle.

JERRY GOOLKASIAN, B COMPANY, 3RD TANK BATTALION

When the Bulge broke, we went up north so fast we wondered if the war was over. I was in the Captain's tank, and our company commander was a guy named Schultz. I only met him when he first joined us since he was a replacement. Usually you were supposed to have three men in the turret, but in our case we had two men in the turret. There was my driver Ziggy Skrobicki. The ball gunner was a replacement from Missouri who was married with a family. The other guy in the turret was named Hildoer who was in the peacetime army. We were driving with our lights on during the trip which was odd. It was one of the few sunny days during my time in Europe. We pulled into Arlon and we were part of CCB. We were then sent into Bastogne around midnight and it was cold. I had two pairs of socks on, my boots, tankers jacket and pants, it was so cold that every time the driver shifted gears the butterfly valves would open that gave air to the radiator and I felt like I was sitting there barefoot it was that cold.[27]

The 10 Armored Division moved by forced march to Belgium. Elements of the division, including the 796th Antiaircraft Battery, entered Bastogne on 17 December to hold that city against the enemy offensive. It was here the weapons of the 796th came into their own against the attacking German infantry. They provided antiaircraft protection to the artillery, with a section and a half in the service trains. When they reached Bastogne, the situation was such that ground defense was more important than antiaircraft defense, so the halftracks were allocated accordingly.

The artillery went into positions about eight hundred yards east of Bastogne. The antiaircraft half-tracks were about two hundred yards further out, in a staggered line running approximately north to south. During the first day and night these positions were under constant fire from the enemy.[28]

MAJOR WILLIAM DESOBRY, 20TH ARMORED INFANTRY BATTALION

We got up the next morning in good time, packed up, and go to the IP. Didn't have any maps, because we were going up to First Army and our maps were all for going in the other direction, going to Mainz. And we didn't have time to issue any maps so we just jumped in our vehicles and hit the IP and they pointed down the road towards Thionville. I had with me two reconnaissance platoons, one from the 90th Cavalry, and my old one. And so I just put the recon platoons out in front, and division, corps and army, put their MPs out and my recon guys would go to an MP at a road block and say the 20th Armored Infantry is coming, which way is it to go and the MP would look at his map and say, take that road. We did that all along the route. When we got to Thionville, I remember vividly standing there at the bridge and watching the task force go by. We averaged three, four men per half-track there. A great many men. So, we went through Thionville and we were told to go on to Luxembourg City, which we did, using this type of system of recon guys out in front and MPs we picked up who knew what was going on. We arrived up on the outskirts of Luxembourg City, a small village, and I have forgotten the name of it.

As the battalion CP, that night we really lived it up. We stayed in the villa owned by the Shell Oil guy for the country of Luxembourg and boy, he had a ball, it was real great. He had servants and we had bath tubs and towels and all that sort of thing. So we had a hell of a good night there and we were getting lazy already. Hell, combat command didn't tell us what we were going to do the next day and nothing came down from them. So, I woke up fairly early the next morning and no orders, so I just got in a jeep and rode over to combat command headquarters and the combat commander, a guy named Roberts, who is now at CCB, was just beside himself. He said where in the heck have you been and this and that, and I told him I was over at such and such a place and we didn't get any orders. And he said, "Well, you got to get on the road right away, we are headed for Belgium," "Fine, what do we do?" "First Army Reserve." "Fine." So, we started out on the road. . . .

O'Hara was now back in the 54th and he was the lead guy. And a guy named Cherry was the second guy who was the third tank battalion commanded and then I followed with the 20th Armored Infantry Battalion and down the road we went. And we are going along at a nice clip and we were sending billeting parties to find a such and such place to spend the night. So we would set up there. We would bring the billeting party back and they would say that you were going to another place and this went on and we were getting kind of exasperated. In fact, we were kind of running out of billeting parties because some of them couldn't get back in time to go to another place. And so I was getting kind of tired of it and I went on up to the head of the column to see what in the heck Cherry knew, and I saw Cherry's jeep parked at a Belgium's gasthause. I guess it was up near Arlon *and so I pulled in and there was Hank sitting in the gasthause and having a Belgium beer, so I joined him and asked him if he knew what was going on. And he said, "Hell no, I don't know a damn thing," Well, there was a radio on and I took enough French in college to sort of semi-translate the news. There was news coming over the Belgian civilian radio that there was a big German breakthrough in the Ardennes and advising people to move and this, that and the other thing. And when I heard that I said, "Gee Hank, do you think we go into First Army Reserve when all hell's breaking loose?" And he said "Well, we better get back to the outfit." So he went back and joined his and I joined mine and later on we got word to speed up the column and that we were going into the town of Bastogne. And so it got dark and I was finally ordered to leave my column and get up to Bastogne. So I did, I went as fast as I could, bypassing tanks and Cherry's outfit and so on, and I got up to Bastogne ahead of my column, a little bit, not much."* [29]

DONALD NICHOLS, C COMPANY, 21ST TANK BATTALION

We moved out in a column on the 17th of December. I know we traveled in the dark with headlights on, most unusual for lights to be on in a convoy in a combat area. I recalled it was raining others say snowing. The Tank Commander had his warm clothes on, as we all did, but he had his raincoat on, buttoned up to his neck and draped around the turret to keep the water from coming down on me and our equipment. We arrived in a city south of or a suburb of Luxembourg and were billeted in one front room of a couple's home. We slept on the floor. We listened to their radio to "BBC" from London and they were playing big band music. It sounded great. [30]

Movement orders for the 10th Armored Division had arrived on the war room ticker at 0330 hours 17 December. Fewer than three hours later, the division was clattering down the road heading north toward Luxembourg. The 20th Armored Infantry Battalion was part of Combat Command B, with tanks from the 3rd Tank Battalion, an engineer platoon, and a reconnaissance squadron. Consequently they were part of General Patton's Third Army. Although many ETO generals were beginning to regard the German army as a spent force General Patton had said, "There are still 6 million krauts who can pick up a rifle, they're not done yet." He had further anticipated the German attack by late November noting, "The First Army is making a terrible mistake in leaving the VIII Corps static, as it is highly probable that the Germans are building up to the east of them." On 17 December General Bradley notified General Patton that at least two divisions would be needed to contain the German attack. According to Patton the Americans were "paying the price for sitting still." The next day he met with Bradley in Luxembourg. As he returned to his base farther south he was notified that the situation in the Ardennes was deteriorating rapidly.

SERGEANT WARREN SWANQUIST, HEADQUARTERS, 3RD TANK BATTALION

It was muddy and cold as hell, I was the ball gunner of the tank that I was in when we traveled up to Bastogne. When we arrived in town it was nice and clean, it was halfway decent looking, and I did not see any civilians. All I saw was a bushel of apples in the window of a store, they were all rotten, but I went in there and got them and ate them.[31]

WALTER LEPINSKI, HEADQUARTERS COMPANY, 20TH ARMORED INFANTRY BATTALION

At times we travelled at a good pace and other times we did not, and we started up after 10AM. When we were going through towards the Bastogne area we saw a column of tanks going south while we were going north, and it stopped. We stopped and my halftrack was just opposite from the main straight and this GMC 6x6 was coming down the hill and when he almost got to me the driver stopped, he came over to my track, asked me if he should get another load of ammunition. I surmised that the Germans were making a big push and that this lone driver was trying to save or salvage ammunition to front lines from a stockpile nearby, he was pretty shook up. But I surmised that there was something big happening and it must have been pretty hairy where he came from.[32]

With the German offensive in the Ardennes going full throttle, CCB commander Col. William L. Roberts received a request from his longtime friend and 28th Division commander Maj. Gen. Norman "Dutch" Cota to provide reinforcements and move CCB to the south of his headquarters in Wiltz. Roberts was unable to comply with this request; his unit had already been earmarked for Bastogne.

WILLIAM RICHARD BARRETT, B BATTERY, 420TH ARMORED FIELD ARTILLERY BATTALION

We pulled out early in the morning and we moved north in our column. I don't know how much was with us but I could only see was what I could see. We spent the night in Belgium in some heavy woods. I stood guard watch that night with another young fella and he was scared out of his wits. He fashioned a knife out of wood and it was so dark that he walked into a tree and stuck a knife in him. It was a little bit scary, he didn't know what he walked into, it could have been me.[33]

STAFF SERGEANT STANLEY E. DAVIS, C COMPANY, 21ST TANK BATTALION
My company, C of the 21st, was assigned to CCB and we arrived around 10:00 p.m. at the village of Merle just outside of Luxembourg City we were billeted there on the night of the 17th.[34]

By 17 December, 1944, allied intelligence had a marginally better idea of the strength and objectives of the attacking German forces. As forward elements of the 10th Armored Division drove and skidded through harsh conditions along muddy, congested roads towards Bastogne, the 101st Airborne had been dispatched at speed to accompany them. The picturesque arboreal countryside of Luxembourg with its steep hills and natural forests would have looked great on a postcard, but to the GIs who had to traverse its narrow winding roads between the high pine trees it was just a hindrance to their progress.

The 10th Armored's CCB was already divided into three teams, each team being named after its respective commander: Team Cherry, Team O'Hara, and Team Desobry.

Carl Moot and the rest of the 420th Armored Field Artillery Battalion would play a key role during the siege of Bastogne. He was a forward observer who served as the frontline eyes for artillery firing missions. As Moot and the rest of the 420th AFA would find out when they arrived in Bastogne, the German army had one more battle left in them.

LIEUTENANT CARL W. MOOT JR., HEADQUARTERS,
420TH ARMORED FIELD ARTILLERY BATTALION
I returned to the 420th Bn. HQ shortly after dawn. Battalion Commander Colonel Browne, most of the Bn. Staff and a number of other officers were there. Col. Browne said that the 420th was to move out as soon as possible, the division was moving to the vicinity of Luxembourg. There had apparently been a German breakthrough northeast of Luxembourg and the Division was to help stop it as soon as possible. There was a flurry of activity preparing to move out and as I recall the Battalion rolled out onto the road within an hour or two. We proceeded towards Luxembourg, I think we traveled 70 or 80 miles and ended up in a small town in Luxembourg about dark. I was assigned as Bn. Duty Officer and spent the night

sorting maps and making up sets of maps for each Observer, Battery CO, etc.[35]

———

As with many 10th Armored Division battalions during the Battle of the Bulge, the 21st Tank Battalion was split up to provide enough tanks to protect both Luxembourg City and the vital crossroads of Bastogne. C Company of the 21st Tank battalion was assigned to Team O'Hara, which consisted mostly of the 54th Armored Infantry Battalion. With the German army poised to break through Bastogne towards the Meuse River, the men of Team O'Hara prepared for the fight at hand. Robert Parker was a gunner in a Sherman tank and he saw the beginning onslaught of the German breakthrough when he arrived outside of Marvie and Wardin just southeast of Bastogne.

ROBERT PARKER, C COMPANY, 21ST TANK BATTALION (LATER ON TEAM SNAFU)

I don't know how many hours we traveled but we got into Luxembourg the day before and we moved into Bastogne and the next thing we knew the enemy was coming upon us.[36]

———

The three German armies were now attacking and wreaking havoc along the entire, thinly held, eighty-nine mile line. Unsurprisingly, the battle was dividing into three distinct areas: the northern shoulder, the center, and the southern shoulder. The Waffen SS formations were operating mainly on the northern shoulder where young, primarily unblooded GI's were facing the wrath of seasoned Nazi veterans, some of whom were disaffected veterans that had served on the Eastern front. At around 1400 hours on 17 December 1944, in the village of Baugnez near Malmedy, eighty-six U.S. Army prisoners of war were murdered by the SS troopers of *Kampfgruppe Peiper*.

At this time CCR of the 9th Armored Division, VIII Corps's armored reserve was fully occupied attempting to resist increasingly powerful, coordinated German attacks, reporting back to HQ in Bastogne that an enemy breakthrough was imminent. General Middleton gave orders to set up road blocks on the main roads east of Bastogne in an effort to prevent further German advances toward the city. Commanded by Col. Joseph H. Gilbreth, the already diminutive CCR was now divided into two task forces, one under Capt. L. K. Rose and the other commanded by Lt. Col. Ralph S. Harper.

Task Force Rose, consisting of a company of Sherman tanks, one armored infantry company, and a platoon of armored engineers, was to position itself at the northern roadblock. Meanwhile, Task Force Harper was to establish a southern roadblock with the 2nd Tank Battalion and two companies of the 52nd Armored Infantry Battalion. Later that day Colonel Gilbreth reported back to VIII Corps HQ that Task Force Rose was as good as surrounded. TF Rose reported that they had counted sixteen German tanks and that the task force was being hit from three sides. Headquarters recommended that they try to fight their way out. To facilitate this they could use two platoons of A/52nd AIB, which was the last rifle reserve in CCR; apparently, everything else was committed. The next report said that hadn't yet committed any of the tank destroyers and were waiting until the over-all plan was made known. Colonel Gilbreth further communicated that he was planning to push TF Rose toward TF Harper's road block to the south If the decision was to stay, then some units would be sent there to help them out.

The corps commander denied TF Rose's request to retire. In the event this was of no matter as Rose's position was already beyond redemption as German troops and armor poured through the intermittent gaps in the American line. As news of the German attack spread to Bastogne the U.S. Army imposed a curfew. All residents of the town had to be indoors by 1800 hours with no exceptions.

Team Cherry after action report:
December 17, 1944
Team crossed IP (Petite Hetange) at 1427 Hrs. March was uneventful and team closed in assembly area at Strassen, Luxembourg at 2030 Hrs. Distance marched 44.7 Miles.[37]

Team O'Hara after action report:
December 17, 1944
On Division order Team O'Hara departed Rettel, France, at 1215 on a mounted march to Leudelange, Luxembourg via Koenigamacker, Thionville, Hettange Grande, Roussy Le Village, Frisange, Bettenbourg.[38]

General Manteuffel with his Fifth Army had planned to be in Bastogne by noon on the 17th. This hadn't come to pass and it was becoming increasingly apparent to him that he was falling behind his intended schedule.

CHAPTER FOUR

MONDAY 18 DECEMBER

Weather report for south Belgium, London
Meteorological Office, Monday 18 December, 1944:
*Dense fog. Overcast, intermittent light snow showers
expected, mild north easterly wind. Temperature: −11°C.*

Combat Command B of the 10th Armored Division was en
route to Bastogne with all haste. The soldiers of CCB still had
little knowledge of the magnitude of the current German attack, which was
gathering momentum as the unsuspecting unit continued northward. General Heinrich von Lüttwitz, commanding the XLVII Panzer Corps, had received intelligence indicating that American reinforcements on the way to
Bastogne, among which was a parachute division. Lüttwitz was openly regarded as an old style Prussian cavalryman complete with monocle and a belligerent manner of speech that suggested an arrogant disposition. Despite
this he had the reputation of being especially altruistic, at least where his
troops were concerned.

Colonel Meinhard von Lauchert, 2ndPanzer Division commander2nd,
didn't know exactly which units had been earmarked for Bastogne, but he realized that time was going to be of the essence if he wanted to take the city
intact. Shortly after 0900 on the 18th, orders were received from 10th Armored Division for CCB to head north as fast as possible to join General
Troy Middleton's VIII Corps. CCB's S-2 liaison officer, Major Johnson, departed immediately for Middleton's headquarters in the former Belgian army
barracks in Bastogne. Simultaneously the column pressed on to Arlon, Belgium, just south of Bastogne, to await further instructions from the corps
commander. Sometime around noon Major Johnson arrived at the corps
headquarters. He was informed that there was still not enough intelligence

regarding the full extent of the German attack, but the VIII Corps line was faltering badly to the east under the weight and ferocity of the German advance.

TECH SERGEANT THADDEUS KRASNOBORSKI, HEADQUARTERS, 420TH ARMORED FIELD ARTILLERY BATTALION

We motor marched from Wehingen, Germany to Luxembourg and entered Bastogne early on December 18th just in time to blunt the German attacks.[39]

420th Armored Field Artillery Battalion after action report:
Dec. 18
Battalion received march order and marched 41.4 miles from Cessingen, Luxembourg to position just west of Bastogne, Belgium. Enemy reported infiltrating civilians across river at some points. Observers joined Teams Cherry, O'Hara, and Desobry. Enemy small arms, mortar and medium artillery fire on battery positions. No casualties.[40]

Reports reaching VIII headquarters were meager and rather incoherent; this was exacerbated by some reports being exaggerated. The only thing that HQ could positively ascertain was that the unfolding situation was fluid and obscure. CCB was ordered to an assembly area just southeast of Bastogne to await orders; they weren't going to have to wait long. As the column had reached Arlon earlier in the day Colonel Roberts had gone on ahead and by 1600 he was receiving the latest news on the situation from veteran commander Troy Middleton himself.

796th Antiaircraft Artillery Battery after action report:
18 Dec.
Moved to Bastogne, attached to the 420th AFA which is part of CCB, 10th AD, to give them AA support, arriving in the early evening at about 18:30.[41]

As 420th Artillery observer Carl Moot moved out towards the Longvilly-area just east of Bastogne to help direct artillery fire for Team Cherry, everything seemed quiet at the moment, but that silence would not last for much longer.

LIEUTENANT CARL W. MOOT JR., HEADQUARTERS, 420TH ARMORED FIELD ARTILLERY BATTALION

We moved out that morning toward the northeast. I remember the Luxembourg people cheering and waving as we passed through some of the small towns. The Tenth Armored Division was formed into Combat Commands that day, however I cannot remember how the Combat Teams were formed. Normally I would have reported to a Tank Bn. HQ for instructions and assignment to a Combat Team. Everyone was moving down the road.

However, along toward dark I had joined the Third tank Battalion, Task Force Cherry and Team Hyduke and was moving along with the point of platoon of tanks. I cannot remember the lieutenant's name who was in command of this platoon of tanks. There were 4 or 5 tanks in the platoon, plus my tank, and I was riding in the middle of the column, third or fourth tank from point, or front tank. There was some Armored Infantry just behind us, but I cannot recall what unit they were from. I had worked with the Third Tank Bn. before, Col. Cherry and Lt. Hyduke, so I was pleased to be with them again.

It was after dark when we moved up near the German position. We went through the little town of Mageret and everything was quiet. At Longvilly we stopped just short of town and pulled off to the side of the road and waited. It is my recollection that we were planning to jump off from Longvilly the next morning. We had always been on the offensive, and I think everyone on the team expected us to take the offensive next morning and start pushing the Germans back.

Shortly after stopping, that night, I started looking for a map of the area. I had a complete set of maps that I had put together the night before. After an hour or two of pouring over these maps (by flashlight inside the closed tank), I knew that I did not have a map of the locality that we were now in. However the boundary of one map was just short of the town of Longvilly. I called the 420th Bn. HQ by radio and informed them of my map problem. They already knew about it and told me that the Bn. had gotten the wrong maps, however they had gotten some maps of the area and would send me a set by jeep as soon as possible.

Later that night some vehicles of the 9th Armored Division began moving back past our tanks, going toward Mageret. Also, later I discovered that there was a battery or more of artillery M-7's of the 9th Armored Division just to our left flank, over a small rise. They were not firing, everything was fairly quiet in the immediate vicinity. Much later in the night (2 or 3 AM) I recalled the 420th Bn. HQ again and asked about the maps, since I had not received any. I was informed that they could not or would not bring them to me and that I would have to get by with what maps I had. This upset and angered me because I needed map coor-

dinates to initiate an artillery mission. A little later I was monitoring the Third Tank Battalion radio channel and learned that the town of Mageret, behind us, had been invaded by the Germans after we went when through, and there was a fight going on to re-open the road through it. I then understood why Bn. HQ could not send any maps to me. I drew in some coordinate lines past the edge of the one map and located the approximate location for Longvilly on them, so that I would have some kind of approximate coordinates to call in if and when I wanted to adjust some artillery fire.[42]

EARL VAN GORP, D COMPANY, 3RD TANK BATTALION

When we arrived in Bastogne it was quite quiet and there were no civilians around.[43]

WILLIAM RICHARD BARRETT, B BATTERY, 420TH ARMORED FIELD ARTILLERY BATTALION

The next morning we mounted up again and headed out. On the way up there I remember seeing a sign on the side of the road, I was in my machine gun position. Corporal Dillon was on the other side of the tank, I said "Dillon that sound like a name that you might find in a history book, Bastogne 14 Kilometers. That afternoon we pulled through Bastogne, people standing around, watching us drive through, pulled out through town and headed out north and east set up in the firing position like we normally did out in a field. We got everything set up and got our ammunition ready to go, no firing mission because it was foggy and you couldn't see nothing. They had a sergeant call there he called all the section chiefs and told them to keep everything together because we might have to move fast.[44]

DONALD NICHOLS, C COMPANY, 21ST TANK BATTALION

The next day, 18th of December we traveled on towards our destination which was to be Wardin, Belgium, passing through Bastogne to get there. We had to pull over to the side of the road during the night to let other units traveling to the rear, to escape the German drive from their front. We asked where they were going but the reply was "Give them Hell Yank," our only communication with the retreating soldiers. We did not know it at the time but the Combat Command split the command into three separate Task Forces, one on to N.E. of Bastogne, one to the east and Task Force O'Hara the Task Force that "C" Co., 21st Tank was assigned to, and one to the south east at the Wardin area. The O'Hara Task Force was in better shape, as far as being up to strength, than the other two. CCB's Commander's information was that the main German forces would hit in that area. Fortunately for the Task Force O'Hara the hardest hit was Task Force Cherry to the north east section. "C" Co., with armored infantry attached, pulled into the Wardin area after dark on the 18th of December, and set up our road blocking area. The night was uneventful.[45]

Late on 18 December, as CCB's lead Sherman tanks, tank destroyers, and half-tracks rolled through Bastogne on their way to the town of Noville, young Maj. William Desobry confidently addressed his hastily assembled task force: "Put those Tank destroyers on point and gather all the ammo you can lay your hands on. Good luck and God be with you". He had no idea of the absolutely "perfect storm" of attacking Germans that was about to break around his small force, but he must have sensed that something big was about to go down because he had incorporated infantrymen and engineers into the team's local defense. The engineers would be vital to setting up obstacles and barricades. Desobry ordered his men to allow armored vehicles pass through the lines and continue on to Bastogne. He figured that additional vehicles would merely congest the streets of Noville and increase his vulnerability to enemy artillery fire. Because the team arrived in darkness they were unable to immediately take full advantage of the natural defenses of the area. A platoon of armored infantry from CCR, which had fallen back into Noville near midnight, gave Major Desobry a vivid picture of the enemy forces moving toward the town from the east. TF Desobry was preparing to make an epic stand against overwhelming numbers. Desobry's Company B was to defend the ridge to the northwest and Company A was allocated to the northeast. The job of Company C was to cover the southern half of the perimeter while the armored group was held in the center of the town ready to strike out in any direction.

WALTER LEPINSKI, HEADQUARTERS COMPANY, 20TH ARMORED INFANTRY BATTALION

We went through Bastogne, and then the little town of Foy, and when we got outside of Noville. In my company I was always the last vehicle in our column, and the column stopped. I heard a German plane, an ME109, evidently a reconnaissance plane, all the sudden I heard a pop and it was a gosh darn flare and it lit everything up like the daylight as it dropped down slowly. I said to myself Dammit, we are going to get a lot of artillery on us. But I did not hear any firing, and it was getting dark fast. After the flare faded, word was passed back to me from halftrack to halftrack that Captain Geiger wanted me to come forward and report to him. That is how I got the message, we did not use radios. I moved for-

ward to report to Captain Geiger, who said to me that he and I were going to go into town and pick the spots to place the platoons and gun positions. Captain Geiger and I left the platoon and walked into the town, it was not very far, and after we passed the first house, which was on the left hand side of the road, we went into town and walked around the area. Once he decided where to place each platoon he called the column to move up to the town. I asked Captain Geiger, "Captain, in the case of a withdrawal, what is the alternate route back out?" He said to me, "Our orders are to stay here and battle to the last man." My heart dropped. At that point there was no firing, small arms or artillery, it seemed so strange. It continued to get dark. I was there with him as he placed each company into positions and I got my men into their position as well. That night my men and I slept on the floor of this schoolhouse that we found on the left side of the town, I didn't know it was a schoolhouse until I saw the desks there. I was tired as all hell and I slept.[46]

THOMAS HOLMES, INTELLIGENCE AND RECONNAISSANCE PLATOON, 54TH ARMORED INFANTRY BATTALION

We were supposed to go in reserve and the word kept coming down that it was a little bigger than it sounded. We had gone close to 100 miles and we closed into Bastogne around 4 o'clock in the afternoon. The man who met us in the center was Col. William Roberts, he was the commander of CCB and he had been an officer in World War I, a wonderful old fella. He told us to go to Marvie. So, Team O'Hara went there. As we spread out that night, the people coming through were scaring the hell out of us, they were saying "you better get out of here, they're coming." Who's coming?" The Germans, they have tanks and tanks." I wondered if anyone was stopping to fight them. We also did not have maps, Col. O'Hara had one, but that was it. When you are a reconnaissance person you need maps. Later in the night I heard about the Malmedy murders, it was mostly scuttlebutt and guys began saying they were not to take German prisoners. It was going through my mind too. I didn't want to be captured.[47]

Earlier in the day General Middleton had asked Colonel Roberts how many teams he could divide his men into? Roberts had answered, "I think I could manage three." Understanding that Bastogne was the major crossroads in the area, Middleton ordered Roberts to use his teams to block the three most important access roads to the city from the east. General Middleton's tone was terse, and his directions were concise: "CCB will move without delay in three teams to counter the immediate enemy threats".

JERRY GOOLKASIAN, B COMPANY, 3RD TANK BATTALION

When we got into Noville around midnight and we got the first call after midnight that the enemy was coming down the road and they fired on the outpost. This was the first connection with the Germans around the area of Bastogne on the night of the 18th. The Germans pulled back because they believed they had run into a bigger force than what they had. The halftrack behind us got hit and that was flaring up all night. Ziggy, my driver, and I got some .50 caliber ammunition from the burning halftrack because we were desperate for ammunition.[48]

SERGEANT WARREN SWANQUIST, HEADQUARTERS,
3RD TANK BATTALION

I was out with Team Cherry on the outskirts because we had enough gas left to get there. I did not get to meet with Cherry. We kept going up to Mageret and we stopped there because we had engine trouble, right at the end of cul-de-sac We were in a field with a fence right in front of us and out about 50 to 100 yards there was a couple of woods, they were separated. Every couple of minutes a German would run from woods to the next. So my tank commander at that time, he said "Load the gun and I'll get one of those guys." And by God he did. One guy ran across and bang! He disappeared. Later on that night, my tank commander said, "You get out Warren, take your machine gun and lay in that ditch over there." Shit there was a dead American in that ditch already. So I had to lay there in that ditch with my machine gun while the other guys took over a house and left me out there in the dark.[49]

So, CCB of the 10th Armored Division was split into three separate teams to help stop the German advance towards Bastogne. The teams were named after their respective commanders and mustered only twenty-seven hundred men in all were dispatched with all haste. Team Desobry led by Maj. William R. Desobry headed north to Noville, while Team Cherry under Lt. Col. Henry T. Cherry wheeled east to Longvilly. Team O'Hara, Lt. Col. James O'Hara's group, shifted southeast to Bras. Colonel Roberts established his CP at the Hotel Lebrun just a few yards from the main square then known as the "Carrefour." Teams Desobry, Cherry, and O'Hara, supported by three batteries of the 420th Armored Field Artillery Battalion, were the first line of defense until reinforcements from the 101st Airborne arrived. CCB initially faced the full force of that German onslaught alone. The rest of the 10th Armored Division was held back in Luxembourg to prevent the Germans from swinging into Bastogne from the south.

Colonel Roberts was a veteran of World War One and he had personally witnessed the massed retreat of American forces from Chateau-Thierry in 1918. He recalled a vital factor from this battle to General Middleton : "Sir there will inevitably be stragglers. I want your permission to use these men." The corps commander immediately agreed to this request.

As the winter dusk descended on the landscape, Roberts met the vanguard of his column one mile south of Bastogne. As the respective teams filed passed him Roberts relayed the orders to their commanders, first to Team O Hara, then Team Cherry, and finally to Team Desobry. After briefly scanning a map and choosing a favorable position for the armored artillery, which was sent into position just east of Bastogne. Eventually, progress through the town was severely impeded by corps personnel and the number of stragglers from the east. Some of the stragglers were used as military police to supplement the MPs already assigned to the combat command. Team Cherry utilized its cavalry to guide the way.

At 1815 hours CCB was placed under the direct control of VIII Corps. Later the 35th and 158th Combat Engineer Battalions were attached to Colonel Roberts's command. Both units were designated to be used as infantry to enhance the defense of the city. The 158th was sent north to the vicinity of Luzery and Foy. The 35th was ordered southeast toward Marvie and Remifosse.

There was no discernible enemy action for the remainder of that night but the devastating effect of the rapid German advance was more than apparent from the number of vehicles now congesting the roads south and west of Bastogne.

No serious attempt was made to halt the progress of these troops because Colonel Roberts didn't deem it necessary to do so. His decision must have been influenced by the confusion and sheer terror that registered on the faces of these survivors, which occasionally bordered on blind panic. One artillery unit had abandoned its guns in the streets of Bastogne, but was forced to retrieve them by an officer in the vicinity.

Maybe fearing the worst, VIII Corps headquarters withdrew to Neufchateau during the night. Despite the blackout regulations and close proximity of the Germans, many of the corps HQ vehicles left Bastogne with headlights blazing.

The advancing German 5th Army probably had intelligence that informed them that many U.S. troops were abandoning the town. It's fair to say that if it were not for the 28th Division's stand at Wiltz and CCR of the

9th Armored Division desperately holding roads east of Longvilly, the Germans could have taken Bastogne that very night.

Meanwhile CCB braced itself for the impending attack and began to anchor their teams in their designated locations. Team Desobry's column moved north through the sleepy hamlet of Foy toward Noville. At around 2200 Team Desobry's advance guard, comprising of Intelligence and Reconnaissance Platoon, 20th AIB, and a section of 1st Platoon, Troop D, 90th Cavalry Reconnaissance Squadron (CRS), entered Noville to find it devoid of any friendly or hostile military formations apart from the occasional lone vehicle that had drifted in from Houffalize, which was nine miles north of Noville and already been overrun by axis forces.

When Desobry arrived in Noville it was pitch dark. Lacking knowledge of the nature of the enemy forces or direction from which the Germans would attack he decided to establish three outposts on the encompassing ridges that were situated about half a mile from the center of the village. Each outpost would be comprised of a section of medium tanks and a platoon of armored infantry although the precise numbers of infantry at each outpost varied slightly. One group was dispatched northeast to cover the Houffalize road, which was the main artery running from Bastogne, through Noville to Houffalize. Another group was sent east toward Bourcy and a third group was sent northwest to the Vaux ridge. Engineers were hastily instructed to establish minefields, but after digging the holes they waited to actually place the mines owing to the number of disorientated American stragglers passing through. In compliance with Colonel Roberts's orders Major Desobry began to incorporate these stray soldiers into his ranks. Later, however, it was acknowledged that these demoralized and in some cases severely traumatized stragglers were of little or no use when the situation began to worsen. There was one exception to this when an officer from CCR 9th Armored division showed exceptional fortitude when the going got tough.

For the soldiers of CCB reconnaissance was paramount so that they could properly prepare for the imminent German onslaught. Platoons of Troop D, 90th CRS were assigned to all three teams. Clair Bennett was with the squadron's Company F and his platoon was assigned to Team Cherry during the defense of Bastogne.

CLAIR BENNETT, COMPANY F, 90TH CAVALRY
RECONNAISSANCE SQUADRON (MECHANIZED)

When we drove onto the road between Mageret and Longvilly we arrived near the town of Longvilly around 4pm to find the entrance blocked with the abandoned tanks of the Ninth Armored Division. After we helped clear the path, my platoon, first platoon, and another reconnaissance platoon were assigned to do recon work around the Longvilly area. The terrain at that time was muddy and swampy which was not a problem for our tanks but the armored cars and the jeep became stuck in the mud and we had to pull them out of the mud all day long. We arrived at village and began to set up our defenses on the eastern outskirts.[50]

PHIL BURGE, C COMPANY, 55TH ARMORED ENGINEER BATTALION

When we entered Belgium I remember going through the town of Arlon in the afternoon of December 18th it was a scene out of a Christmas card. It was snowing, but the Christmas lights were on, people were shopping and it was about the prettiest scene you could ever imagine. After passing through Arlon we made a turn in the road and the truck headlights showed a sign saying Bastogne", white letters on a dark blue background. I had never heard of Bastogne, but something told me that it was a name that I would never forget.

We drove through the snow and reached Bastogne by 7 or 8 PM, we spent the first night in the railroad station.[51]

STAFF SERGEANT STANLEY E. DAVIS,
C COMPANY, 21ST TANK BATTALION

We left early the next morning expecting to be billeted in Mageret, Belgium the night of the 18th. I had not realized it at that time but CCB was now on its own and the rest of the 21st Tank Bn and the rest of the 10th was going to be completely involved in an entirely different part of the "Battle of the Bulge."

We arrived at the southern outskirts of Bastogne late afternoon on the 18th and our officers went into Bastogne to get our orders. When they returned we learned that Mageret had been or was about to be occupied by the advancing German forces. CCB was divided up into three teams which were to move rapidly to the Northeast and the East of Bastogne on the main approaches to the city, set up defensive blocking positions, prevent the advancing enemy forces from capturing this key city, and to hold "at all costs." C Co. 21st Tank Battalion was assigned to Team O'Hara, commanded by Lt Col. O'Hara who was the Battalion Commander of the 54th AIB. Team O'Hara was the second team into Bastogne and we were assigned a sector along the Bastogne-Wiltz road and set up its defensive position along this road sound of Wardin and prepared for the assault from the East.[52]

MAJOR WILLIS D. CRITTENBERGER, HEADQUARTERS BATTERY, 420TH ARMORED FIELD ARTILLERY BATTALION

On the 18th we continued on up to Bastogne, one of the exciting things was we were given a goose egg, which was taking a grease pencil on map and drawing circles around different points which we find out. We sent a reconnaissance party into Bastogne which had been corps headquarters for the Red Cross, they had stripped their classified maps off the wall but they left the 1/100,000 which are similar to Esso road maps and that is what we used to fight with. We were on the east side of Bastogne when we arrived, we had plenty of ammo, and refitted some of our weapons including adding a second machine gun onto our halftrack We were in a position that we could fire support for the three task forces: Desobry, Cherry, and O'Hara. We knew it was going to be tough fight because the maps were so large, and we sent a chief messenger to each task force to see what was going on and two of the messengers were fired on with small arms and they got out. We fought that night and put a mine field out in front of our battalion just in case the Germans kept coming.[53]

ROBERT PARKER C COMPANY, 21ST TANK BATTALION (LATER ON TEAM SNAFU)

There were a couple of divisions that had been overrun and they were retreating back through our lines. They had been quite mauled. We had set up a roadblock and the next thing I knew I saw, something similar to our halftrack or a truck, I shot it and I hit it. We lost a couple of tanks that first day. I think we had three left in our platoon at the end.[54]

MAJOR WILLIAM DESOBRY, 21ST ARMORED INFANTRY BATTALION

They said that O'Hara had been sent out to the southeast to block a road coming to the town of Wiltz which was a high speed road, and Cherry was moving out to the town of Longvilly to block that road, and I was going due north to a town of Noville and I was to block that road. They really didn't know what the situation was, except the Germans had broken through the 28th Division and somewhere to the east of us; that Germans were using American equipment and some of them were dressed in American uniforms and some of them civilian uniforms. So you had to watch out for that. We didn't know the situation in the 28th Division and they didn't know. There were a lot of Corps engineers deployed out there as their last line of resistance, but they didn't know exactly where they were. They were out there some place. They didn't have any maps because they hadn't been there long enough. And I was to go to this town of Noville and if there were any Germans in it, I was to knock them out; and seize the town. If there weren't, I was to hold the town, the town of Noville. And I asked, "Well, if I get into trouble, can I withdraw or the like?" And they said, "No, you are to stay there." So, I said, How in the heck do I get to Noville?" And nobody knew how to get through Bastogne to Noville and so I sent a guy off to find an MP and he found a Corps MP. I met him outside and I said, "I [have] to go to Noville and I'd like him to lead me up there." And he said "He wasn't about to leave Bastogne." And I said, "Well can you get me through Bastogne and get me headed on the road to Noville?" And he said, "Sure, I'd be glad to do that." So the column came in and the MP had a vehicle and we jumped in the vehicle and we took off. He led the column through the town of Bastogne, the winding roads, and we got to the outskirts and he says, "Stop here." And we did and he said, "Noville is two towns up, straight down the road." So, we sent the recon platoon on out to get up there first and take over the town, and if Germans were there, just deploy and then we'd come in and start the fighting. And then we came behind them, a few minutes behind them moving about five miles an hour. And we went up the road and we saw stragglers, but we didn't see any Germans. We went through the town of Foy, which was the first town, and then we came to Noville. And there were no Germans there. The town was deserted. We got in a bit after midnight, we deployed around the town, and set up the defense of the town with outposts and with all of the things that you do. Then we proceeded to try to get some sleep. And we did. And the Germans hit us about 4 o'clock in the morning. So we were sort of out on a limb. During the night a number of small units came back into our lines and a lot of stragglers. They essentially told us horror stories about how their units had been overrun by large German units with lots of tanks, Germans in American uniforms, Germans in civilian clothes and all sorts of weird tales. I had been given the authority to take into my outfit any stragglers and units that I . . . wanted by Colonel Roberts, the Combat Commander. Initially it was my idea to take them all in, but I found out very quickly that as individuals came through in either one person, two or three that their physical condition and mental condition was such that it would be more of a burden than they would a help and so we just passed them on back to the rear.

However, we did pick up one engineer unit with remnants of a platoon with an officer and then we picked up one complete armored infantry platoon from the 9th Armored Division that had been fighting out to the east. We particularly wanted engineers and armored infantry because our rifle squads that came into Noville were under-strength. We had one rifle company and a headquarters company, which is really a heavy weapons company. We only had three or four men per squad and so we wanted engineers and armored infantry. The engineers turned out to be a minus. They worked with my engineers during the night, but they just weren't effective. So in the morning, before the fight started, I released them and sent them on back to the rear. We couldn't use them.

I think I got one hour of sleep that night which doesn't sound like much but it is a God send under conditions such as this.[55]

Team Desobry consisted of fifteen medium tanks, five light tanks, a company of infantry transported in M3 half-tracks, and a platoon of 5 M10 tank destroyers. There were accompanied by a unit of mechanized cavalry in three armored cars and six Willy's jeeps. Unbeknown to Team Desobry, heading in the direction of Noville was the entire 2nd Panzer Division, commanded by Colonel Meinrad von Lauchert. The 2nd Panzer had already dispersed the 28th Division's 110th Infantry Regiment at Clervaux, about seventeen miles to the east and hammered the task forces of the 9th Armored Division's CCR. Now Lauchert's panzers were planning to meet up with Gen. Fritz Bayerlein's feared Panzer Lehr and General Kokott's 26th Volksgrenadier divisions, which were approaching Bastogne from the east. Team Desobry had no idea of the magnitude of the task ahead of them.

COMBAT MEDIC ROBERT KINSER, 3RD TANK BATTALION

On December 18, 1944 at 9:00 p.m. we rolled into Bastogne, it was pitch black and we could not even see the next vehicle. We were to go to the next town but found out it was filled up so we stopped at Bastogne for the night. We had no idea how far the front was, about half the column went on to the next town, "Noville," they were cut from us, most of it was lost and part got back into Bastogne, two days later.

The Germans were 9 kilometers from Bastogne, we stayed at a big church, we found the MPs were living there, they were not sleeping. That night all were sitting by the phone waiting, we ate "C" rations about 10:00 p.m. and got to bed about 11:00 p.m.[56]

At around 1800 hours on some high ground just east of Wardin, Team O'Hara stopped for the night. A couple of outposts were established to secure the area but no concerted effort was made to establish real defenses. The bitterly cold night was relatively quiet save the sounds of the occasional straggler passing through the lines, most of whom were the badly mauled remnants of 28th Division that were holding some 15 miles Wiltz south east of Bastogne.

LIEUTENANT COLONEL JAMES O'HARA,
54TH ARMORED INFANTRY BATTALION

On the evening of the 18 Dec 44 Team O'Hara composed of 22 officers and 372 enlisted men from Bn HQ/54, HQ Co/54, B/54. C/21, Sqd C/55, Plat D/90, having 17 medium tanks including the forward observer, four 75 mm assault guns, and sundry small arms and vehicular weapons, occupied this forward slope of the high ground west of Bras, southeast of Wardin as ordered.

An outpost to the flank in Wardin consisting of two medium tanks and one rifle squad, went into position at 182200 Dec 44. To insure prior notice of the enemy's direction of attack, Troop D of the 90th Cav. Rcn. Sqdn. (Mecz) and the reconnaissance platoon of the 54th Armd Inf Bn. were placed well forward at key intersections. The necessity for these precautions was caused by our exposed flanks.[57]

Team O'Hara after action report:
  December 18, 1944
  At 1140 Team O'Hara departed Leudelange, Luxembourg, moving forward to Arlon. At 1320 team commander was given an assigned assembly area, vicinity of Wiltz. At 1630 orders were received to seize and hold high ground southwest of Wardin, due to enemy's swift advance. Occupied and consolidated positions as ordered 1725.

———

The same evening that Desobry arrived in Noville, Team Cherry moved out towards the village of Longvilly. This role had been designated to the team for two reasons: They were the best equipped outfit, and there was an impending threat of Germans advancing rapidly from the east towards Bastogne.

Team Cherry had been the first of the reinforcements to arrive in Bastogne. Now, after detaching the trains at an assembly area near the city it divided into two teams under the respective commands of First Lieutenant Hyduke and Captain Ryerson. They were immediately ordered to move out and engage the enemy forces that were advancing from the east along the road from the direction of Clervaux. The Team Cherry consisted of a tank battalion, a company of armored infantry, a platoon of combat engineers, and an armored cavalry squadron. During the evening the Team Cherry moved out towards Longvilly. They had been told to expect to see elements of Combat Command Reserve of the 9th Armored Division's CCR along the way. When they arrived in Longvilly they found the whole village gridlocked with CCR vehicles that were retreating in disorder. Trucks and halftracks laden with stragglers heading for Bastogne reported having seen the enemy about six miles east of Longvilly.

The retreating CCR soldiers and vehicles caused a difficult traffic situation on the narrow road as Team Cherry tried to move up to the line while the remnants of moved to the west. The retreating 9th Armored Division soldiers had survived a heavy fight against vastly superior numbers and suffered terrible casualties in their valiant effort to stem the German advance.

———

In the absence of commanding general Maxwell Taylor, who was back in Washington, Brig. Gen. Anthony McAuliffe had assumed acting command of the 101st Airborne Division. The Screaming Eagles were originally designated to go to Werbomont on the northern shoulder to check the advance in that sector, but were redirected to Bastogne when the All Americans of the 82nd Airborne got on the road in front of them. McAuliffe drove ahead of his column and went straight to the VIII Corps headquarters at the Heintz Barracks to talk with Lieutenant General Middleton. Colonel Roberts was already there.

RALPH K. MANLEY, 501ST PARACHUTE INFANTRY REGIMENT, 101ST AIRBORNE DIVISION

I was in Paris on a twenty-four-hour pass after we just returned from Holland, and a loudspeaker came on saying, "All [soldiers] report to your units immediately, as quickly as possible, any way possible." So, we returned then from Paris back to our unit and immediately got on what clothes we had. I still had on my class A, of course, for being in Paris, and we loaded onto port battalion trucks—these semi-trucks that had four-foot sidewalls on them and open tops—loaded onto those without overcoats and without overshoes and headed toward the Bulge, and it was very cold.

We met troops that were coming out, wounded (this, that, and the other), walking as we crossed paths, us going in, and them coming out—those who were disenchanted, having been overrun by the Germans and so on—a truck with maybe a series of bodies on it, and as one rounded the corner, some of the pieces of bodies fell off the truck. At that time they had grouped together clerks, anybody who was a soldier, to go to the front, and some of those not having seen that just keeled over in their halftracks because they had not seen that type of wartime before.

We did not know actually what was going on. As we got back to our unit in Mourmelon, France, then we got our equipment and our guns, and what have you and were on trucks in minutes, headed off to Bastogne. We didn't know the situation, we just knew it was cold, and we had to go as we were without overshoes or overcoats. Again, with zero degrees, you can imagine—in open-air trucks, going there, put in like cattle you might say, on trucks that weren't covered. They were actually port battalion trucks that were used to haul merchandise from the ships out to the warehousing areas, so that's what we rode to Bastogne on. Once we got there, of course, it was just dismount and head up the road to the city, on foot. We just missed others as they were coming out—both wounded, disabled, and what have you, who were hobbling and going out in trucks coming out hauling bodies that had been killed and so on. That's what we met as we were going into Bastogne.

Being a demolitionist, I was out on the edge, in a foxhole. In this case, the ground was frozen, but we were in a barn lot with all the feces and cattle stuff that was coming out, so it was easier to dig a foxhole there. You can imagine what I must have smelled like. We disabled some tanks that were coming through with the bazooka, but they got very close. Often times you maybe had two in a foxhole, but in this case it was just one because the ground was so hard to dig, at least on the surface with the snow. Also, you didn't want to reveal your position because of the black dirt on top of the white snow, so you had to get snow and cover over the soil that you had dug out of the foxhole.[58]

Meanwhile as large open trucks were arriving in Bastogne with their loads of Screaming Eagles, 28th Division commander Dutch Cota had established his headquarters nearby at Wiltz, Luxembourg, just a few miles east of Bastogne. Reports were reaching him of desperate attempts being made by his division in the direction of the German border with Luxembourg. The town of Clervaux had already fallen and the situation was deteriorating by the hour as German forces succeeded in preserving their momentum as they pushed west.

The 101st had spent almost fourteen freezing hours exposed to the elements in the trailers of the port-battalion trucks after being hurriedly sent north from their base in Camp Mourmelon France. They were ill provisioned at all levels. Brigadier General McAuliffe had put the 501st Parachute Infantry Regiment (PIR) at the head of the column. When McAuliffe entered the city he took up residence at the former VIII Corps HQ at the Heintz Barracks as he now assumed command of the defense of Bastogne.

———

At approximately 1920 1st Lt. Edward P Hyduke, commanding Company A, 3rd Tank Battalion, halted the lead elements of his force just west of Longvilly. The village, which nestled in a depression between several adjacent hills, was congested with vehicles of CCR, 9th Armored Division. Lieutenant Colonel Cherry and his S-3 went forward to ascertain the intentions of this outfit and to learn what he could of the enemy's advance. With one battalion of infantry, two batteries of artillery, and supporting tanks, CCR had set up roadblocks east and north of the village and had been the target of several attacks during the evening. At that time they had no orders, no plan, and did not know whether they should pull out or remain in Longvilly. At this very moment the Americans were completely unaware of the German columns that were circumnavigating the town to the south. Cherry returned to his column, refueling along the Bastogne road. He directed Lieutenant Hyduke to reconnoiter the ground west of Longvilly and occupy it with his forces before dawn.

Ryerson's forces were to remain where they were until there was a change in CCR's situation. Cherry then returned to Bastogne via Mageret to report his findings to Colonel Roberts. Along the route he observed CCR's trains moving to the rear, a clear indication that they had made a decision to retreat. Colonel Roberts directed Cherry to cover this force if it withdrew, but in any case to hold Longvilly.

Troop D, 90th Cavalry Reconnaissance Squadron (Mechanized) after action report:

18 December

On December 18, 1944 the Troop assembled at Arlon, Belgium where it reported to and for attachment to CCB. Troop D was ordered to precede CCB to the vicinity of Nothum and bivouac for the night. While enroute our orders were changed and the Troop, less the third platoon, assembled at Bastogne with CCB. At this assembly the Troop was given the following assignments: The 1st platoon was assigned to Team Desobry, the 2nd platoon to Team Cherry, and the 3rd platoon to Team O'Hara. The Troop headquarters remained with CCB Headquarters in Bastogne. Between 2000 and 2200 all three platoons moved to the objectives of the three CCB teams: 1st platoon to Noville, the 2nd to Longvilly, and the 3rd to the vicinity of Bras. All moves were completed by 2400 of December 18.

During the night the following patrols were sent out: 1st platoon sent a mounted patrol which proceeded along the main highway from Noville to Houffalize. The patrol encountered no enemy along the route. It also sent a dismounted patrol to the south and west through Cobru-Recogne and Longchamps.

When Team Desobry arrived in Noville the outpost for the town was turned over to him.

The 2nd platoon sent a patrol to investigate the woods 1000 yards directly north of Longvilly the patrol reported the woods clear of enemy.

The 3rd platoon was given the mission of out posting the town of Bras. No patrols were sent out from this platoon during the night.[59]

————

CCR had begun to withdraw at around 2339. Lieutenant Colonel Cherry received word from Lieutenant Hyduke after midnight that his and Captain Ryerson's forces were holding Longvilly alone. This rather unwelcome news was supplemented by the report of a wounded tanker who had been hit near Mageret. This told Cherry that the Germans were getting behind his position and that he was in danger of being surrounded. Another unidentified source reported that he had witnessed a strong German presence in Mageret. The Germans were now occupying the road between Cherry and his CP in Neffe.

Captain William F Ryerson, commanding Company C, 20th AIB, was directed by radio to dispatch a patrol westward from Longvilly to reopen the road to Neffe. Two squads or armored infantry reinforced with a tank destroyer, which had been requisitioned from the 9th Armored Division, for the duration set out on this mission. East of Mageret they dismounted and cautiously approached the village. Within moments near the crossroads of the village they had observed what appeared to be a company of Germans accompanied by several tanks. The patrol concluded that the opposition was too great for their small patrol and promptly scurried back to Captain Ryerson with their report.

This was the general situation on the night of 18 December. The three teams had made it to their pre-allocated positions intact. The problem was that they were too widely dispersed and their lines of communication were over extended. Their overall situation was impeded by a glaring lack of infantry support. Heading in their direction were aggressive and highly motivated German Panzer columns, eager to seize Bastogne and still glowing from their initial successes against the allies. Fortunately for the allies the Germans had adopted the ricochet tactic often employed by armored units of veering from left to right of the center of resistance as they progressed toward the river Meuse.

———

Lieutenant Colonel Henry T. Cherry, Jr. Cavalry
(3rd Tank Battalion) Silver Star with Oak Leaf Cluster citation:
On 19 December 1944, in the vicinity of Neffe, Belgium while commanding a task force, he was informed of an enemy force hitherto undiscovered was approaching his position for an unprotected flank. Undaunted and with an indomitable fighting spirit, Lieutenant Colonel Cherry personally engaged the enemy with submachine gun and pistol fire. His fire dispersed the estimated twenty-five man group and permitted his own force to organize and meet the enemy attack. Later, when his small force was compelled to evacuate its position, Lieutenant Colonel Cherry moved forward and sprayed the enemy with sub machine gun fire, reducing the enemy fire to enable his force to proceed with less harassing fire. The high degree of leadership, extraordinary fidelity and untiring energy displayed by this officer were a constant inspiration to the personnel throughout his command and materially contributed to the successful accomplishment of the mission of the 101st Airborne Division. His actions were in according with the highest standards of the military service. Entered military service from Georgia.[60]

———

Team Cherry after action report:
December 18, 1944
Weather and visibility—Poor, Rain, Cloudy
C/3 detached at Strassen and attached to CCR, 10th AD. Team Cherry subdivided into two teams: Team Hyduke—(A/3—1 Plt) (1 Plt & 1 Sqd C/20) (D/3—2 Plts) (1 sqd 3/C/55). Team Ryerson—

(AG[assault gun] Plt) (Mortar Plt), (C/20 AIB—1 Plt & 1 Sqd) (1 Plt A/3) (1 Sqd 3/C/55) marched from Strassen, Luxembourg, to Longvilly, Belgium. Team Cherry in order of March, Team Hyduke, Team Ryerson, Trains, left Strassen at 1130 hours and head of column reached Longvilly at 1930 Hrs. Distance marched 41-5 miles. Column halted closed up on road from Bastogne to Longvilly with head of column at Longvilly. 2/D/90 became attached to Team Cherry when column reached Bastogne and led column to Longvilly where contact was made with CCR, 9th Armored Division. Team trains went into assembly area at Bastogne. Bn CP was located at Neffe. Battalion Commander Col. Cherry and Battalion S-3 went forward to CP, CCR 9th Armored Division. Road blocks manned by elements of CCR 9th AD were then in the process of being by-passed by the enemy. Information obtained of friendly and enemy troops was vague. Team Ryerson and Hyduke were ordered to remain in their present positions and to make a reconnaissance as soon as possible in their immediate vicinity for defensive positions. At 2339 elements of CCR, 9th AD and 28th Inf Div started withdrawing from Longvilly.[61]

Lieutenant Colonel James "Smilin' Jim" O'Hara was the commander of the 54th Armored Infantry Battalion. His nickname was Smilin' Jim as he always seemed to have a smirk on his face. His Team O'Hara led the initial defense of the Marvie and Wardin area southeast of Bastogne. O'Hara was awarded a Silver Star for his leadership during the battle for Bastogne.—*courtesy National Archives*

Don Nichols was the loader in a Sherman 105mm howitzer tank in Company C, 21st Tank Battalion. Nichols fought in the Wardin and Marvie area with Team O'Hara and is credited with knocking out a Tiger tank and a Panther tank during his time in the Battle of the Bulge.—*courtesy Donald Nichols*

The 54th Armored Infantry Battalion officers are pictured here in August 1944 before the 10th Armored Division was shipped over to Europe. Several of the notable officers in this photo are Lt. John Devereaux, Lt. Col. James O'Hara, and Maj. William Desobry. Desobry was originally in the 54th Armored Infantry Battalion before being transferred to the 20th Armored Infantry Battalion before the Battle of the Bulge.—*courtesy National Archives*

Lieutenant John Devereaux commanded Company B, 54th Armored Infantry Battalion. Devereaux was known for his theatrics from his days on Broadway but he proved to be a capable leader who led his men against a larger German force in the Wardin area, southwest of Bastogne. He earned the Silver Star for his leadership during the Battle of the Bulge. —*courtesy National Archives*

Major William Desobry was the leader of Team Desobry during the battle of Noville, north of Bastogne. Desobry was originally assigned to the 54th Armored Infantry Battalion, but took command of the 20th Armored Infantry Battalion right before the Battle of the Bulge. Desobry's soldiers helped hold the Germans off in Noville long enough for reinforcements from the 101st Airborne Division to arrive. Desobry was wounded when an artillery shell hit his CP in Noville. Subsequently he was taken prisoner and sent to a German POW camp.
—courtesy National Archives

Lieutenant Colonel Henry Cherry Jr. was the commander of the 3rd Tank Battalion and also commanded Team Cherry during the Battle of Bastogne. Cherry was a hands-on commander who was seen driving down the Neffe-Longvilly road, constantly checking on his troops up until his chateau CP burned down during a German attack on 19 December. He was awarded the Silver Star for holding off the German attack against his CP and for reorganizing his men.—*courtesy Roland Gaul, Musée National d'Histoire Militaire Diekirch*

Major Willis D. "Crit" Crittenberger was a senior officer in the 420th Armored Field Artillery Battalion who, along with commanding officer Lt. Col. Barry Browne, kept the unit running smoothly as the artillerymen fulfilled the difficult task of providing supporting fires for the encircled defenders of Bastogne, to every point on the compass. He took over the battalion after Browne was mortally wounded on Christmas Eve.—*courtesy National Archives*

Captain William Ryerson was the commander of Company C, 20th Armored Infantry Battalion. As a part of Team Cherry, Ryerson led his men in firefights throughout the Bastogne area. On January 14, 1945, as Ryerson led a group of Company C men in an attack against a group of Germans northeast of Bastogne near Bourcy, an Allied fighter plane dropped a bomb short of its target, and killed Ryerson.—*courtesy Gail Ryerson Parsons*

Phil Burge was with Company C, 55th Armored Engineers. As a member of the supply company he tried to find food and supplies for tankers and paratroopers trapped in Bastogne. Burge saw firsthand the difficulties the average soldier dealt with in Bastogne—having cheese and crackers for Christmas dinner and using 101st Airborne commander Maxwell Taylor's generator to keep warm.—*courtesy Phil Burge*

Walter Lepinski served with Headquarters Company, 20th Armored Infantry Battalion. He was in Noville manning a .50 caliber machine gun on a halftrack. He was awarded an Oak Leaf Cluster for his Bronze Star for helping his fellow tankers find different targets that were closing in on the town.—*courtesy Walter Lepinski*

Belgian volunteer nurse Augusta Chiwy was one of the two civilian nurses who served along with 20th AIB surgeon, John "Jack" Prior; the other was Renée Lemaire. Chiwy worked without proper anesthetic or other medicines in a makeshift aid station near the center of Bastogne. She even accompanied Jack Prior on a mission to retrieve wounded soldiers off the battlefield. She was in the aid station when the bomb destroyed it on Christmas Eve but survived.—*courtesy Martin King*

John "Jack" Prior, surgeon for the 20th Armored Infantry Battalion, treated multiple casualties during the combat in Noville. He volunteered to stay with the wounded as Combat Command B, 10th Armored Division, and 101st Airborne pulled back to Bastogne, but he was ordered to return because he was the only surgeon available. He received the Bronze Star for saving patients from a burning ambulance.
—*courtesy Jeff Prior*

Irving Lee Naftulin was the dental officer for the 20th Armored Infantry Battalion during the Battle of Bastogne. Naftulin was not trained in medical procedures beyond oral surgery and first aid, but he learned quickly how to treat serious wounds as the only trained medical doctor in Bastogne other than Battalion Surgeon Jack Prior. Naftulin distinguished himself by saving many wounded soldiers lives when the aid station was bombed on Christmas Eve.—*courtesy Donald Naftulin*

Stanley Davis served in Company C, 21st Tank Battalion, with Team O'Hara during the Battle of Bastogne. Davis fought primarily in the Marvie area southeast of Bastogne. He later fought in January 1945 during the counter-offensive by the 101st Airborne and Combat Command B attacking east out of Bastogne. Davis received a Bronze Star for knocking out several German vehicles on 23 December.—*courtesy Howard Liddic*

Known for his hands-on approach, Lt. Col. Barry Browne was the commanding officer for the 420th Armored Field Artillery Battalion during the Battle of Bastogne. He was mortally wounded by a German shell burst while visiting one of his batteries on Christmas Eve. Browne was posthumously awarded the Distinguished Service Cross.—*courtesy of Jan Newsome*

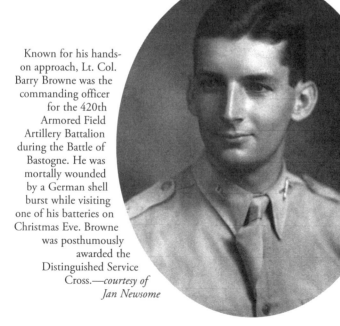

CHAPTER FIVE
TUESDAY 19 DECEMBER

Weather report for south Belgium, London
Meteorological Office, Tuesday 19 December, 1944:
Low lying mist in the hills and wooded areas. Cloudy,
ground frost remaining dry, mild north wind.
Temperature: −9°C.

A battalion of freshly arrived paratroopers from the 506th commanded by Lt. LaPrade had been ordered up to Noville to provide support for Team Desobry. So far the perimeter of Bastogne had been
held for a full eight hours by CCB and the remnants of CCR, 9th Armored
Division, and the 28th Division pending the arrival of the Screaming Eagles.
At their headquarters in Noville Major Desobry and Lt. Col. James L.
LaPrade, 1st Battalion, 506th PIR, had not decided who should be in overall
command of the combined forces, a detail that would shortly become super-
fluous. At around 0430 the stream of battle weary CCR soldiers passing
through the village dried up quite abruptly. This was a glaring indication to
Desobry and LaPrade that the next soldiers to arrive would probably be
speaking German. Their expectations were met when first contact with German troops was made at 0530 when a group of German halftracks rumbled
along the Bourcy road east of Noville. The GIs at the roadblock weren't sure
if they were American or German. No mines had been laid on that particular
road and the American tanks were a few hundred yards to the rear of that
position. Therefore there was no serious opposition in place. Suddenly one
of the vehicles ground to a halt in front of the roadblock and the GIs heard
something in German. That was their cue to shower the halftracks with
grenades, many of which hit their intended targets and exploded inside the
vehicles. Screams of agony echoed out into the pitch dark night as the sur-

73

viving Germans leapt from the halftracks and took up positions in ditches beside the road. A ferocious firefight ensued that lasted around twenty minutes until Sergeant Leon D. Gantt, realizing that he was up against a numerically superior force, gave the order to withdraw a hundred yards or so. This would at least place him out of range of the potato masher grenades the Germans were hurling at him and his men. Meanwhile members of Headquarters Company of the 20th AIB were busy with other issues in the center of Noville.

WALTER LEPINSKI, HEADQUARTERS COMPANY, 20TH ARMORED INFANTRY BATTALION

It didn't seem that I slept at all when all of the sudden all hell broke loose. Small arms, burp guns, and artillery, everything was going on outside the window of the schoolhouse. I jumped up and told the men that we needed to get out of here. My halftrack was parked alongside the building facing away from the main street. I manned the .50 caliber and it was gray outside with a lot of fog out. The first room in that house facing the street was the battalion headquarters, and the room behind it in the same building was the headquarters company headquarters. The artillery fire was constant and some of our halftracks and some of the flames were so high from them. We were in a staggered formation in that area and the half-track to my right had two buildings or sheds in front of them and he would fire between the two buildings. The road north of my position was sloped down and on the road that ran parallel to the road we were on had a column of German tanks that were lumbering towards where we came from, they never fired, but we kept losing them in the fog. The fog kept rising and falling, and when I could see I lined up my barrel over a hedgerow, that was 15 feet in front of me, so that I could see my tracers bouncing off the tanks. Even when I could not see them I could continue to fire since I was lined up. It was one hell of hectic time, a lot of fire and smoke. I sat up there like a duck in the pond, nothing to protect me, but most of the fire came from the other side of the street. When the 101st Airborne came in they looked very similar, except for their pants pockets, to a regular foot soldier. I did not have any contact with the 101st Airborne at all. Most of them were in the outskirts on the line, I did not see many of them in Bastogne either.

Later on that afternoon Captain Geiger called for me to come see him. He told me that there was a halftrack down the bottom of the street, towards the north, it was a machine gun platoon halftrack and he could not get it started. It had a radio in it and they had to have it. He told me go down and get it. He told me that the battalion headquarters halftrack was dead, and their radio, which was the biggest radio that we had, could not be used. I grabbed some tools into my pocket and instead of running down the street I ran down behind the buildings. There was a space of maybe 50 to 75 yards of no houses, except one house that was standing alone and that halftrack was standing against it. The driver of that halftrack had dug a foxhole fairly close to it up the street. I went to start it to see why the hell it wouldn't start, and I put the hood up and turned the starter to see that there was gas moving. I looked at the battery to see if it still worked. I discovered that the driver took off the connectors, which were made of brass, on the carburetor and he cross-threaded it and I took some soap, it was similar to the soap my mother used to wash clothes, and I smeared it on the connectors wrapped with my goddamned handkerchief and sure enough it started. I was in a hell of a hurry and I backed it out and I came galloping at full goddamn speed in second gear up that street. Unbeknown to me I parked that vehicle in front of the CP where I ran in with the battery and I placed it on a window sill, jumped through another window and brought the battery through to the dead battalion halftrack. Captain Billet, from company B, and another 2nd Lieutenant were leaning on the wall near the window I had the battery on and he said to me, "Sergeant, where are you going with that battery?" I told him that it was for the battalion halftrack, and he replied, "What? Salvage now?" I never knew that it was for such an important purpose. I then went in to talk with Captain Geiger. So I took off and as I came out of the CP I started to walk over to my halftrack, a Lt. Schnicke, yelled "Sergeant!", who was red-faced and really mad, he really chewed me out saying "Why did you not tell anybody that you were going down to get that track?" I said, "Nobody told me why I shouldn't, I was told to get it and bring it up to the CP." He told me that there were halftracks facing up the street that had been used by troops who were overrun by the Germans that entered the Noville area and that Captain Way in a 75 howitzer tank was ready to touch one off and almost fired a shell at me. Thankfully he halted Captain Way from firing at me. He was madder than mad. I told him "Sir, I had no idea," Shortly after I heard that Lt. Schnicke got killed after he went down to a cellar and Sgt. Fields was manning a bazooka there. A German tank was coming up near the cellar and Fields went to fire on it, as I heard, Schnicke took the bazooka from Fields, but due to the movement a projectile came through the window and killed Schnicke.[62]

First Lieutenant William Schnicke, 20th Armored Infantry, Posthumous Silver Star citation:
On 20 December 1944, in the vicinity of Noville, Belgium. He discovered that the ammunition of his assault gun was depleted. Without hesitation and with complete disregard for his personal safety,

Lieutenant Schnicke secured a rocket launcher and took up a position in a ditch to await the oncoming tanks attacking the vital defense of the village. He fired two rounds at a close range stopping the lead tank and knocked it out with the third round. However, by this action he exposed his position and was mortally wounded by machine gun fire from the second tank. By his devotion to duty, daring courage and exemplary leadership, Lieutenant Schnicke aided materially in retarding the attack and preserving the defense of Noville. His actions were in accordance with the highest standards of the military service. Entered military service from Ohio.[63]

Staff Sergeant Walter R. Lepinski, 20th Armored Infantry,
Bronze Star with Oak Leaf Cluster citation:
On 19 and 20 December 1944, in the vicinity of Noville, Belgium, from an exposed position, Sergeant Lepinski directed fire on enemy tanks with a .50 caliber machine gun mounted on a half-track. While he was directing fire, the enemy were attacking within from three to five hundred yards, using 88mm guns, machine guns, and mortars. By his courage and complete disregard for his personal safety, Sergeant Lepinski assisted in knocking out at least four enemy tanks thereby enabling his unit to save important vehicles and equipment. His actions were in accordance with the highest standards of the military service. Entered military service from New Hampshire.[64]

The two medium tanks that were supposed to be supporting the outpost did not fire due to the lack of visibility and fear of hitting their own men. As soon as Leon Gant's men had pulled back the Germans remounted their vehicles and drove back up the road. At 0730 the GIs abandoned their roadblock and fell back to Noville as previously instructed by Major Desobry. The German group they had encountered was a lead element of the 2nd Panzer Division, which was now heading toward Noville.

First Lieutenant Herman C. Jacobs, Headquarters Company,
20th Armored Infantry Battalion, Silver Star citation:
On December 19, 1944 in Noville, Belgium, braving intense enemy fire, First Lieutenant Jacobs, adjutant, voluntarily advanced through five miles of enemy held territory to succeed in obtaining reinforcements and supplies for his besieged unit.[65]

About half a mile away some of Team Desobry's men out on the main Houffalize road were listening with growing trepidation to the fervent exchange of arms occurring at the Bourcy road. The firing had only just begun to subside when three tanks approached their position. Sergeant Jones of the 20th AIB was in a foxhole on a sloping bank beside about seventy-five yards up the road from the roadblock. He thought that the tanks sounded like M4 Shermans and assumed that they were more stragglers coming in. He shouted "Halt" and fired a few rounds from his BAR over the lead vehicle which came to an abrupt halt. Then the sergeant thought that he could hear heard American voices but within moments machine gun bullets were whizzing past his ears. Then he heard someone shout, "Cease fire they're friendly troops." Two Shermans that were supporting the roadblock fired a couple of rounds at the approaching vehicles, which immediately returned fire, knocking them both out. This ultimately determined the identity of the approaching vehicles and a firefight ensued that lasted for over an hour before the defenders fell back on Noville.

THOMAS HOLMES, INTELLIGENCE AND RECONNAISSANCE PLATOON, 54TH ARMORED INFANTRY BATTALION

In the morning I was called to O'Hara's house, and he wanted me to go on a recon to find where the enemy was. I asked "Where do you suspect the enemy is?" and he said "We don't really know." At this time both Noville and Longvilly were in position, but yet the communications were not there to tell me that they were already having evidence of harm there. In fact, I found out later at 10 O'clock in the little town of Wardin, which was off to our left flank, about several hundred yards, the Germans had come there, the Panzer Lehr Division. I was told to go up the highway that led up to Wiltz. I asked how far I should go?" Until you make contact, and O'Hara said whatever you don't become engaged." I had never heard that before other than it meaning my girlfriend. Before we left I saw paratroopers marching in coming down from the main street in Bastogne, where they came from I was not sure. I was glad to see them, but they came in and they did not seem to me that they had anything and word got around that we had to give them anything we could spare. It didn't sound right at the time but we didn't know the whole story. I felt that with them here we now had a chance.

As we rode down the Wiltz Road, we ran into parties of people along the way and they were soldiers and civilians. They were a mixed group. Some of the soldiers didn't have arms in some cases and didn't look much better than the people, who were distraught. Later that day we heard about the killings that happened

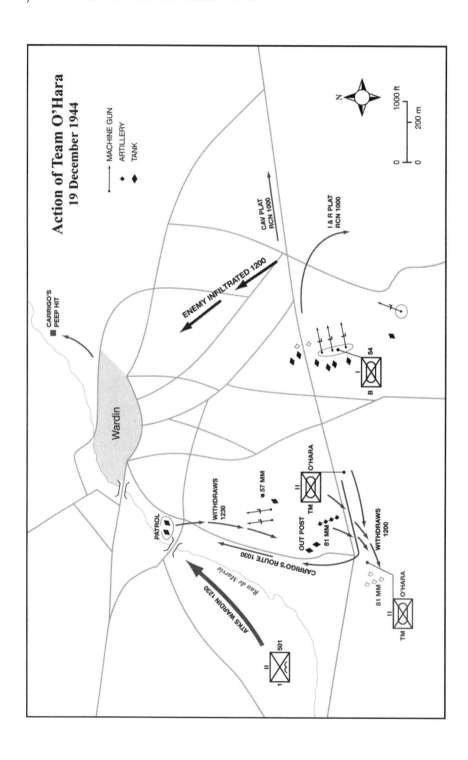

Action of Team O'Hara
19 December 1944

up north of us, we wanted to know more, it was interesting that even with the lack of communications word of something like that spread like wildfire. The men quit coming and we had the road to ourselves. And we were proceeding towards Wiltz, it is about 12 miles from Bastogne, as we neared it we could hear gunfire. As we eased down, we crept as quietly as possible. We were on the high ground on the west side of the river which flows into and through the town of Wiltz. We were observing the troops, Americans leaving on one side, the Germans coming in on the other side over a bridge. The guys were after me about what we could do to knock the bridge down. I said, with a 37mm gun in an armored car, it's idiotic, and I said I told the old man we would come back and report and not become involved here. They wanted to become involved and some of them fired a few shots at the Germans coming across the bridge. I decided to get the hell out of there, so we came out, we had a pretty good idea of the types of troops they were, we started back on the road. Because of the situation, I sent one jeep back and told them to tell O'Hara everything we had seen there. We had three jeeps and an armored car at this point. The armored car had a big radio in it, I had a radio in my jeep. I sure as hell did not want to be in that armored car, I had claustrophobia. We headed back from Wiltz and we came to a three way situation in the road on the way back. I told my men to set up here and anchor the road to keep an eye on things. I put one jeep so that the machine gun had a sweep of the road coming in and the armored car was on the main road so that he could shoot down the road we had just up on. While we're setting up and I was just getting the armored car in the position that I wanted it and Bingo! Here is a German Volkswagen in the center of the road stopped, they're looking at us and we're looking that them, I'm looking that them. It is hushed, no one is saying a word, they are not saying a word, it was weird. All of the sudden someone hollered, hey! They're Germans! We opened up and unfortunately for them it was a trap and it worked like a charm. We were right in the middle of it. The vehicles following them, a Mark IV tank, a big personnel carrier, we had never seen one for real, it had tracks in the back, and it was loaded with infantry people. The guy with the machine on the jeep is firing on them, I had an M1 in my hand and I'm firing, but I'm thinking, let's get the hell out of here. So I'm hollering to them, get out! My jeep came and picked me up and got out of there. We stopped one more time to get a shot at them, and the guy in the M8 fired one round, he missed and we got out of there. The town that the intersection was at was called Bras. When I reported back that night, they seemed to be more interested in Bras than they were in Wiltz. Headquarters was in a very stout house on the high ground in Marvie that looked down on the main road. They had gotten shot out on December 19th, by a shell that burst and spread shrapnel on them, our interpreter was killed and my buddy John McCambridge from New York had been wounded as well. Our machine gun platoon had been overrun and they called us up to regain the position.[66]

At 0730, as weak crepuscular light began to hesitantly illuminate the village of Noville and the surrounding area, an all-encompassing fog descended, restricting visibility to just a few yards. Moreover the Americans had to contend with some serious probing attacks from the Germans. Captain Gordon Geiger, 20th AIB, established a thin screen of infantry around the perimeter of Noville. They were mainly armed with automatic weapons, a few tanks, and assault guns, all strategically placed at key entry points around the village. The infantry were placed to the north and northeast while the lone tanks covered the southern approaches. Even though this was a weak perimeter defense it afforded a decent redoubt to the GI's who were forced to retreat from their roadblocks.

On the road running north towards the village of Vaux, German armor began lumbering down towards one of Captain Geiger's roadblocks.

JERRY GOOLKASIAN, COMPANY B, 3RD TANK BATTALION

The next day, we spotted three tanks on the horizon on the road towards Vaux, the junction that met the main road at Noville. Hildoer, he was a good shot, fired the 75mm, and shot four rounds out there and the fourth round caused the tank to stop. The other two tanks surprising enough turned sideways and with one shot we stopped the second one, and two more shots we stopped the third one. A half-track came down the road, after Captain Schulze congratulated us after taking out the German tanks, so we hopped into our tank and obliterated it.

I was concerned naturally with the amount of shells being fired, it was never ending. The 101st came up around noon, we saw them walk up the road and we turned our turret around because we were told not to be expecting any more ammunition or fuel. This fact did not make us feel too well because we assumed we were going to be surrounded. We turned our turret around because we were not expecting any reinforcements. We knew they were America paratroopers because we trained at Ft. Benning at the same time as they did. The 101st dug in around us, and the shelling continued the rest of the day into the night.[67]

*Private Delmer D. Hildoer, Armored Infantry
(3rd Tank Battalion), Bronze Star citation:*
On 20 December 1944, in the vicinity of Noville, Belgium was gun-

ner in the command of tank acting as the commander. In an attempt to infiltrate into the village, the enemy launched a counterattack against his position. During this attack, by his skill and valiant attempts he was responsible for disabling three enemy tanks. After being wounded seriously about his face and legs as a result of enemy artillery fire, he continued to perform his duties as tank commander until his tank was disabled by enemy fire. The judgment, inspiring leadership and unerring sense of duty displayed by Private Hildoer are in accordance with the highest standards of the military services. Entered military service from Pennsylvania.[68]

Staff Sergeant Calvin O. Jarrell, 420th Armored Field
Artillery Battalion, Posthumous Bronze Star citation:
On December 19, 1944 in the vicinity of Mageret, Belgium, he was assigned as a forward observer with a column of tanks and armored infantry cut off from the main body of his organization. The only possible route of return was through the village of Mageret which was held by the enemy. A plan was made to seize a corner of the village and pass the column through. Sergeant Jarrell was adjusting fire on the village when a shell exploded ten feet from him knocking him down. Dazed and blinded for several minutes, he recovered and dragged the wounded to safe position nearby. He returned and adjusted fire on the village in support of the attack, at times adjusting defensive fires within fifty yards of his own position. These adjustments were made at night in a heavy fog and from a position where his own fire fell between him and his guns. In spite of these difficulties, his fire was so successful that the larger enemy force was prevented from taking that corner of the village then in friendly hands, thus allowing the column to break through to the main body.[69]

With Colonel Cherry setting up his command post several hundred yards south of the small village of Neffe, he sent Lt. Edward Hyduke with tanks from the 3rd Tank Battalion towards the town of Longvilly while Capt. William Ryerson was sent to the town of Mageret. Under the leadership of Lieutenant Hyduke, the tanks of the 3rd Tank Battalion moved towards Longvilly and set up defense of the village. As with the members of Teams Desobry and O'Hara, the tankers had no idea how big of a force they would be facing.

EARL VAN GORP, COMPANY D, 3RD TANK BATTALION

As we went out to Longvilly, we never had communications directly with Col. Cherry, I was under a Captain and some Lieutenants. They never told us what was out there. We had snow on the ground and it was cold, the tank did not provide much heat in there. The town of Longvilly was a smaller town and it was deserted. There was the 28th Infantry there and as they were coming out and we were coming in and said "You'll be sorry" and that was it. We first ran into artillery, there were a lot of trees there and the artillery bursts hit the trees with shrapnel coming down. In our platoon we were spread out and not close to one another at all. We fired mostly with our 50 caliber machine gun, we could see the Germans and pick them off. There were three light tanks together most of the time in Longvilly.

It was in this area that my tank was hit right in the slope(armor) in front by a big shell, it didn't really come into the tank but it spoiled all the wiring and stuff. I was stunned for a minute or two but I was not wounded. My assistant driver was killed by shrapnel when the shell hit. We couldn't drive over one mile an hour out of there but we drove a little while and stayed with the tank. There were other people who saw we couldn't get away and they took care of us and got us out of there. One of my best friends, who was a tank commander too, his tank was hit by a bazooka and burned up while out in Longvilly.[70]

PHIL BURGE, COMPANY C, 55TH ARMORED ENGINEER BATTALION

The next morning it continued to snow and I saw paratroopers from the 101st Airborne Division marching in. They had come in by truck, since it was impossible to drop them in by air. Eventually the whole division of the 101st Airborne was in Bastogne. But we were there first, by a matter of hours.

Since I was with the headquarters, supplies were an issue since they were very low. The 101st set up quarters in a hotel which was already being shelled by German artillery and since we needed supplies, my friend Ray "Flash" Villard and I were ordered to go to there to see what could be done to get us needed supplies. On the way to the 101st's headquarters, I saw something I could not imagine. Remnants of the 28th Division from Pennsylvania were going to the rear, opposite the direction that we were going. Many of the soldiers were wounded and were bandaged up and almost all of them looked like there were in shock!

When we arrived at 101st Airborne's Headquarters I saw General McAuliffe, a one star general at the time, chewing out some paratrooper who apparently was not in proper uniform. It was something about the tie or neckerchief he was wearing. "Who is this guy?" we both thought, not knowing that he would be a national hero for telling the Germans "Nuts!"

After we left the 101st Headquarters the shelling in Bastogne became much more serious and my buddy "Flash" Villard, who was a very devout Catholic, insisted that we stop at a Catholic Church so that he could make peace with his maker. He said to me, "Burge, this is our last day on earth, and I'm going to church, no matter what." So he and I went to church, which was crowded with civilians, even though it was early in the evening. They knew more than we did about the German offensive, since they were all in church. [71]

WILLIAM RICHARD BARRETT, BATTERY B, 420TH ARMORED FIELD ARTILLERY BATTALION

On the 19th we moved back through town and we were moving alongside two story buildings and we had some shell fire and they hit a building and that wounded two or three people. We moved out of our position on the north side of Bastogne. When we left, we left at night. We set up our firing position but we did not have a lot of firing missions because our forward observers can't see anything. You don't know with that bank of fog if you are looking at the muzzle of an 88 or a squad of infantry. So, you're a little on edge, finally we got a few missions. Then we got back to where we were but we were too close, we gotta back up, we had to get high so our shell will drop back on the point we want to put it.

We were firing between our tanks the paratroopers came in on trucks, in our course of combat, we had been to a lot of battlefields and we found a lot of extra equipment. Most of our guys would rather have an M1 Garand than their carbines that they carried because you wanted [a gun you could depend on.] So we had a lot of extra guns. The 101st come in and some of them were picked up off of leave. One paratrooper jumped off a truck wearing his dress uniform and carrying a .45, he jumped off into the snow. We chucked down extra blankets, digging out these extra guns, our sergeant said load up everything, we had extra ammunition and we had extra everything and we were more than glad to share it, and we did share it. From the 19th we had firing missions all around and our observer told us that our last mission that day was for the road we came in on. We had to move since the enemy was getting close, so we backed off a mile or so. . . . We fired everywhere we could in support, and we were running low on everything since we were there for so long, we were waiting for the weather to clear and hearing stories about help breaking through. We heard that Patton was supposed to be coming up from the south with a unit to breakthrough to us, we were sending out a unit to get through the lines to get help.[72]

420th Armored Field Artillery Battalion after action report:

Dec 19

Enemy armored columns reported advancing. Teams Desobry and Cherry heavily engaged. Were alerted for counter attack by American tanks, manned by Nazis GI clothes. Excellent supporting fire given by Battalion FO (forward observer), Lt. Hamer. Lt. Hamer's tank receives two direct hits and burns; three members of crew escape. Lt. Hamer reported as wounded and evacuated and one member of crew last seen inside burning tank. Team O'Hara engaged in afternoon. Elements of 101st Airborne Division pass through to relieve pressure on Teams Cherry and O'Hara. 73rd Armored Field Artillery Battalion of the 9th Armored (less captured and destroyed elements) attached. 58th Armored Field Artillery Battalion reinforcing our fires. Lt Greene, Battery "B", wounded while directing artillery fire. Harassing fires continued all night on known and suspected enemy targets. Corps Commander praises CCB for good job done. Battalion forms infantry and bazooka squads for defense of position. Casualties: 2 Officers and 1 EM(enlisted man) wounded; 1 EM-MIA.[73]

SERGEANT WARREN SWANQUIST, HEADQUARTERS, 3RD TANK BATTALION

The next day we were on the outskirts of the town and a German halftrack came charging in there, they must have thought they still had the town. The halftrack came in and we shot at them but we let them go. There was supposed to be three tanks coming with us, but the 105s (artillery) came in and helped us. I saw many of their panzers including a Tiger. All we could hear were German tanks clamoring around inside the town, they came in and they just turned around and went out, thank God. I was so damn cold I thought I was dead. I had the guys dig me a hole behind the tank and I put my shelter half on the bottom with my rain coat and I told them to back the tank over me and boy did I sleep well that night.[74]

Back in the village of Noville the situation was growing more difficult by the minute. Literally moments after most of the roadblock crews had returned to the village a German 88mm gun began firing out of the fog from the road that ran north from the village to Houffalize. The Germans were aware that this road ran straight through the center of the village and that their artillery was bound to cause havoc there. Within half an hour of the commencement of the firing they had destroyed three halftracks and jeep.

Miraculously no American personnel were killed in this *preliminary* bombardment, preliminary because worse was still to come. Suddenly, at about 0830, two Tiger tanks appeared menacingly out of the fog just twenty yards from Geiger's machine gun positions. Supported by an M4 Sherman and a 51mm gun the Americans opened fire in the direction of the Tigers with everything they had. Both Tigers burst into flames and as the crews attempted to evacuate the roasting hulks they were riddled with a hail of lead. There was some German infantry advancing behind the Tigers, but on seeing what happened to their comrades they melted back into the fog from where they had come. About an hour after this action, at 0930, German armor attempted to infiltrate the thin line from the west. This was where the line was at its most vulnerable. The officer in charge of this sector, 2nd Lt. Eugene Todd, was now in action and felt that the whole German Army was bearing down on his position. When he respectfully requested permission to withdraw Captain Geiger told him to "Hold your ground and fight." Lieutenant Todd reluctantly but courageously complied with this order.

> *Private Ronald F. Sheller, 20th Armored Infantry, Silver Star citation:*
> On 19 December 1944 in the vicinity of Longvilly, Belgium, he was accompanying a group of tank men and infantry men who were attempting to gain entrance to the town. The town was partially in the hands of the enemy and the group was pinned down by enemy artillery and small arms fire. Private Sheller, in an attempt to knock out the enemy gun which was harassing his comrades and preventing their progress, killed an enemy sniper and crawled to a point where he could observe an enemy machine gun emplacement. Advancing under enemy fire, he wiped out the enemy gun single-handed killing two members of the crew and taking the third prisoner. His actions were in accordance with the highest standards of the military service. Enter military service from California.

Battery B, 796th Antiaircraft Artillery Battalion after action report:
19 Dec.
Remained in AA positions around the Artillery and prepared to act in our secondary role as ground defense.[75]

Troop D, 90th Cavalry Reconnaissance Squadron (Mechanized) after action report:

19 December

1ST PLATOON:

At 0400 the town of Noville was attacked by infantry and tanks. The platoon took up defensive at the south end of town of close-in defense. The attack came from the north and north-east, and was repulsed. At 1400 the same day the town was again attacked from the north-east by enemy tanks. One enemy tank was knocked out at 900 yards by a 37mm manned by Tech 5 George S. Coward Jr. The tank burned and the attack was repulsed.

The patrol sent out the evening before to Longchamps, consisting of Sgts James A. Martin and Joseph Crews, was attempting to return to Noville at the time the enemy launched its attack. It was driven back form the town by enemy fire and forced to remain in the woods between Longchamps and Recogne during the day. That night it re-entered Longchamps and returned to Troop Headquarters at Bastogne.

Two more enemy tanks were discovered on the main road north of Noville. Both were driven off by 37mm fire. At 1700 an enemy tank appeared on the crest of the hill north-east of Noville and started to fire into the town. This tank was driven from its position by fire from Tech 5 Coward's 37mm gun.

2ND PLATOON:

At 0300, 2nd Lt. John K. Irvine [platoon leader] took a 1/4 ton with Tech 5 Paul W. Israel, as driver, and Pvt. William A. Beckwith, as gunner, to return to Team Headquarters in the vicinity of Neffe for further orders. Lt. Irvine and Pvt. Beckwith have not been heard of since. Tech 5 Israel was evacuated at Neffe having walked approximately two miles after being wounded. Near Neffe Tech 5 Israel was met by Lt. Col. Cherry and Lt. Treacy who were heading for Longvilly in 1/4-tons. Tech 5 Israel warned them of an enemy ambush in Mageret. Had they not been stopped by Tech 5 Israel they probably would have encountered the same enemy fire.

As dawn broke the platoon vehicles were moved to daylight positions. As the morning progressed things were comparatively quiet. A few intermittent rounds of enemy artillery fell and two dismounted enemy could be observed on a ridge approximately 1,800 yards to the east.

Three enemy soldiers in a house were reported by civilians and men of the platoon apprehended them.

At 1000 Staff Sgt. Paul J. Curran, platoon sergeant, became worried as to the whereabouts of the platoon leader and called Troop headquarters on the FM radio but Lt. Irvine had not reported there. At 1030, S Sgt. Curran and Sgt. Sidney A Balck took a 1/4-ton and started back down the road to find their platoon leader.

As they were about a half mile from the town direct fire from enemy tanks commenced to set afire and destroy tanks and vehicles along the road. Their vehicle off the road, and between two burning tanks, the two sergeants dismounted and attempted to use the radio in the 1/4-ton to warn the platoon of the surrounding dangers. The radio was damaged by fire and no contact could be made. The two sergeants went to high ground where they saw three German tanks on the ridge 1,800 yards east of Longvilly firing into the town and along the road. German infantry was flanking the town form the east and south.

The sergeants then made their way back into the town under the enemy fire and found that the platoon had tried to withdraw their reconnaissance vehicles and after arranging with friendly TDs [tank destroyers] to destroy the equipment, had started to move back to the parent unit in Bastogne.

At 1330, S Sgt. Curran and Sgt Black, certain that all the men had gotten out of Longvilly, started out and dismounted for Bastogne. While going through the woods they found Pvt. Trower, from this platoon, who was lost, and 10 unarmed medics, and led them back to Bastogne. The sergeants reported to the Troop Commander at 1900 and found that Sgt. Jossi, Tech 4 Metzger, Tech 5 Curran, PFCs Moskowitz and Prunier, Pvts Auld and Vaughn were safely in. These men had reported in at 1800, so that 10 men were accounted for at 1900.

The remainder of the platoon under Cpl. Donald W. Everett had joined with an infantry platoon and under Cpl. Everett's gallant leadership aided in cleaning the town of Mageret of enemy.

3RD PLATOON:

Early in the morning one armored car from this platoon was attached to the Intelligence & Reconnaissance platoon with Col.

O'Hara. This patrol proceeded to the town of Doncols and returned. Again the platoon was called on to furnish a 1/4 ton to accompany two of the I & R 1/4-tons to check the crossroad on the main road east of Doncols. Upon reaching the crossroad the patrol began to look for fields of fire because it was reported by civilians that the enemy was in the vicinity. While the patrol was in the vicinity a German personnel carrier appeared at the crossroad. The machine gun in the I & R 1/4 ton started to fire but jammed. The crew of that vehicle then opened up fire with their M3 submachine guns. The 3rd Platoon 1/4-ton then pulled up and opened fire on the vehicle to cover the withdrawal of the I & R 1/4-ton. The enemy vehicle was knocked out and one German soldier was killed.

About 0800 civilians who were entering Bras reported enemy tanks approaching from the north and east. The platoon leader, 2nd Lt. Hubert Schlietinger, took a Machine Gun peep [jeep] and started to check the report of enemy tanks approaching from the north. When he reached about 800 yards north of Bras he could hear the tanks approaching from the east. He returned to the platoon and ordered them to withdraw to Team O'Hara's position immediately, with the peeps first and the two armored cars covered the withdrawal. The platoon leader with his peep remained with the last armored car and before they could leave, the first tank came into view of the fog at about 100 yards range. The tank was unbuttoned and the armored car opened up with 50 cal Machine Gun fire and six rounds 37 mm Anti-Personnel rounds and got way before a return shot was fired. The platoon joined Team O'Hara's position and warned them. The platoon accompanied Team O'Hara when it withdrew to the high ground in the vicinity of Marvie.[76]

Under the cover of a shroud of fog the menacing rumble of approaching tanks and vehicles gave the defenders of Noville the distinct impression that a buildup was underway and that a major attack was imminent. Suddenly, at 1030, the fog lifted like a theatre curtain to reveal a landscape literally covered with German tanks and support vehicles. Some eyewitness accounts state that they saw between 50 and 60 tanks coming in their direction. This was convincing evidence, if it was needed, that, lamentably, Team Desobry was in the path of a whole German division. The fog returned and dissipated intermittently throughout the day adding a further element of jeopardy to the furious encounters that were occurring around Noville. The defenders put every gun they had to the attacking Germans. Even .50 cal machine guns that were completely ineffective against armor were firing continuous streams of tracer rounds that clanged like hailstones on a tin roof as they ricocheted off their targets. The mandibles of perdition were gaping ominously and it did indeed now feel as if the entire German army was descending on Noville.

Theodore Yri, Headquarters Company,
20th Armored Infantry Battalion Bronze Star citation:
Noville, Belgium December 19, 1944
Tech Sergeant Yri, a halftrack driver, dismounted the machine gun from his vehicle and moved it to a forward position where he could cover his platoon front during an enemy attack in the vicinity of Noville, Belgium. He remained in this position constantly for twenty consecutive hours, despite repeated attacks and heavy hostile fire and so skillfully directed his fire that he eliminated a hostile machine gun squad and materially aided in repulsing the enemy with heavy losses.[77]

While Team Cherry was battling it out at Longvilly, Team O'Hara was struggling to gain the upper hand in Wardin, which had the advantage of being closer to Bastogne than the locations of the other two teams. Initially Team O'Hara withdrew slightly to more advantageous and defensible ground when they dug in on the southeastern approach road to Bastogne. They established position in a sector that was between the 501st PIR and the 327th Glider Infantry Regiment (GIR). Team O'Hara was in desperate need of information so to facilitate their intelligence gathering they organized reconnaissance patrols to move forward into the dense fog southeast toward Bras and northeast to Wardin. The 54th AIB approached Bras at around 1140 and observed a lone Volkswagen driving along the main Wiltz – Bastogne road. The patrol commander correctly assumed that this was probably a point vehicle for a column because as the vehicle neared the patrol he ordered his men to open fire. His assumptions were validated when two Mark IV tanks and some halftracks loomed menacingly out of the mist. The patrol did not have suitable weaponry to effectively deal with the German armor so they relayed the information to O'Hara and withdrew as artillery shells from the 420th Armored Field Artillery Battalion began raining down on their targets. Meanwhile, just a few miles east of Bastogne, O'Hara had sent out another patrol. A Willy's jeep containing two GIs approached the tiny village of Wardin. They emerged from the fog, drove to the center of the village near the chapel and stopped the jeep. A few wary villagers left the safety of their cellars and approached the two Americans. Captain Edward A Carrigo and 1st Lt. John Devereaux were out doing a bit of recon for their boss Lt. Col. James O'Hara when they ventured into the Wardin. Carrigo was second in command to O'Hara and the 54th's S-2, and Devereaux commanded the battalion's Company B. A few moments later they parked their vehicle beside the small church in the center of the village as a number of curious locals crept out of their cellars and assembled around the stationary jeep.

Never one to disappoint a gathered host and miss an opportunity to perform Lieutenant Devereaux, an educated man and a noted thespian, mounted the hood of the jeep and began to speak theatrically: "Have no fear" he said in quite good French, "the U.S. army is here to stay. You have nothing to fear, we shall protect you". He concluded with a low Jacobean bow that almost caused him to lose his footing on the stationary vehicle. The impromptu audience cheered, waved and even attempted to embrace the gratified actor and his companion. Well pleased with the result and with the sound of his audience still ringing in his ears Devereaux and Carrigo got back into the jeep and drove east back into the fog from whence they came. Suddenly their attention was diverted by the sound of approaching heavy engines. A shell burst onto their intended path followed by a burst of machine gun fire. The two captains looked at each other in astonishment as muzzle flashes punctuated the grey gloom and machine gun bullets now tore up the ground around the jeep. Then they could make out the silhouette of a vehicle but couldn't ascertain whether it was an American or German one until they heard the voices.

"My God those are krauts," exclaimed Devereaux wrenching the gear leaver into reverse and pressing the gas pedal to the floor. Within seconds they were whizzing back through Wardin at full speed with Devereaux shouting to the locals "Get out of the way you morons the krauts are coming!" A little while later the two officers were reporting their findings to Lieutenant Colonel O'Hara. He listened assiduously as Carrigo described the recent events and then thoughtfully turned to Devereaux with paternal advice. "Lay off the theatricals for the time being son, it's distracting for the locals." Lieutenant Devereaux remained a popular and respected member of Team O'Hara for the duration and he didn't have to prove his worth under fire. He'd already done that.[78]

First Lieutenant John D. Devereaux,
54th Armored Infantry, Silver Star citation:
On 19 December 1944 in the vicinity of Bastogne, Belgium he was in command of a task force in a defensive position when subjected to strong attack by superior enemy forces. After defending the position during the entire day, he received orders to withdraw his men and take up new positions. Executing the movement with conspicuous skill, Lieutenant Devereaux held his new position against numerous attacks by strong forces of enemy infantry and armor. During this defense, his unit destroyed seven enemy armored vehicles and inflicted heavy casualties on enemy infantry. Throughout the action, Lieutenant Devereaux exposed himself to enemy fire in order to personally check the positions and fire of his men weapons. The heroic courage and skillful leadership of this officer was an inspiration to his men and contributed in a large measure to the defense of Bastogne. His actions were in accordance with the highest standards of the military service. Entered military service from New York.[79]

Team O'Hara noted that by noon the fog was beginning to clear a little. Second Lieutenant Theodore Hamer, a forward observer from the 420th AFA, moved his tank to the crest of a hill in front of O'Hara's main position. There were already five tanks on that position but Hamer wanted to get a better view of the enemy so that he could relay the coordinates back to the artillery. Suddenly a high velocity German shell exploded on the front of his tank as he took a direct hit. Another tank on the crest took a shell to the turret that killed the gunner outright. It promptly reversed away from the crest and became stuck in the mud at the bottom of the hill. Failing to identify the source of the German artillery the other tanks also sped down the hill and abandoned the position.

O'Hara expected the Germans to attack westward on the Wiltz-Bastogne road but they had already chosen to bypass this route and move north through the village of Wardin. To accomplish their objective the enemy set about infiltrating O'Hara's front line with small groups of infantry. They used the cover of a small gully to get up close to their intended targets. American artillery would have normally had no problem in breaking up this attack but they were preoccupied with providing support for Team Desobry to the north in Noville. The Germans kept up the pressure on O'Hara's position virtually unimpeded for the remainder of the afternoon.

STAFF SERGEANT STANLEY E. DAVIS,
COMPANY C, 21ST TANK BATTALION

The night of the 18th and the early morning hours of the 19th passed relatively quietly with the stragglers mostly from the 28th [Division] coming through our positions until 10:00a.m. C company went into the battle with close to a full company of three tank platoons of five tanks each commanded by a lieutenant. I was a Tank Commander in the second platoon. On the morning of the 19th we had the second platoon to the south of the Wiltz road and the third platoon on the north of the road with platoons of B Company 54th AIB dug in positions with the first platoon a couple of hundred yards to our rear and the 105mm assault gun in the position with the third platoon. In the morning after a breakfast of K rations I walked across the Wiltz road to talk with a good friend of the mine, Pat Corcoran in the third platoon area. He was very concerned about what was going on but I knew that O'Hara had sent out some recon elements when the stragglers had stopped coming so I was not too worried at that time. While we were talking an infantry anti-tank crew pulled up on the road just a little east of us and set up their 57mm anti-tank gun as part of our defense. But shortly after that they came back, hooked up their gun and headed west to Bastogne. I decided at that time that I had better get back into my tank and we had all better get ready to fight a battle. Later in the morning one or more German heavy tanks came towards our position on my left and set fire to an artillery FO tank in the third platoon area and hit one of our tanks in which my friend Pat was the tank commander. Don Nichols, the gunner of our 101mm tank remembers knocking out a German tank at this time. The source of the German tank fire was not visible at this time. The source of the German tank fire was not visible to the second platoon at this time. Corcoran fired his 75mm at the attacking tank and hit him but he [the German tank] kept firing and hit Corcoran's tank in the turret killing his gunner and wounding him [Corcoran]. This caused his driver to put it in reverse and back up until the vehicle bogged down and the crew was able to get out.

The second platoon was under attack from the woods directly to our front about this same time from varying strength of forces but we were able to hold our ground without suffering any losses and the Germans started swinging around to our right flank. Early in the afternoon a strong infantry force came up to our left rear in uniforms a little different from ours but they turned out to be I Company of the 501st Parachute regiment of the 101st Airborne Division. They were ordered to take Wardin but about the time they got into town a strong tank infantry force of Germans forced them to pull back as best they could. A couple of C Company tanks repositioned themselves to cover the exits from Wardin. With strong forces to our front, nobody on our right flank and heavy attacks on our left flank Lt Col. O'Hara obtained permission to pull back to a better defensive position on the high ground just east and north of Marvie. This position better aligned us with the total defensive positions on our right and left. The second platoon of C Company and a platoon of infantry from the 54th AIB served as rear guard and we pulled back without any more losses. The German forces made many attacks on this new line but they never got any closer to Bastogne on the Wiltz road. The 420th Field Artillery Battalion provided excellent cover for this pullback.[80]

TECH SERGEANT THADDEUS KRASNOBORSKI, HEADQUARTERS, 420TH ARMORED FIELD ARTILLERY BATTALION

We started firing, on the 19th, as soon as the batteries were in place. Targets were being called in at a fast rate. My plots showed (I was HCO in the Fire Direction Center) the enemy fanned out in front of us.

Each successive set of coordinates called in by the FOs had ever-decreasing ranges until the enemy was just yards in front of our guns. This necessitated extreme elevation of the howitzers and we needed to move back to give our guns more freedom to bear down on their targets.[81]

DONALD NICHOLS, COMPANY C, 21ST TANK BATTALION

At daybreak a very heavy fog had moved in and visibility was very limited, 75 to 100 yards. About 10 A.M. the fog would lift and come back down. At this time when it lifted again the forward observer tank, about 75 yards to my right front, burst into flames. Sgt. Bulano, the loader, climbed out of our turret running towards this burning tank to help its crew. Due to the enemy fire at this time we yelled for him to return as we needed him also. The tank to my left front about 75 yards was hit as it was backing up and its gunner was killed. It stalled out as it hit a small building behind it and its crew bailed out and went to the rear.

No one in my tank had observed any enemy tank or force. We were slightly hidden as the terrain was not completely flat but slightly rolling like farm country is. As mentioned the fog would rise and fall. At one point in searching with my gunner scopes, I saw a Tiger tank point its nose out of the pine woods about 600 yards to my front, fire and back up.

I told other crew members but they were unable to see or identify it. After several times of this happening, the tank commander told me to fire at it and adjust my own fire. My first round was a littler short and he, the Tiger, backed up again. My next rounds were over or ricocheted off the trees. One hit the Tiger turret, bounced off but did not explode. These were high explosive shells. I finally told the loader, Sgt. Bulano, to load the HEAT (high explosive anti-tank), fired and hit the Tiger as it was rolling back into its pine tree hideout. Saw black smoke and figured it was out. Did not see it or hear from it again. Kill was later confirmed.

More and more enemy fire was coming across our front at the 500 yard distance from a hidden position. We had other "C" Co. tanks ahead and to my right front. To my left front at several hundred yards was a line of trees that hid another road or trail. I began to see vehicle movement but the vehicles were too obscured to identify who's they were.

We reported by radio and were soon told to move our position to the road and to the rear. Probably moved about a mile or less back and set up a road block on the side of the road with the other "C" Co. tanks joining us. We could still see the smoke and explosions from the burning forward observer's tank.

After a short while, there was a German tank firing his 88 shot down the road narrowly missing our tank. Eighty-eight near misses sound like a freight train passing by at high speed. We were ordered to pull back to a new position of Marvie which was a small village close to and east of Bastogne. We were posted on one of the main roads into Bastogne. Task Force O'Hara was located in a farm house across the road close to where my tank was positioned, to guard that road. One other "C" Co. tank was posted next to me and across the road several more were posted.

Not much activity the rest of that day or the next as the Germans were trying to gain access to Bastogne on the other routes. Within a couple of days, probably 20th or 21st, they mounted an attacking force on Marvie. This was on the other side of the road from me in more of a hidden position and some trees between me and that battle. Although I could hear it I could not see it.

One of our tanks was hit and knocked out with casualties. However the enemy column of a couple of tanks, half-track with infantry was destroyed. One German lead vehicle was able to get into Marvie but had to retire from there. Meanwhile we, or Bastogne, were being surrounded and some of our tanks were deployed to other hot spots for defense of that area. There were more "C" Co. casualties of men and materials.

One of my friends that was in the area and his tank had to report to O'Hara's command post for orders and came over to see me and wanted to know if I knew that we were surrounded. I said, "Yes". We talked for a few minutes and decided we should feel sorry for the "Poor Bastards" that had us surrounded. We got a laugh out of that.[82]

———

To the east, along the Belgian-Luxembourg border, German troops had scattered the American's hurried defensive positions. To the north of Bastogne the entire 2nd Panzer Division, along with elements of the 116th *Windhund* (Greyhound) Division, was currently bearing down on Noville and the U.S. line was faltering badly. General Middleton had hoped that the CCB, 10th AD, teams would be able to impede if not entirely halt the German advance, but as previously mentioned the German panzers were adopting secondary routes and avoiding the main ones. The VIII Corps commander had quite seriously overestimated the potential of these teams to fulfill their tasks and at the same time underestimated the force and vigor of the German attacks. Despite this substantial disparity in Middleton's expectations and reality, the meager American forces were able to quite a large extent confound the momentum of the German advance.

LIEUTENANT CARL W. MOOT JR., HEADQUARTERS, 420TH ARMORED FIELD ARTILLERY BATTALION

Just before dawn the flow of vehicles and soldiers coming back past our tanks increased continuously. There were all kinds of vehicles from jeeps and I & R cars to halftracks and medium tanks. After daylight this column toward the rear was jammed up, bumper to bumper, and moving very slowly. Some of the soldiers going by asked us what we were going to do and we told them we had come up to help stop the Germans. They said we were crazy, that there were thousands of Germans just behind them. Most of them appeared to be badly demoralized and just trying to get away from the fighting. Shortly after dawn the fighting started, and we began receiving mortar and/or artillery fire along with some rocket fire and a lot of small arms fire. Soon there was an anti-tank gun or two firing into the jam of vehicles from a direction about northeast of Longvilly. However I could not see these anti-tank weapons and I could not determine their position close enough to direct any artillery fire on them. I think it was purely luck that our tank platoon had stopped and pulled off to the left side of the road the night before, in a place where the anti-tank guns could not fire on any of us. They were, however, knocking out vehicles on the road about 50 yards in each direction from our nearest tanks. A medium tank pulled off the road opposite our tanks toward the east (away from us) and was knocked out after he got stuck about 100 ft. from the road. There were a lot of men on foot about this time heading toward the rear, many of them from vehicles that had been knocked out or abandoned in the traffic jam. Some of the M-7's from the artillery outfit on our left flank started trying to move out and back down the road. I don't think any of them got out, but it is possible some of them made it.

Shortly after the anti-tank firing started, which was fairly early in the morning, German infantrymen could be seen coming over a hilltop to our northeast, moving toward Longvilly. They came over the hilltop standing up in full view. One of them, apparently an officer, was standing on the highest point and looking down all around. This was my first artillery target. The other tanks with me began firing on the hilltop, mostly machine gun fire, with a few high explosive roads from their big guns. Using my improvised map I finally got an artillery round that I could identify, adjusted it on the hilltop, and called for a battalion barrage. This was fairly early in the morning and I got the entire 420th Bn. (18 guns). The artillery fire covered the hilltop, and this stopped all visible movement over the hill. I did not see any Germans on it again. From our position, jut southeast of the town of Longvilly, we could not see the buildings in town below a level of six to eight feet above the street level, but we could see the upper parts of nearly all the buildings in town.

I thought we had some armored infantry men from our team in the town, but I was not sure of this. There was a lot of small arms firing in town, both German and American machine guns could be heard, but it was impossible from my position to tell how the fighting was going. I never saw any of the 10th Armored Div. infantrymen that day, so if they were in town they were apparently killed or captured. Periodically some German soldiers were seen to our right front or northeast, they were gunned down or driven back by our tank machine guns while still several hundred yards away from us.

By late morning (10 or 11 AM) most of all of the troops that were retreating past our positions had gone on by us so that our tank platoon was more or less alone. One side of the road was jammed up, bumper to bumper, with knocked out or abandoned vehicles beginning about 50 yards past our position and extending down the road to the rear as far as I could see. Many of them were burning. At this time, I do not think there had been a single casualty in the tank platoon I was with. All of the tanks were firing steadily mostly machine guns. We had not seen any German tanks. Sometime in this period I fired another artillery barrage, but I cannot remember what the target was. I was monitoring the 420th Bn. fire direction radio channel continuously. Since I first fired the Battalion Artillery early in the morning, the calls for artillery fire had increased steadily. It seemed like every officer in the battalion had a target. The fire direction team had been split so that the second time I requested fire all I could get was one battery (6 guns). The other two batteries were each busy firing on other targets.

Apparently we were causing a big problem for the Germans because the incoming mortar, artillery and rocket fire began to increase steadily along with firing of flares by the Germans. I thought at the time that this was mostly rocket fire because there was a lot of blast or explosion, but the shell fragments seemed to be small or light weight. The medium tanks were very rarely closed up tight (buttoned up), usually the tank commander kept his hatch open and looked out over the top of the turret. This was because vision was very limited out of our periscopes. At that time the aerial bombardment kept increasing in intensity until I could not see anything but dust and smoke, then I buttoned up the hatch on my tank. The intensity of the bombardment increased until no individual explosions could be distinguished, it was one continuing solid sound of explosion. This went on for what seemed like a long time but was probably only a few minutes then it all stopped suddenly.

I immediately opened my hatch and looked around. I could see nothing but smoke and dust. This began to clear off shortly and the first thing I saw was the nearby road sign that said "Longvilly". The sign was cut all to pieces by shell fragments, and was barely legible. I could also see that my tank was covered with dirt form the blasting, and our duffel bags that were on the back deck of the tank were all tattered and torn by shell fragments. However, my 50 Caliber machine gun (mounted just in front of my hatch) was not damaged. The smoke and dust cleared in a few minutes and it appeared that none of the other tanks with me were seriously damaged either. None of them were on fire.

When the smoke and dust was about cleared a wave of German soldiers came over a hill to our right flank or to the east and slightly south. The hill top was not too close to us, possibly 200 yards or more. About 10 or 12 Germans came running as fast as they could toward us. They were carrying only panzerfausts and were apparently trying to get close enough to knock our tanks out with them. This was a disastrous mistake for them. All of our tanks were still fighting, and the Coaxial 30 Caliber machine guns were very accurate at that range. All of the German soldiers were killed more than 100 yards from us, before any of them could fire his panzerfaust.

Not long after the artillery barrage stopped I remember that a lone German soldier came toward us from the town of Longvilly to our left front. He did not seem to realize what was going on. He carried a light machine gun casually under his army with the barrel pointing into the ground. Our coaxial machine gun was pointed away from him, toward the panzerfaust attack so I tried to hit him with my 45 submachine gun (grease gun). I emptied a clip of ammunition without hitting him or even rousing him from his casual stroll. He was getting close to us and I was about to have my gunner traverse around and get him, when one of the other tanks cut him down. I remember he acted very surprised as the bullets hit him, at that time he was only about 100 ft. from me.

Sometime in the early afternoon I saw some German vehicles moving, quite a distance away to my right or to the east. Visibility was not good, but I could see vehicles passing on a short stretch of road. I directed my last artillery barrage at that target. By that time there were so many artillery fire missions that the batteries had been split into platoons and each platoon was firing on a different target. For this fire mission all I got was one platoon (2 guns, from "B" Battery I think). Visibility was so poor that I could not see if I had knocked out any vehicles. I did get the artillery adjusted on the place I wanted it however.

As time passed we continued to be attacked by the foot soldiers carrying panzerfausts, over the hill on our right flank, always over the same hill and only a few men at one time (no more than twelve). This seemed to be a very foolish thing for the Germans to do, because those soldiers did not have a chance to make it as long as we could still fire our machine guns. All together there were four or five of those groups of soldiers who came over the hill at us in the same manner. Each time they were all cut down by our machine gun fire before they got close enough to fire their weapons. Not a single panzerfaust was fired. At the end, the hillside was quite a grisly scene with approximately 40 or 50 dead Germans laying out there. Our machine gun ammunition belts contained tracer and incendiary bullets and a lot of the bodies had their clothing burning and smoking from these bullets.

As the afternoon progressed our position became more and more insecure. The town of Longvilly was in German hands and we were receiving small arms fire from there. Also the sound of battle now extended back along our flanks, well to the rear of our position. No other American troops could be seen other than those in our tank platoon. Apparently everyone else had retreated at least a quarter of a mile behind us. The Lieutenant in command of the tank platoon came over to my tank and we discussed the situation. We both thought that we would soon be cut off from the rear if we did not do something. We were getting very low on machine gun ammunition also. The Lieutenant said he was going to request permission to retreat, and returned to his tank.

He could not contact anyone in command and returned to my tank, and I tried to contact Lt. Hyduke or Col. Cherry on my radio without any success. He then decided to take the responsibility to retreat back down the road if possible. We had to use the road because it was too muddy to go overland. At that time all of the tanks in the platoon were still in fighting condition, there may have been some casualties, but all the tanks were firing and capable of moving. All five of us in my tank were untouched.

In a short time the tanks jockeyed around and the lead tank started back down the road toward Mageret, with just enough room to get by the other knocked out vehicles on the road. As the first tank came out of our protected position, he immediately came under fire from the anti-tank gun across town. Before he got more than 100 yards he was hit and the tank started burning. The engine kept running and the driver tried to get the tank off of the road, but the fire became too intense and the burning tank was left squarely blocking the road,

Shortly after this the Lieutenant in charge told me that they were going to abandon the remaining tanks and attempt to get out on foot. My crew and I discussed abandoning the tank. We could see no way to drive it out. We checked for something to disable it or destroy it so the Germans could not use it. There were no thermite grenades, but we had some smoke and fragmentation grenades. The sure way would have been to put thermite grenades in the gun, ammunition compartment, and on the engine. I decided to use a fragmentation grenade and try to set it on fire. We got out submachine guns (grease guns) and proceeded to leave the tank. Shortly before or after my crew (4 men) left the tank, I fired the last of my 50 cal. machinegun ammunition into the town of Longvilly. I was the last to leave the tank and before I got out I opened the gasoline valve on the gasoline generator (little Joe) inside, and left gasoline running out into the tank. As I left I threw the grenade back down into the hatch, hoping it would start a fire. I immediately came under small arms fire, and to this day I do not know if the tank caught fire or not.

As I hit the ditch on the west side of the tank it seemed like a hundred riflemen were shooting at me, however, I really think it was only one or two rifles and possibly a burp gun (German submachine gun). I crawled down the ditch about 100 yards or so with the rifle fire hitting the shoulder of the road just a few inches above me. By then I was opposite a line of disabled vehicles on the road, bumper to bumper. I looked back toward Longvilly and I could see that I was wide open to the small arms fire, the ditch was too shallow. The bullets were hitting into the road shoulder inches above my helmet and only inches from my face, which was flat on the ground. I decided to run for the knocked out vehicles in the road, and try to get behind them away from the rifle fire. As I raised up to run I was hit in the left arm and left buttocks by bullets.

Neither wound was very serious and I made it behind the vehicles without further injury. My assistant tank driver (don't remember his name) had seen my predicament and he was waiting for me there, he was unhurt. After seeing that I could move OK we started down the road, behind the vehicles and away from the small arms fire. One of the other tanks came up behind us and we moved in front of it for more cover. An anti-tank gun began firing at this tank, but only high explosive ammunition, apparently they were out of armor piercing ammo.

We came to the burning tank that was blocking the road and stopped. We were talking to the tank crew when a round of high explosive hit in the road behind the tank and shell fragments came through under the tank and hit my assistant driver's foot, injuring it so that he could barely put any weight on it, but I was not hit. The tank crew said they were going to try to get their tank out that they would not abandon it. We said we were leaving, they were still OK and trying to get past the burning tank the last time I saw them. We could not get by the burning tank so we ducked through the other vehicles and back down into the ditch again. At that point we were almost out of range of the small arms and the ditch was deeper. No small arms fire was hitting close to us as we crawled back down the ditch. Soon we came to a culvert in the road where there was water running and a hole of water about 2 ft deep. Rather than expose ourselves, we stayed in the ditch and got all wet.

The Lieutenant who was in command of the tank platoon was lying at the edge of the water hole near the culvert. He had been shot through the body and was badly hurt. He said he was too badly wounded to go on and he did not want us to try to help him. He asked us to send the medics for him if we ever caught up with them. We left him there and went on down the ditch. Water was running in the ditch there and I remember being worried because there was gasoline on the water from some of the vehicles along the road, and also some of them were burning. I was afraid the ditch would catch fire, but it did not while we were there. Soon we came to a place where there were a few houses (one or two on each side of the road). We were well out of range of the small arms, however a round of high explosive artillery fire hit the bank some distance from me and a shell fragment cut across my right boot and cut a gash on the top of my foot, but not deep enough to be a serious injury. My assistant driver was ahead of me. The ditch ended at the houses and there was a big jam up of vehicles on the road between the houses.

The vehicles were knocked out and completely blocked the road but none of them were burning. The assistant driver jumped up into the road and disappeared into this traffic jam. In a moment I followed him and came out on the other side to find him sitting in a jeep that had been abandoned. He had the engine running and said, "Get in Lieutenant and lets get the hell out of here!" I got in and we wormed out way through the other vehicles and moved quickly back toward Mageret. In a short distance we cleared the disabled and abandoned vehicles, the road was clear and we had seen no one, Germans or Americans.

As we came over a rise we found the American soldiers that were trying to get back through Mageret. There were quite a few soldiers and vehicles just on the outskirts of town I did not know the Captain who had taken command and I do not know if he was a 10th Armored Division Officer or from one of the other units. The soldiers were a mixture of several units. We talked to some Medics about going back after the lieutenant we had left in the ditch, but I do not think they made any effort to do it.

I think it was probably about 5 PM when we got back to the soldiers at Mageret, because it was not long before it got dark. We gave the jeep to someone and got into a half-track with some other wounded soldiers and laid down. There was a lot of gunfire of all kinds going on around us, with the most intense of it in Mageret as darkness set in. The group we were with was trying to fight it's way around Mageret on the northwest side, on some poor dirt roads as I remember it. The vehicles were fairly close together, and we were on the edge of town shortly after dark when suddenly a medium tank, only about twenty feet behind the half-track we were in, was hit by an antitank round. Only one round was fired, but the tank immediately burst into flames, burning all over and lighting up the area like daylight. All the other men in the half-track left immediately, but my assistant driver was asleep or nearly passed out and I had trouble getting him up and out of the half-track. All the time I was expecting the next round of anti-tank fire to hit us. However we got out and there never was another round fired.

The tank was the only vehicle hit. The two of us struggled up the column about 100 yards and got back into another half-track. We had quite a bit of trouble moving, my assistant driver's foot was really bothering him, he could barely walk and I was pretty weak from loss of blood and lack of sleep. The rest of the night is rather vague. We moved around looking for a route around Mageret, hitting road blocks, detouring and trying another route most of the night.[83]

MAJOR WILLIS D. CRITTENBERGER, HEADQUARTERS BATTERY, 420TH ARMORED FIELD ARTILLERY BATTALION

The next afternoon after we had been fighting there for 18 or 20 hours, the 101st Airborne Division dismounted and started marching along and we saw them marching by. These guys walked into battle with no helmets or overboots, and some of them didn't even have weapons so we tried to help them. They were gung-ho fighters but so were we! The first couple of days we had support from the rear and we were resupplied. They liked the armor a lot because we had tanks, jeeps, trucks, and gasoline. We had a good relationship with the 101st.

We were lucky in the armored division, we had gasoline and an engine so you could stick your C-ration on the manifold to warm it up, it was the poor infantry who had it tough.[84]

Out in Longvilly Team Cherry were experiencing severe problems. Granted they were the best equipped of the three teams but they had no idea what was waiting for them at their predetermined destination. They had expected to link up with CCR and block the advancing German divisions but things didn't go exactly according to plan because within a few short hours they realized that the task was going to be more difficult than they had anticipated. That morning encircled commanders out at Longvilly were coming under so much significant pressure from repeated German attacks that they decided to attempt to fall back on the village of Mageret, unaware that this place already had been overrun by the Germans. Consequently the forward elements of the team fought a rear guard action while the main body attempted to move back to the west. As the column pulled back they were joined by the 58th Field Artillery Battalion who provided artillery support and aimed their guns at German tanks that were at that moment in hot pursuit. Falling back on Mageret was easier said than done because vehicles from the 9th Armored Division's CCR were still blocking the westbound roads. In the course of the afternoon the situation went from bad to worse when the rear guard was attacked by the 26th Volksgrenadier Division's 77th regiment from the southeast while the 2nd Panzer Division came at them from the northeast. The retreating column now found itself stuck on the road with its vulnerable right flank prone to enemy attack. Then the situation deteriorated even further when Panzer Lehr, supported by units from the 26th Volksgrenadier, began emerging from the fog and hitting the column from the south. The team attempted a fighting withdrawal but by now the road west was completely blocked with abandoned U.S. vehicles. About an hour after the initial German attacks on the column remnants of the team somehow managed to reach the outskirts of Mageret.

During the ensuing battles, with the main column leading, elements of Team Cherry arrived in Mageret and attempted to clear the road to Bastogne. Savage house to house fighting ensued as they tackled the significantly larger German force that had occupied most of the village. At 0300 on the morning of 20 December after sustaining heavy losses, with the support of airborne troopers laying down covering fire, the remnants of Team Cherry managed to stagger into Bizory then Foy before finally making it back to Bastogne.

———

In an attempt to completely envelop the village of Noville the Germans had launched a concerted all-out attack. The defenders managed to repel the first wave but they correctly sensed that more was on the way. The enemy then changed tactics and arranged their armor in a semi-circle on the higher ground beyond the village perimeter. Once in place they unleashed a crippling barrage of shells that rained down on the defenders. Earlier on Desobry had requested permission to retreat to Foy but this had been denied by Colonel Roberts who informed him that the situation demanded resilience. Roberts could have granted permission for a withdrawal but he based his decision on the possible improvement in the situation that would probably occur when the paratroopers got up there. He'd initially been reluctant to respond to Desobry's request. That was until the CCB commander was on his way to consult with General McAuliffe and he encountered the 101st assistant division commander, Brig. Gen. Gerald J. Higgins, and explained the developing situation to him. Higgins ordered the 1st Battalion, 506th PIR, under Lt. Col. James L. LaPrade, to proceed directly to Noville. He then placed the 2nd and 3rd battalions in reserve to the north of Bastogne on the road to Noville.

With this under his hat Roberts returned to his CP and relayed the information to Desobry. He instructed Desobry to use his own judgment concerning the withdrawal but assured him that reinforcements were on their way north as he spoke.

MAJOR WILLIAM DESOBRY 20TH ARMORED INFANTRY BATTALION

Along about 4:00 in the morning off to the east at one of our outposts we heard a heck of a fire fight start up on the road from the town of Bourcy to Noville. There was a real racket and it lasted oh about 15-20 minutes or so. I went out to the crossroads where the road from Bouresches came in and stood by the church there, along with my S-3, and in came the outpost pulling back into town. Now that was in accordance with orders. We had three outposts out and their instructions were that if the Germans came down the road that they were guarding to . . . take them under fire and stop them, but as soon as they could to pull back into the defensive line in the town.

Anyway they came up and that saved us because now the artillery could fire coordinates, off maps rather than guess or by God. We did call for artillery support, but we didn't get very much. Now the reason we didn't get very much is that while we were fighting at Noville, off to the east of us at a town called Longvilly, about 10 miles away, Task Force Cherry, part of our Combat Command was engaged

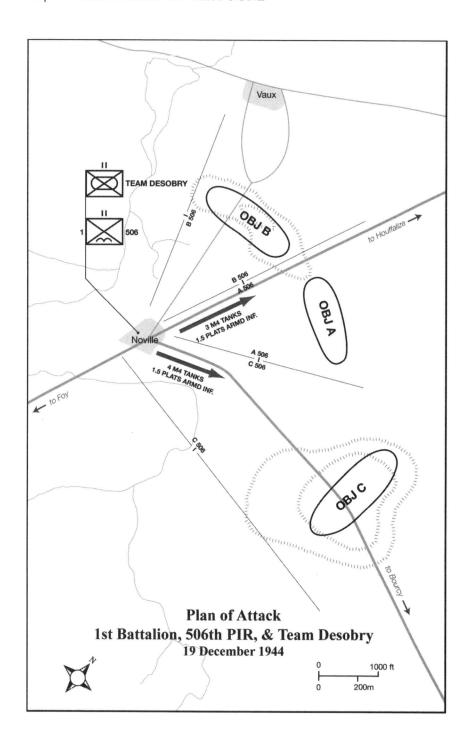

Plan of Attack
1st Battalion, 506th PIR, & Team Desobry
19 December 1944

in a desperate fight, which I will describe later on and they required artillery support. To the south of Cherry, about 6 or 7 miles, was Task Force O'Hara and although they weren't heavily engaged, there were some Germans down there and they had requirements for artillery. So basically we were competing for the fires of the 420th Field Artillery Battalion with Hank Cherry, Jim O'Hara and of course, myself. So you get what you can get in a situation like that. Now, Cherry was actually having at the point in time, more desperate straits than I was. But anyway we did get some artillery fired, but not like what were used to normally. When we fought down in the Saarland and northern France, it was not uncommon for my task force to be supported by 5 or 6 field artillery battalions when I got into a fight. They would all shoot for me—155s and 8-inch guns. Now we were really down to the bare bone. We could hear the Germans starting this attack and it was coming from the north in the fog and a little bit to northeast. You could tell there was a lot of them out there. Well, as the rounds got closer to us, the fog started to lift a little bit. The ground fog starts to burn off a little bit from the sun in the morning and that was happening, lo and behold, we looked out there and the whole hillside in front of us was literally covered with German tanks and half-tracks. This huge attack was taking place and we started to fire at what we could see and so on. This attacked lasted just about all morning. One German tank got into the town—got in that close—others got within 50 meters, 100 meters. The fight by the way, from where we could see on the ridge to where we were, was a distance of about 700 meters. But everybody and his brother took the Germans under fire and we brought the tank destroyers out and they took them under fire and after about an hour, two hours of very intense fighting the Germans broke the attack off and moved back right behind the ridge. We continued fighting them. What they would do then was to start probing us. We would get an attack down on the Bourcy road by small units and we would knock that off; and then we would get an attack from the northeast across the ridge line and open terrain and we would knock that off; and then we would get one from the northwest and we would knock that off. We did not get a concerted attack like the first one, where their entire force, whatever it was, came at us. The German artillery oddly enough and I found out later why, wasn't all that intense in the first big attack. There was a lot of mortar fire and things like that, but not all that much artillery. But later on it really started to come in on us. Since we were concentrated in a small village town, all they had to do was shoot at the town and they would hit something and so we started to take a lot of casualties from mortar fire, artillery fire and so on. Then the Germans were firing an awful lot of automatic weapons down the roads into the town and so we were under intense fire almost continu-

ously. As I say we were taking a lot of casualties and so we had an evacuation problem. We started losing right off the bat, vehicles, particularly half-tracks—tanks no, but half-tracks, which were vulnerable to artillery and mortar fire. We started losing those and there were a few of them burning around the town. So we brought our maintenance guys out. Our service company was, back in Bastogne and we brought our maintenance guys with the tank recovery equipment and started evacuating the shot-up vehicles on back to the rear. We did that all during this battle and all day long. So this was the type of fighting we were doing; an attack from the north and knocked out, an attack from the northeast and knocked out. This went on and on. We had radio contact and also CW contact with Combat Command whose headquarters was back in Bastogne, oh! About twelve miles away I guess. There was a big ridge running behind us which sort of made our voice radio sort of sporadic. We were in contact with them and I got a weird radio message from the exec back there, a lieutenant colonel. After we had knocked off this big attack and this attack to the north—and we had reported all this—he got me on the radio and instructed me to send a patrol to the town of Houffalize, which was about 20 miles to the north of us. I said, "My gosh we have been fighting the Germans who are blocking the road to Houffalize and he insisted that I send a patrol. If I sent a patrol to Houffalize, I would have had to go through the whole daggone German Army to get there, but anyway I was getting crazy orders like this all the time. Well, with the losses that we were taking and the fact that we were being attacked from the north and from the east, and there was nothing behind us and nothing on the flanks, and with visibility being sporadic, I realized that the town of Noville was in sort of a bowl, almost a semi-bowl. We were on low ground and all around us were these ridgelines about 700 and 1000 yards away and the Germans controlled these ridgelines. That made us extremely vulnerable to the Germans, particularly tank fire, artillery fire and mortar fire. To the rear of us, a couple of miles back, was the little town of Foy and it had a huge dominant ridge behind the town, very high ground. It was a about 8-9 miles from Bastogne and that appeared to us, from where we were sitting, to be excellent defensive terrain where we would then be positioned on the high ground. Anybody trying to attack us while at that position would be on the low ground and would reverse the situation. I asked permission, because I had been told to hold Noville, to withdraw to the ridgeline behind Foy and I was told to wait. Then I was told shortly after noon, "No, I had to stay where I was and was not allowed to come back." So there we were. Shortly thereafter our Combat Commander, who was obviously worried about us, asked what we were fighting. I told them a reinforced tank battalion because that is all I could imagine; I couldn't imagine beyond that.

And so we were told that a parachute battalion from the 101, who arrived at Bastogne was on the way to reinforce us. I was asked at that point in time what we would do. Well, since I had been denied the permission to go back to the high ground at Foy, and I knew I was in an untenable position in the town of Noville, and taking a lot of losses from this fire that was coming from these ridgelines and if I was going to defense this place, I had to get out and knock those Germans off the ridgelines. There was no way I could stay in Noville and stay forever. It was going to be case of either taking the ridgelines or I was just going to run out of men if I stayed there. Even if they didn't overrun us in their attacks. So I said, "Well if this battalion will come up, "and as I said, I thought we were fighting a tank battalion plus, "and if the battalion commander would agree, we would counterattack and drive the Germans off this ridgeline and set up our defense up there." So they said, "OK," or whatever they say in a case like that. They left it up to me and I was told that the parachute guys were walking up from Bastogne since they had no transportation.

It was a helluva of a long walk. So I sent a jeep back to get the Battalion Commander, so I could give him the situation on where we were and what we wanted to do and they brought him up very quickly. He was a wonderful guy. His name was LaPrade. A big tall guy and very confident. He brought with him a couple of officers and I went over the situation with him and showed him the German positions and you could see them. The Germans were attacking at the time. He agreed that we couldn't stay in Noville and that we ought to go ahead and launch an attack and take that ridgeline. So we dreamed up a scheme to put his paratroopers with some tanks and armor infantry and one outfit would go out to the northeast and get that ridgeline, and two other companies would go out to the north and northwest and secure this whole ridgeline. We estimated that the earliest that we could attack, taking into consideration the length of time his column would take to get up to us, would be 1400. So then we sent more vehicles back and brought his company commanders and people like that up and I took them on a reconnaissance of the area, the company commanders. That was real hairy. There were about six of them and we jumped from one building to the other, dodging artillery barrages and mortar barrages and so on. We completed the reconnaissance with the troops still marching up. I learned from LaPrade that these guys had come out of Holland from that big Holland jump at Nijmegen and were back at a rest area near Paris, down near Paris, to be refitted. They had lost a lot of equipment and were getting replacements and then they had been suddenly pulled out and rushed up here. A lot of their guys had been on pass in Paris, like they normally would, and they came back off pass and jumped on trucks for Bas-

togne. So a lot of their guys still needed equipment and some didn't have weapons. A lot of them who had weapons had no ammunition. Some of their officers who were on reconnaissance with me, and some of them who came up later, were even in the old pinks and greens. They didn't have time to get into their battle uniforms. Some had low quarters shoes and these guys were marching up the road. Well, if you will recall before we came up here, we had been getting set to go on a big offensive to the Rhine River and having had considerable combat experience by now, we really didn't have all that much confidence in the supply system. So in our service company, we had overloaded those two and one-half ton trucks with spare weapons, ammunition, fuel, you name it – we were really loaded. Now that was fortunate as heck because here we were in this situation. We sent for the service company and moved their vehicles up in the vicinity of the town of Foy, out in front of this column. They put their vehicles on each side of the road. As these paratroopers marched in single columns on either side of the road, like they always marched in those days, a guy would come by the truck and yell that he needed an M-1 rifle, he needed a BAR, or he needed a carbine or whatever or ammunition and my guys would toss him the weapons and ammunition and maybe a helmet or whatever the heck they needed and so on and that's the way we re-equipped the battalion. Here is a battalion coming out of Bastogne on the approach march to make an attack and this is the way they are getting some of their equipment. Well, these guys marched on up the road and we had convinced the Combat Command for this attack to fire a brief artillery preparation along the ridgeline since it was exposed and the fog now at this time was sort of lifting and coming back and lifting and coming back. We figured that we needed to smoke that ridgeline so we could get out of town. So the paratroopers did come in and instead of going into the assembly area they went in the attack right off the approach march. They hit it just about on the nose and we had the artillery preparation. They didn't do all this sort of stuff that you normally would do in preparation for an attack and it was a great attack. They spread out across the fields and those guys when they attacked, did it on the dead run. None of this fooling around like you see on television—walking and so on—these guys did it on the dead run. They would run for 50 meters, hit the ground, get up and run and so on and that sort of thing. Our tanks moved out with them. But much to our surprise, and I guess these things happen, but it sure was a rough one, the Germans also picked 1400 to launch a major attack. So when we came boiling out of town and when the smoke cleared form our artillery preparation, out of the smoke came the Germans, over the ridgeline. So here we were engaged in a head-on clash with whatever was out there. We did get one company out on the ridgeline to the northwest. The other elements that went to the north and northwest almost got to it, but it was impossible. They took a lot of casualties. This fight lasted from 1400, 1500 into about 1600. A very desperate fight. By that time towards the end of it, LaPrade and I realized that if we did take the ridgeline we were fighting too big a fair to actually hold it. We were taking a lot of casualties with guys exposed out there and the guys to the northeast who had the ridgeline were radioing that they were under severe attack by tanks and panzer grenadiers and they didn't think they could hold it. So we said, "OK, good try, but let's pull back into the town," and we did. They worked their way back and that takes time too.

You just don't get up and turn around in the face of enemy and walk back. So by 1700 in the evening we were coming back into Noville to set up our defense. In the meantime, the Germans out to the east, towards Bourcy, were putting on a heck of an attack. I went out to Bourcy Road and fought them out there with my tank destroyers. We would sneak out with our tank destroyers from behind a building in a village and would see the German tanks and would take a couple of shots at them and get back behind the building in a defensive position – in and out sort of fighting. The Germans were doing the same thing. It started getting fairly dark at that time and it was getting hard to see. We were kind of tired. We had been fighting since 4:00 o'clock in the morning, I guess and it's at that point in time when you are tired you sort of loose your zip and so forth. So I just said to the guys, "OK, let's just knock this off—stay in your defensive—stay in your defensive position—keep them under fire and when it gets daylight in the morning we'll go back at them when you can see them better. " So we knocked that battle off and I got word that LaPrade wanted to talk to me back in CP, which was back in town. I went back there and met him in CP. Unfortunately my guys had put the CP up in a house alongside the road in the middle of the town, a very small house, on the first floor. When I got in there and took a look at it. I was a little bit worried and so we took a great big huge Belgium schrang, and put it up against the wall, off to the north. We did this for added protection. I guess that would not protect us too much, but we always think things like that might help. So we did that. Then LaPrade and I got over a map on a little table and he was showing me where he intended to put his paratroopers in the defense for a night. I agreed that well, if you put a company in there, I'll put some tanks in there and so on. While we were working on this defense, the maintenance officer, who had been evacuating crippled vehicles back to Bastogne, drove up in a VTR, a recovery vehicle which looks like a tank, and parked it outside this CP. He came in to tell me that the job had been completed and that he was going on back to his company in Bastogne. He made the fundamental error, which we are all taught not to do, of driving any ve-

hicle right up to a CP because that just shows whoever might be watching where the CP is. The Germans that I had been fighting to the north of town and a little bit before apparently saw that VTR in the dark and they started shooting at it and as it normally is they missed the VTR and hit the building. When they hit the building they really took it down. And they killed LaPrade, I guess probably 10 to 12 guys, and I was badly wounded, hit in the face, head and the eyes. The guys took me down into the cellar and when I came to they told me I was badly wounded and the doctor said that I had to go back to the hospital. So I said, "Well, I want to go back and talk to Colonel Roberts, the Combat Commander, because I was convinced that we couldn't stay in Noville, and we had to get back on that ridgeline at Foy where we could do a much better job. But I wanted to go back and tell him. He hadn't come up to see us. The only ones that would come up to see us during the day were General Higgins from the 101st and Colonel [Robert F.] Sink, the [506th PIR] regimental commander, nobody from the 10th Armored. They knew what the situation was and they had agreed with us that we ought to go back to Foy. They didn't have the authority to say that though. So I wanted to go back and see Roberts and so I asked that they get my jeep and take me back there and so the jeep driver went out to get the jeep and he never came back.[85]

At 1800 an 88mm shell hit the team's command post and struck down both the infantry and the armored commanders. Lieutenant Colonel LaPrade was killed outright, and Major Desobry was wounded so severely that he was immediately evacuated. Major Robert F. Harwick, executive officer, 1st Battalion, 506th PIR, assumed command of the combined force; Major Charles L. Hustead took over the armor.

WILLIAM J. STONE, BATTERY B, 321ST GLIDER FIELD ARTILLERY BATTALION, 101ST AIRBORNE DIVISION

On the morning of the 19th we moved out with the 1st Battalion [506th PIR] to Noville which we were to defend along with TEAM Desobry, CCB, 10th Armored Division, which had been defending the village since the previous evening. During the march we met soldiers of the 28th Infantry Division who were moving to the rear toward Bastogne. They told us that the Germans had fired at them using tanks captured from the 9th Armored Division. We began to understand just how serious the German attack was. None-the-less we maintained the esprit and confidence typical of soldiers of the 101st.

Noville is seven kilometers northeast of Bastogne. Two and one half kilometers southwest of Noville is the hamlet of Foy. Noville lies in a saucer-like depression with high ground all around it except in the west. This made it difficult to defend against the German attack from the east as we did not have the high ground. Between Noville and Foy the ground sloped from east to west with the high ground on the east. Noville was critical because it contained the junction of roads important to the German movement westward. It was also important to the Germans because, if they choose, they could drive on Bastogne from the north along the axis of the Noville–Bastogne road. Our defense of Noville also gave the remainder of the 506th time to occupy and improve positions behind us to the south and to tie into the 501st Parachute Infantry Regiment on the right flank of the 506th.

While talking with the officers of the company with which we were working, Canham learned that they had no ammunition for their carbines. As artillerymen we were armed with carbines and had enough ammunition to share with them which we did. In addition, the riflemen did not have sufficient ammunition for their rifles and there was a shortage of hand grenades and rocket launcher projectiles. This was remedied somewhat just as we were entering Noville. The S4 of the 1st Battalion came riding up with a jeep trailer full of ammunition, which he passed out to the riflemen as they entered the village late in the morning. [Second Lieutenant George C. Rice, the] S4 of TEAM Desobry also managed to obtain ammunition, which he distributed.

We stayed in Noville for a few hours but that afternoon we left and spent the night with another battalion of the 506th near Foy. To this day I do not understand why we were ordered to leave the 1st Battalion. Shortly after we left, it attacked out of Noville along with TEAM Desobry in an attempt to gain the high ground to the east. This attack was supported by the fires of the 420th Armored Field Artillery Battalion, which was in direct support of the team. Regardless, the fires of the 321st would certainly have enhanced the possibility of success for the attack which did not achieve its objective. [86]

Second Lieutenant George C. Rice,
Armored Infantry Bronze Star citation:
During the period 19 December 1944 to 2 January 1945, his unit was engaged in the defense of the town of Noville, Belgium. On the success of this defense depended the defense of Bastogne. Throughout the action enemy tanks and infantry attacked relentlessly, forcing the defenders to expend large amounts of ammunition. As the action progressed, a serious shortage of ammunition occurred. Despire direct enemy tank fire, Lieutenant Rice made repeated trips to rear areas in order to obtain ammunition and other vitally needed sup-

plies. Through the keen foresight and courage of Lieutenant Rice, his unit and other units who were engaged in the fighting in that sector were constantly supplied with sufficient quantities of ammunition and other essential items. His actions were in accordance with the highest standards of the military service. Enter military service from Illinois.[87]

———

After the Battle of the Bulge, German Fifth Army commander Hasso von Manteuffel said that the initiative had been lost as early as 18 December. This may have been the case on the northern shoulder but around Bastogne the German's were still hoping to break through and take the city. At Noville they still enjoyed numerical superiority and if the axiom of war states that the attackers only need a three to one advantage to have a realistic chance of obtaining their objectives, then the Germans definitely had the upper hand. The problem was that thanks to the vagaries of the ever-shifting fog, neither side was ever entirely sure how strong the other was. As the fog occasionally lifted it became apparent that the Germans had a whole panzer division in the area, but initially there was a lot of muscle flexing and posturing from both sides as they established who had what and who was where.

On 19 December at around 0700 General Bayerlein launched his Panzer Lehr Division in an attack against Team Cherry in an effort to get through to Bastogne. As the Panzer Lehr approached Neffe they were intercepted by heavy fire from the 1st Battalion, 501st PIR, which had arrived on the scene just a few moments before the attack commenced. Two platoons of German infantry, supported by two Panther tanks, then turned their attention to the large chateau that Lieutenant Colonel Cherry had been using as his CP. Eventually it was on fire and under simultaneous attack from three sides. Despite their desperate situation, however, the defenders refused to abandon Chateau Vanderesken until late that evening, after the German attacks had died down. As the hours passed the paratroopers consolidated their positions and continued repelling attacks made by the Panzer Lehr. American artillery further frustrated German attempts to head west by shelling all roads leading to Bastogne from that area.

ROBERT KINSER, COMBAT MEDIC, 3RD TANK BATTALION

We were awakened by the M.P.'s at about 4:00 a.m. they were leaving, and we got up at 5:00 a.m. and they told us the Germans were 2 kilometers from town.

We moved out of the church to a Boy Scout building and set our aid station up. About 6:00 a.m. the stragglers came in, it was not good to see in a way, about 2 out of every 10 had no gun at all and a lot had no helmets. They walked by in a steady stream, everyone who passed that had no gun or helmet would ask us if we could give them one, but we had none. That afternoon the Germans threw artillery at us, we were on the main street and the 88s came down the street like it was a bowling alley. The house we were in was right at a turn in the street, it seemed like they were all being shot at us, the first one to hit our building was a 240mm. We had one of our peeps parked in front of the house between a half track and the house, the shell hit the peep and blew it up so bad that even the tools in it were twisted in every way. There was a window right over the peep and a pool table even with the window. I was lying on the table and dozed off when the shell hit it, and blew all the glass out of the window onto me and blew off the table to the floor. I didn't know if I was hit or not, I got up and seemed to be OK. That was one of the luckiest times in my life. The next morning I went outside and looked around. There was hardly anything left of the peep, if the shell had been three feet higher up it would landed right on me.

All that day the tanks and trucks of the 9th Armored Division kept retreating thru Bastogne, the 10th Armored tanks kept going to the front, we did not know what was really going on. Then the town was surrounded, cut off from all sides and we knew we could not get out. The airborne casualties came in so fast we could not take time to eat. The first day we took care of over 200 by ourselves. We were dead tired but had to take turns staying up with the wounded men.[88]

Two GI's were just sharing a cigarette when a tank approached their foxhole. The ground rumbled and shook under the weight of the approaching vehicle. The sound of the tank motor sounded familiar to the two men. They thought it was American. When the tank was in close proximity one of the GI's yelled, "Halt!" and fired a quick burst with his BAR over the turret as it came to a halt about 20 yards from the foxhole. He heard the occupants conversing in English. Then fire from the tank's machine gun broke around the foxhole, only missing their heads by inches. Suddenly there was a cry of "Cease-fire, cease fire, they're friendly troops!" They couldn't determine if the voice had come from in front of them or from behind them but it was enough to arrest the small-arms fire. Then German fire started up again in earnest and they were pinned in their foxhole once again by fire and this time it was from enemy guns. Across the road two damaged U.S. half-tracks, which were in line behind the some destroyed Sherman's, had reinforced the road block.

The position of the ruined tanks not only prevented the enemy from coming down the road but also allowed the half-tracks to turn their .50 cal. machine guns against the approaching enemy column. Under these deadlocked conditions the two forces continued to slug it out almost face-to-face while the fog swirled around them and at last closed in so thickly that they could scarcely see the muzzles of their guns. Despite this the GIs maintained their rate of fire and kept their heads low.

ROBERT PARKER, COMPANY C, 21ST TANK BATTALION

I could see that I hit another vehicle or tank because I had a telescopic sight, the tank commander was able to turn the turret which I could not. I would use the sight to zero in on it and shoot. I personally did not take out any German tanks, but I mostly shot at infantry and infantry vehicles. We lost a tank in our platoon and it was still in gear and it was heading towards enemy lines. So we fired on our own tank to stop it from being captured by the enemy. I fired the gun quite frequently, I did see Panther tanks, but thankfully we did not have to contend with them much. I fired on a Panther but I did not set it on fire, but it moved away quickly.[89]

In Noville evacuation of the many injured had been virtually impossible. They did manage to load four patients onto a halftrack at one point and just as it lumbered off it received a direct hit from a German tank and burst into flames. GIs fought through the flames and unloaded the four injured soldiers and carried them to the aid station under the view of the German tank commander. Captain Jack Prior, battalion surgeon, worked without cover during the action on the road ahead patching the wounded on their open carriers. Many of these casualties incurred further wounds due to the occasional small arms and mortar fire from the enemy east of the highway. Prior was himself struck by a mortar fragment but remained dutifully at his post, caring for the more seriously injured.

Team Desobry was becoming increasingly frustrated by the fog and close proximity of German troops and armor. Visibility was down to fewer than ten yards and, in the confusion, fire fights had even broken out between friendly forces.

MAJOR WILLIAM DESOBRY, 20TH ARMORED INFANTRY BATTALION

Later on they discovered, as I was told, the jeep was found on a small roadway up against the building overturned and no sign of the jeep driver. What happened to him I don't know, to this day I don't know. So there we were. Shortly after that, a 101st Airborne Division ambulance jeep came into town. Those were the jeeps that would carry a couple of wounded at one time. The doctors insisted that I got back in that. I got in the front seat and we drove back to Bastogne. When we got to the little town of Foy, where I wanted to go back to, we were stopped by what was apparently a German patrol, but when they saw the wounded, we were all bloody, they said, "Awk, go on . . . " and back we went. So that tipped me off that the Germans were behind us and in the town of Foy. Later on, I learned that it was the 26th Volks Grenadier Division. Back to Bastogne, I went to this regimental aid station. They checked me out and sent me further back, to their division medical installation which these days I guess you would call a MASH. This is a fairly large medical complex with tents, surgical tents, surgeons and so on. I remember going into the tent and doctors talking to me. Before they operated on me they put me out and when I came to I was in an ambulance, moving down the road. I was lying there and the ambulance would move and then stop, move and then stop, and then I heard the Germans. My first reaction was, "My gosh, we sure captured a lot of German prisoners." A little later I heard some more Germans. Instead of just German conversation, they were yelling, "Achtung–Halt," and all these things and I thought Oh! My gosh this doesn't sound like German prisoners. So I asked the ambulance driver what the heck was going and he said, "Oh, Gee, we have been captured for about 7 hours." So, I asked him, "well, what was going on?" He said, "Well, we were moving down between German units and a lot of German tanks and soldiers all over the place." I asked him if he knew where Bastogne was and he said well he saw road signs every once in a while, Bastogne. And I said, "Well the next time that you come to a road that says Bastogne that goes off to the left or right or whatever just pull into the thing and get going." And he refused to do it. He said, "No, there are too many Germans around." Well, I had been wounded at night and by that time it was daylight and we travelled all that night before and we travelled the next and the next night. The guys that were in the ambulance with me were terribly wounded and we finally halted someplace. I was the only one of the four wounded to get out of the ambulance alive. The others died in the ambulance. They took us into what was obviously a German aid station and there were lots of German wounded there and quite a few American wounded who had been captured. They took me out of a barn of some type and into another room, which was an operating room. They just finished operating on a guy when I came in. They sat me on a table and I watched them with one eye since the other eye was all shut up. I couldn't see out of it and then came my turn. It was really hairy because of the way the Germans were doing it.

They didn't have all this fancy equipment. They gave you an anesthetic by taking a piece of gauze and dipped it in what was obviously ether, or something similar to it, and a guy just slapped it over your nose and when they figured you were unconscious they went to work on you. That was rather hairy watching that. They put me on the operating table and this German doctor started probing around my head wounds and into my eye. I couldn't understand German and after a short time of checking me out he just went "ah" and motioned me to get up and get out of there. Luckily he didn't mess around and the reason he didn't was that it was obvious that I had been operated on an Army medical facility and had been given excellent medical attention. In fact, that is what saved me because the Army medical facility gave me sulpha, blood and all the rest of it and that was what I needed to get me over any infections during the year and one half as it later turned out.[90]

[After being severely wounded in Noville and despite his extensive injuries, Maj. William R. Desobry asked to be taken to Colonel Roberts at the CCB command post in Bastogne. From there he was taken to the division clearing station of the 326th Airborne Medical Company, located north of Bastogne at Barriere Hinck. On arrival he was sedated and immediately attended to.

At approximately 2230 hours 19 December 1944, an enemy force consisting of six armored vehicles supported by a hundred infantry attacked the 326th's clearing station. During a lull in the fighting a German officer approached the station and questioned Division Surgeon Lt. Col. David Gold, the senior officer present. After a discussion with the enemy officer, Doctor Gold surrendered the 326th Airborne Medical Company.

————

Back at his CP in Bastogne Colonel Roberts instigated plans to catch stragglers from various units who were drifting back to Bastogne. He instructed his Headquarters Company to organize the serving of hot food throughout the day at a central point in Bastogne. Roberts then sent a detail stood by to retrieve these men from other units and billet them at a various locations around the city square not far from his CP. MPs were stationed at the road crossings in the south of Bastogne with instructions to stop every soldier who was trying to get away from the battle and turn him back to the Combat Command B area. Roberts managed to assemble around 250 men, some of whom were from CCR of the 9th Armored with most from the 28th Division. This is how Team SNAFU (Situation Normal All F****ed Up) came to be and over the next few days the ranks of this ad hoc unit swelled to number around 600 GIs. Team SNAFU was intended to be used mainly a reservoir for the defending force. It was a temporary home for stragglers and other units were allowed to draw from it when they needed to.

GINNY KRUTA, GRANDSON OF WILLIAM S. GREENPLATE SR., TEAM SNAFU

My Grandpa Greenplate didn't tell stories. When we asked, he talked about the Christmas he spent in a Belgian family's basement eating C-ration canned spaghetti. He didn't tell us that he had left his wife and three young children [Alvin, William F. Jr., and Liz] back in Delaware. He didn't tell us that his unit got surrounded in Bastogne with the 101st Airborne during the Battle of the Bulge, one of the most brutal campaigns in the European theater. He didn't tell us about the railroad tracks that stood perpendicular to the ground after the bombings, looking like ladders to nowhere. He didn't tell us that he was part of the self-named "Team Snafu," a mismatched group comprised of those who had survived the constant onslaught of Germans. While Team Snafu did have a few soldiers like my Grandfather, who was a tank mechanic and an expert marksman, they grabbed anyone who could handle a rifle. These men were thrown together into a makeshift combat unit as a last desperate attempt to keep the Germans from taking Bastogne. He didn't tell us about marching in to liberate the concentration camps. He didn't tell us about the carts overloaded with the emaciated bodies of those they were too late to save. We pieced all of those things together from photo albums and documents found in his home after he passed away in 1994.[91]

LIEUTENANT COLONEL JAMES O'HARA, 54TH ARMORED INFANTRY BATTALION

At approximately 1138, 19 Dec 44, the reconnaissance troop reported a strong enemy armored column approaching our position, moving on the Wilt-Bastogne road. At 1145, the reconnaissance platoon of the 54th Armd Inf Bn. reported it has knocked out a Volkswagen, the point of a larger armored unit, at 1142. It was approaching the Wiltz-Bastogne highway from the south, vicinity. Out gunned they were forced to withdraw. At 1155 the patrol in Wardin, and officers of the battalion who were inspecting our installations in the town, reported a column moving on the town from the northeast. At 1200 a Volkswagen approached our hasty minefield in front of our position. They withdrew under small arms fire and it is believed casualties were inflicted.

The enemy attacked with infantry and armor. They drew first blood, knocking out the forward observer's tank. Several individual small arms fights developed as the enemy continued to feel out our lines by fire. They withdrew, placing artillery fire on our positions.

This concentration of artillery and coordinated movement of enemy armor towards our position revised the plan of defense. The reconnaissance by fire, by the enemy, made the forward slope untenable. Baker Company withdrew to prepared positions on the reverse slope. The patrol was withdrawn from Wardin and now occupied the high ground to the south. Medium tanks were placed with infantry so as to insure the left flank.

Without previous notice, troop movement on our left flank moving toward Wardin, was the first outside units other than our own were in the ready to engage the enemy. Liaison proved this unit to be Company E 501st Airborne Regiment.

The action was hampered by a slinging fog that reduced visibility to less than 75 feet. All fire was directed at flashes. Enemy infantry tried an assault at approximately 1400, but were discouraged by machine gun fire before they started.

The airborne boys had entered Wardin, destroying an enemy patrol, but were counterattacked by infantry and armor. They were virtually annihilated. This was learned from wounded stragglers who were picked up by our outposts at 1600.

For the first time enemy artillery direct fire 88's from the high ground on the left flank and nebelwefers were brought to bear. This proved to be a preparation before an attack by infantry and armor at 1700 hours. The enemy after being engaged withdrew, but the casualties were heavy. Feeling that he could not stand another attack of these proportions with his troops spread so thinly to protect his flanks, the team commander requested permission to withdraw. Permission was granted. Hasty reconnaissance of the line Marvie, high ground north of the bend, was made. The engineers prepared demolitions to blow trees and placed hasty minefields. Protective fires were planned with the artillery to cover the noise of our movement.

At 2100 the reconnaissance elements and light tanks plus Headquarters Company, 54th Armd Inf. Bn. were given the mission to secure and prepare the selected ground for occupation by our forces. To contact friendly units, if any, on our flanks. At 2200 the movement was started and by 2340 everything was once again in readiness to repel the enemy. This movement was accomplished without the loss of a man. The artillery delivered one round every minute upon enemy positions.

The retrograde movement proceeded as follows: a platoon of infantry followed by a platoon of tanks from our right flank position. A platoon of infantry followed by a platoon of tanks. Battalion Headquarters and the anti-tank platoon of Com-

pany B, 54th Armd Inf Bn. A platoon of infantry and a platoon of tanks from our right flank position were the last to leave. Time period between infantry-tank teams—five minutes. Between infantry and tanks within the team—two minutes. This spacing of movement reduced any confusion or noise on our forward positions and was responsible for our ability to move into the newly selected position with ease.[92]

Team O'Hara after action report:
December 19th
At 0830 Company B's sector was attacked by a superior force of armor and infantry after an artillery preparation on our position. By 1000 the attack had been broken and developed into a series of small fire fights. When H, 501st Regiment on our left flank was virtually annihilated in the vicinity of Wardin, our right flank being open, we prepared for an all around defense. At 1730 orders were received from CCB to drop back approximately 1500 yards to the line Marvie, high ground north of the bend, and to harass Wardin all night by patrols and fire, and to make contacts with units moving in on left and right. Withdrawal was made under cover of our artillery fire beginning at 2200. The action was completed without the loss of a single man. Our engineers installed roadblocks with mines and felled trees. We occupied ground as ordered, outposted Marvie, consolidated fires with the unit on our left, planned harassing fires on the town of Wardin, and artillery fires for FPL.[93]

———

The 969th Field Artillery Battalion was an African American artillery unit equipped with five medium howitzers that had inadvertently joined the defense of Bastogne. They were originally assigned to support the 28th Division. Finding themselves stranded within the perimeter, they were assigned by General McAuliffe to provide artillery support. They were one of two African American units in the city, the other being the 333rd Field Artillery Battalion, which had moved to Bastogne on 16 December at less than full strength. This battalion sustained heavier losses defending Bastogne than any other VIII Corps artillery unit: 6 officers, 222 enlisted men, nine guns, thirty-four trucks, and twelve weapon carriers.

South of Wardin Team O Hara established a road block on the high ground but the elevation did not give them any real advantage due to the fog-restricted. Meanwhile in nearby Neffe the 501st had dispatched a company from the 3rd battalion southeast towards Wardin who had managed to link up with Team O Hara in the early afternoon. The team had been forced to reposition after coming under attack from the Panzer Lehr. Supported by tanks provided by Team O Hara the paratroopers moved into the village of Wardin with the intention of covering the Wiltz—Bastogne highway. The ensuing fight became so desperate for the Americans that after sustaining heavy casualties they were forced to withdraw. They were so heavily impaired by their losses that as they pulled back towards Marvie that they could not even assemble a platoon of men from the widely dispersed unit. Unbeknown to these men the Panzer Lehr was equally exhausted by the day's exertions and consequently couldn't push home the advantage at the time.

———

At 0630 the 3rd Tank Battalion's reconnaissance platoon, outposted at the command post in Neffe, was attacked by enemy infantry and tanks. The battalion CP was alerted and organized Chateau Vanderesken for defense. The two headquarters tanks were sent into the center of town to reinforce the platoon. The recon platoon knocked out one of the enemy tanks with a bazooka and the HQ tank section accounted for another enemy tank. Then one of the headquarters tanks was knocked out with a *panzerfaust* at 0700. The recon platoon with the remaining tank were forced to withdraw from the center of town back to the battalion CP at the chateau on the outskirts of Neffe. At this time the CP became completely cut off from the rest of Team Cherry.

At 0830 Team Ryerson was ordered to return to Neffe, by way of the Longvilly-Bastogne Road. Upon reaching the outskirts of Mageret at a little before 1000 Captain Ryerson's men encountered enemy small arms, tanks, and antitank fire. An hour or so later the team Ryerson destroyed an enemy tank used as a roadblock about three hundred yards east of Mageret and then called for artillery fire on the town. At 1130 the CP was assaulted by a hundred or more German infantry, four panzers, and an armored car. The CP fought off the attackers for the next four-and-a-half hours until it was forced to fight its way back to Mont. The defenses at Mont had been hastily organized by elements of the 101st Airborne Division. The stand made by the 3rd Tank Battalion CP at Neffe gave the Screaming Eagles time to move into Mont and establish their positions.[94]

———

Team Cherry after action report:

December 19, 1944

Weather and visibility—poor, rain, foggy.

At 1307 Team Hyduke was ordered to return to Neffe by way of the Longvilly, Bastogne Road and join forces with Team Ryerson. Team Hyduke at this time was receiving attacks from both flanks by enemy tanks, small arms fire and being shelled by enemy artillery. Team Hyduke reached Team Ryerson just West of Mageret and the two (2) teams consolidated at 1500. (Note: hereafter his consolidation of teams will be known as Team Ryerson). At 1900 Team Ryerson now consolidated with Team Hyduke entered and held part of Mageret. At 2145, Team Ryerson was attacked again by enemy tanks and infantry. Continuous attacks were beaten off again by our forces in Mageret.

Bn Trains were moved at 1200 from Bastogne to Magerotte by way of the Neufchateau Highway.[95]

CHAPTER SIX

WEDNESDAY 20 DECEMBER

Weather report for south Belgium, London
Meteorological Office, Wednesday 20 December,
1944: *Persistent fog, heavy snow showers expected on
the high ground. Cloudy, overcast, mild north easterly
wind. Temperature: −15°C.*

On the morning of 20 December General Middleton personally
summoned Colonel Roberts to announce that CCB was now
attached to the 101st Airborne Division. Middleton told Roberts "Your work
has been quite satisfactory. I'm attaching you to the 101st, because I have so
many divisions that I can't take time to study two sets of reports from the
same area". Roberts immediately reported to General McAuliffe to organize
the command liaison, and remained at his headquarters for the duration of
the siege. CCB was assigned the mission of mobile reserve, to be held in Bastogne in readiness to counter attack when called upon to do so.

Meanwhile, on the same day action resumed with a vengeance in the
Noville area. At around 0730 two German tanks came storming through the
fields adjacent to the Houffalize road. As they approached the buildings on
the edge of town they ground to an abrupt halt and opened fire on the village.
One jeep was hit and demolished. A bazooka team that was only ten yards
from the attacking tanks returned fire and with their first rocket they set
ablaze one of the tanks. Staff Sergeant Michael Lesniak, a tank commander,
dismounted from his vehicle to reconnoiter the situation on foot. Peering
around a building he ascertained the exact position of the remaining enemy
tank before returning to his own tank and rotating his turret in the required
direction. He alerted his gunner, drove directly into a small street into the
path of the German tank and with one swift round he blasted the surprised

foe. Before Sergeant Lesniak knew it another enemy tank that had been lurking on the road beyond in the fog appeared. Apparently its mission had been to support the first two tanks or to provide cover for them in the event of a hasty withdrawal. It fired a round in the direction of Lesniak's tank and struck its turret, damaging the traversing mechanism so he was unable to rotate his gun to the left. Fortunately none of Lesniak's crew were injured.[96]

WALTER LEPINSKI, HEADQUARTERS COMPANY, 20TH ARMORED INFANTRY BATTALION

It was the next day that they told us that we were withdrawing, they did not tell us when. The Germans thru out one hell of a barrage onto the road, those 88s, they used armor-piercing shells, and I feared for tree bursts, luckily they used the armor-piercing. I did not get hurt by the shells. The goddamned screaming sound that those 88s have, you could hear it long before it arrived. When we were on our way towards Foy back to Bastogne, the column had stopped, but we had no idea why we were stopped, but there wasn't that much firing coming to us at that point. We stayed there for a little while and a lot of the 101st Airborne soldiers were in a ditch to the right side of the road quite a ways up. The Captain sent word back that I had to report to him. He told me to go back up the column to tell them to be ready to move out. I don't know why, but that is what he said. And we did move out. We were going fairly slow in the convoy and we stopped again. On the left hand side it was open field. When we stopped there were two German soldiers coming across that field with their hands on top of their head, they didn't have helmets on, just the soft hats on. It just so happened that they came in line with my halftrack and they came to it. I dismounted and came around and frisked them, they didn't have anything on them and put them into the halftrack. Eventually the column started to move again towards Foy where we went through without a hitch. Then we came to Bastogne, the Bastogne sign was there on the right, and the column stopped towards the main street of Bastogne. The main street went uphill on an upgrade with all cobblestones. The Captain told me to dismount, and stay, then count, and check every vehicle that comes through after they move out for any men of our company who might be in another vehicle and have them stay with me, and then eventually find the Company's CP. So I stayed there and the whole column went by, and there were all kinds of small arms fire coming from the left side. Not one goddamned man was in the vehicles from our company, and then I heard the 88s coming in and it got louder and wham! It hit right nearby, one after another and another hit and I needed to take cover as quickly as I could. There was a house nearby, the first house entering Bastogne, it was a long house it had a piazza in front of it. I started to run to try and get inside that house for cover. God was with me that they were only armor piercing shells and they would ricochet off the cobblestones with sparks flying around from the projectile. I was trying to run but I couldn't hold my legs and I flopped down with my legs going out from underneath me, I probably fell down a half dozen times, I couldn't help it my mind was way the hell in front of my legs. I tried to get into the house, on the piazza side they had all the windows barricaded, whole bureaus outside in front of them. I took my rifle butt and broke the windows and I was able to move one of the tall bureaus. I got into a room and across that room there was a light on the bottom of the door, so I knew there was someone in the room, not knowing if there were Germans inside, so I kicked the door open and there was table, similar to a picnic table, with a long bench on each side. On the opposite side of the table sat an elderly man with a long black coat, his face was white as can be and he was very feeble. To his left there was a little boy and to the left of the boy there was a young woman in her early 30s. This kid was about five years old, and the minute I kicked that door in and I stepped in and that kid jumped right up and put his hand forward in front of me and said "Heil Hitler!"

I said "Nix, American Soldat."

The woman took the kid and hugged him after I said that. This woman spoke French and she said that the man is sick. I said to her where was the cellar? She pointed to a door and there was a door and another door, which was where the cellar was. I opened the door and I looked inside and there was a bedroom. It had a thick feather bed there and only a couple of candles for light. I found some quilts which I put down the cellar and I told the woman to make up the bed. I carried the old man down to the bedroom. From earlier experience I discovered that pocket watches were popular in Europe but I had never seen a gold one, I saw one on the mantle of the house and put it into the old man's pocket so that it would not get taken if someone else came into the house. Some other soldiers, three or four came into the house, and things seemed to quiet down around the house and it was silent outside. I did not hear any incoming shells. I decided to find my company, I did not even know if they were in Bastogne and I found them up the hill on the main street in Bastogne when I saw a guy I knew up in the square who pointed me to the building. It was dark out when I went into that building and the Captain said "Sergeant, am I ever glad to see you," and that was it. I never got to tell him about the house or anybody for that matter.

I heard that the Battalion Commander had been hit but not that badly.[97]

———

MAJOR WILLIS D. CRITTENBERGER, HEADQUARTERS BATTERY, 420TH ARMORED FIELD ARTILLERY BATTALION

When the Germans kept coming in we had to raise our artillery high to hit them so we moved across Bastogne out to the west to a small town called Senonchamps. We could reach the whole perimeter from there. It was a good location. The Germans trying to get by the armor and the airborne on the east side of town, they started to come around and they tried to come in the back door and that was where we were. We had two or three firefights everyday, we could hold them off since we had machine guns on our halftracks and vehicles, we also had a battery of triple A self-propelled, four [.50 cal. machine] guns mounted on a track; we called them woodchoppers because when they swept the woods, the trees fell down. We had those, 105mm howitzers and halftracks. We could handle the Germans until the 101st came.[98]

420th Armored Field Artillery Battalion after action report:

Dec 20

Battalion moved to Senonchamps under heavy mortar and artillery fire. During march from Bastogne a "B" battery ammunition trailer was hit by enemy artillery. Sgt. Packard, "B" Battery ammunition sergeant, jumped from half-track behind and without a moment's hesitation took his fire extinguisher, tossed burning ammunition onto the pavement with his bare hands, thereby protecting vehicles and personnel in the rest of the column and saving ammunition. 58th Armored Field Artillery Battalion relieved from attachment to 420th Armored Field Artillery Battalion. 73rd Armored Field Artillery Battalion became separated, location unknown. Battalion alerted to expect attack at any time, led by Sherman tanks. Casualties: 7 men wounded—one killed.[99]

JERRY GOOLKASIAN, COMPANY B, 3RD TANK BATTALION

I heard voices coming over the radio, which were German. I learned later it may have been tanks from the 9th Armored Division that the Germans had taken early in the onslaught of the Bulge against us. As the morning of the 20th broke I heard the revving of German tank engines. It was foggy. I woke everyone up and I said we better get busy; something is not right here. As the fog lifted and we saw a lot of German infantry coming up the slope in front of our tank, Hildoer got up on .50 cal. and started firing the 50, I grabbed my M3 and shot what little .45 I had, and I assume the ball gunner was firing his 30. We did a pretty good job of stopping them. At that point our .50 got hot and was only firing single shots. We carried a spare barrel and Hildoer asked me to change the barrel and he would get some more ammo. I had the good barrel in one hand and I unscrewed the other barrel off in my other hand. Just then I got hit. I had no pain; I was in shock, because the nerves in my arm were just gone. . . . The blood was pouring out of there, but I had no pain at all, and I figured I better get out of here. Hildoer came up out of the inside of the turret with stuff coming out of his helmet thinking he had been knocked out. I yelled at Ziggy in the driver's seat that Hildoer and I had been hit and he should stay in the tank. I went on the front of the tank to slide down and I took my grease gun with me, and I had heard all the horror stories of being taken prisoner, so I figured I would take someone with me; I still had a good right hand. When I got to the front of the tank as the fog lifted, not even a hundred yards away was a German tank pointed at us. At that point I jumped off the top of the tank, landed on my behind, and I no sooner landed there another explosion lifted me in the air, blew off my right shoe, nicked my finger, and in my nose. Then I figured I was done. Meanwhile there was a dead GI under the tank, he must have been killed during the night. Then all of the sudden out of nowhere was a guy. I had never met him. He was a paratrooper, an infantryman not a medic. He asked if I could make it. I got up on one leg, got my good arm around his neck and limped on my other leg down twenty-five yards to a stable. He dragged the dead guy, too. Two big shots came through the stable, big chunks of cement. He asked if I wanted to go the aid station, and I said it was better than getting killed by cement. I hobbled with him up to the aid station, which was in the church in Noville. The walking wounded were coming in by the dozens, both paratroopers and 10th Armored alike. The doctor—I don't know who it was. He might have been from the 20th [AIB]—was calm as cucumber, cut my clothes off, gave me two shots of cognac, and a couple bottles of blood. They were going to send me back to Bastogne on a jeep. Well the guy came in and said that the jeep was on fire. So they shoved me on the back of halftrack—it wasn't a medic's halftrack—along with three other guys. I still had no pain because the nerves were gone. I was wide awake and on the way back to Bastogne—I don't know where these guys came from, but they heard a burp gun go off, jammed the brakes on the halftrack, and piled out, leaving us laying there. I said, "It's only a burp gun; it won't hurt you; keep going!" A mile down the road same scenario took place all over again! Back in Bastogne around noon I was in a large tent, I finally fell asleep, there was a bunch of wounded in there, dozens of them. The nurse came over and tried to put more blood into me, but she could not find a vein on my right arm and naturally nothing doing in my left. I said to myself, thank God she's gone.[100]

Jerry Goolkasian was not the only tanker who faced the continued German artillery and tank fire. Even after his tank's turret was damaged, Tank Commander SSgt. Michael Lesniak stared down a Tiger tank.

By 1000 hours the fog had thickened to such an extent that visibility was reduced to under ten yards. Another Tiger tank rumbled down into the village. The Tiger didn't realize that he'd come so far down the road and immediately drew to a halt directly in front of the building used as the CP of Company B, 20th AIB. Slowly the big 88 rotated to cover the door, so long it practically touched the entrance. The soldiers in the CP endured a few tenuous moments as they braced themselves for the Tiger to fire. Once again Staff Sergeant Lesniak came to the rescue. Rotating his crippled turret slightly to the right he fired three rounds in rapid succession into the Tiger. Although the rounds didn't appear to do any damage to the Tiger, the German crew were undoubtedly stunned by the impact of the M4 Sherman's rounds and, unable to determine the source of the volley, immediately began backing up. As it did so it rolled over a stationary jeep, reducing it to a flattened pile of junk.[101]

> *Staff Sergeant Michael Lesniak Armored Infantry Silver Star citation:*
> On 19 December 1944 in the vicinity of Noville, Belgium, not being able to give fire orders from his position in the turret of his tank, he dismounted under intense enemy tank and automatic weapons fire and moved to a position from where he could give his gunner orders. This enabled the tank to knock out three enemy tanks, thus crushing the enemy's attempt to enter the village. Even after the tank which Sergeant Lesniak was commanding received a direct hit from an enemy tank, by his outstanding leadership he rallied his crew and again manned his tank, accounting for the last two of the three enemy tanks destroyed. By his devotion to duty and courage Sergeant Lesniak exemplified the highest standards of the military service. Entered Service from Pennsylvania.[102]

THOMAS HOLMES, INTELLIGENCE AND RECONNAISSANCE PLATOON, 54TH ARMORED INFANTRY BATTALION

We were told to patrol on a road that was south of Bastogne and Marvie. O'Hara wanted us to take that road and see how far they [the Germans] had come. We went down that road and one of the first things we ran into was a gas truck coming alone, actually he was behind us, he had a trailer as I stopped and was looking

*at him, and I hailed him to stop. In the process he had another truck that was fol-
lowing him and I don't know if the brakes failed or whatever but they ran into
the back end of the deuce-and-a-half that was in front. We had to get them
straightened around and I said to them that they could not go down the road.
They told me that they were on their way delivering gasoline to the 28th [Divi-
sion]. I told them they're falling back. We left them and about fifteen minutes or
so, further down the road we ran into Gen. Norman Cota. Because of what we
had heard and everything, my machine gunner radio operator, he was nervous
and jerky, he said this guy is one of those damn people going through lines in American uniforms. I told him to cool it, just cool it, "Let's find out." Here he is, the
general of a division. He was spent; the man was tired obviously and distraught.
He said to me, have you seen any of my men? I said, what men are you talking
about, sir. He replied, the 28th Division, I am the commander of the 28th Division. At the time I didn't know him from a barrel of hay, he had one man with
him, his driver. The machine gunner, Garrity, he's got his arm draped on the 30
cal. pointing right at the General. We're asking him for some identification, and
he's fussy about it, he said I am who I am. He whipped out something that was an
identification thing. I told him, "Okay sir, but we have to be careful. We've had a
lot of your men come through here." He said, "That's what I want; I want to know
what you can tell me about my men" I told him that I had been down to Wiltz on
the 19th. He had left there sometime in the morning of the 19th, and he went to
a town called Sibret. He had established it as his headquarters. He asked me to
send any of his men who I run into over to Sibret. He asked about Colonel Roberts
and the 101st Airborne people. I told him that I didn't know about the 101st Airborne people but I know that Roberts maintained his own headquarters and they
had theirs. Cota told me that he wanted to talk with Roberts, that he wanted any
of his 28th men to be sent down to Sibret. I told him how to get to Bastogne and
that there were MP's there who could direct him to Colonel Roberts.*[103]

---

*Private First Class Frank V. Keeney, Headquarters Company,
20th Armored Infantry Battalion, Bronze Star citation:*
Noville, Belgium on 20 December 1944.
After his radio was destroyed by enemy artillery fire, PFC Keeney,
radio tender, courageously returned to his unit command post
through intense enemy artillery, small arms, and mortar fire and secured another radio with which he reestablished communications
for forward observation post.[104]

In Noville, they were running short of armor-piercing shells. In Bastogne, General McAuliffe was wondering whether Noville was worth holding on to. The time had finally arrived for the U.S. forces there to pull out and get back to Bastogne.

Battery B, 796th Antiaircraft Artillery Battalion after action report:
December 20
The 796th AA had orders to try and break through to Noville to relieve pressure on our besieged troops there an enable them to withdraw. In the event a breakthrough was impossible, they were to report to the nearest unit needing assistance.

On reaching a point outside Foy, they learned that that town was in enemy hands, and three enemy tanks were astride the road from Foy to Noville. Realizing a breakthrough was impossible, Capt. Walker reported to the C.O. of the 3rd Bn. 506th 101st AB. The C.O. gladly accepted the platoon and incorporated it in his plan to retake Foy.

The three M-15s, along with all the trailers and one M-16 with motor trouble, dispersed in a wooded area to strengthen the 506th and support the attack. The other halftracks, three M-16s, lined up on the road waiting to jump off with the infantry. When the attack began, they moved off two hundred yards in front of the advancing infantry. They soon received direct 88, mortar, and machine gun fire. Not being able to fire over the cab they were forced to fall back and wait for infantry. Halftrack and infantry pressed steadily forward and forced the Germans to withdraw from the town. During the attack, no ammunition was expended by their halftracks.

After entering the town the 767 AA gun crews, using small arms, facilitated in cleaning out houses, barns, and other hiding places, and then assisted in the capture of some forty prisoners.

For the time being the halftracks dispersed in Foy and awaited further orders. Remnants of the 1st Battalion, which had been trapped at Noville, started to come through Foy on their way back to Bastogne. The attack on Foy had relieved the pressure at Noville enough to enable them to withdraw.

In order to strengthen the defense of the newly-won Foy and to the northwest, Recogne, which we held but which was threatened, the three M-15s went into position around Foy, and Lt. Nell and the three M-16s were sent to Recogne to contact the C.O. of Company "G", 506th. The one M-16 with motor trouble was sent back to the Battery C.P. at Senonchamps.

At Foy, the M-15s went into position for a ground defense: Halftrack 131 set up near the crossroads, just out of town; 141, about three hundred yards up the road to the west; and halftrack 232 went into position on the edge of a sparsely wooded area just west of town. Orders for these halftracks were to support the infantry against ground attack and if necessary, withdraw with them. They were cautioned not to fire at night unless absolutely necessary.

Halftrack 232 went into position accompanied by eight infantry men. These infantry men set up a machine gun outpost about thirty yards in front of the halftrack. At about 0300 next morning, Dec. 21st, enemy artillery fire forced them to withdraw. As soon as the fire died down, the halftrack again made its way into position, this time with ten infantrymen. Again they encountered heavy artillery fire and were forced to pull out.

Twice more before 0900 attempts were made during lulls in firing to get back to the position. On attempts, the third and the fourth, squad leader was accompanied by fifteen infantrymen while the halftrack remained back toward the middle of the woods. The squad leader figured if he could make the forward foxholes with the infantry, he could observe any enemy movement and call back for the halftrack if he needed it. No sooner had they reached the holes on both of these attempts, however, then fierce artillery and mortar fire forced them to turn back.

Halftrack 131, meanwhile, stayed in position about three hundred yards southeast of Halftrack 232. The orders were to fire at enemy ground troops only. At dawn the enemy launched an attack using tanks and infantry. the line was held until approximately 1000 when a tiger tank broke through and the halftrack came under direct fire and had to withdraw with the infantry.

Just south of the crossroads, Halftrack 141 had turned into a position where it was subject to heavy mortar and 20mm fire. The 20mm had set up near some buildings about two hundred yards distant and was firing down the north- south road leading through Foy. The halftrack was in such a position its guns couldn't be brought to bear unless it pulled out into the line of fire.

About 1000, a tiger tank was sighted about three hundred yards up the road, and the sergeant was ordered by the infantry officer to "pull out and stop that tank." There was a T.D. sitting short distance from the halftrack and the sergeant called the officer's attention to it, explaining while the halftrack couldn't pull out on the road. The officer went over to the T.D. but for some reason could get it to engage the Tiger Tanks. Shortly afterward, the tank was driver off and the 20mm neutralized. The infantry decided to withdraw from Foy to better positions. All three halftracks were ordered to the Battery C.P. at Senonchamps.

Meanwhile upon arriving at Recogne, Lt. Nell was ordered to put one M-16 at each of the three roads leading into that town. These positions covered road blocks and were chosen to include a commanding view of the surrounding terrain to guard against possible enemy infantry attack. Bazooka teams were placed with the M-16s.

Before they went into position, all members of the three squads were shown the route out of town back to Bastogne in the event of a withdrawal. Their orders were to support the infantry and cover their withdrawal if necessary. This policy of orienting the troops on the situation as soon as possible really paid off in this case. Two of the three halftracks had to find their way back, one squad on foot.

From 1800 until 2100 that evening of December 20th, the town was under heavy mortar and artillery fire. At 2200, a strong enemy patrol infiltrated through our lines into the town to harass defenses in the rear. At approximately 2400, the crew of Halftrack 142 made contact with the patrol. The driver of the halftrack cut loose with his tommy gun, killed four and wounded a fifth. The wounded man lay out in the night moaning. A German medic went out to help him but, after blundering around in the dark for half an hour, couldn't find him. Rather than let the medic get back to his lines with possible information, the crew of the halftrack took him prisoner. An hour or so late, the town was raked with machine gun fire from enemy outposts.[105]

WILLIAM J. STONE, BATTERY B, 321ST GLIDER FIELD ARTILLERY BATTALION, 101ST AIRBORNE DIVISION

Early on the morning of the 20th we were ordered to return to Noville and rejoin the 1st Battalion, [506th PIR]. The Germans were trying to take Noville by attacking from the east and northeast. When the initial effort failed, the enemy continued to attack Noville while attempting to by-pass the village to the north and south. The Germans moving around Noville to the north were meeting with more success than were their fellows moving south of the village. To the north, there were no American troops. To the south were the 501st and the 506th. The enemy was trying to slip between their forward lines and Noville in an attempt to surround Noville and the going was slow. Within our FO party we knew nothing of this. We knew only that we had to get fire on the enemy north of Noville. In order to accomplish this, Canham selected a stone barn on the northeastern outskirts of the village as our observation post. He and Plummer went to the second floor from which they could observe through an open window. I set the radio up at the other end of the barn just outside a door on the first floor and ran a wire to Canham and Plummer so that we could send fire missions to the Fire Direction Center (FDC) of the 321st in Savy.

At this time Noville was taking a beating. The Germans were pounding the village (and us) with everything they had. The piercing whistle of incoming projectiles followed by the sounds of their explosions assaulted our ears. Their blasts buffeted our bodies. The sharp, bitter smell of the exploded powder invaded our nostrils. Buildings were severely damaged. Wounded were walking or being carried to the battalion aid station. If the enemy could take the village quickly he would have freedom to continue his advance to the west, where he was ordered to seize crossings over the Meuse River, or a straight road into Bastogne provided that he could break through the other battalions of the 506th. Still, the riflemen of the 1st Battalion and the men of TEAM Desobry, aided by the fires of the 321st, held. For now, there was to be no road through Noville for the 2nd Panzer Division. The defense of Noville gave the other battalions of the 506th time to occupy and improve their positions astride the Bastogne-Noville Road just south of Foy. Despite the vigorous German attack, from the narrow perspective of our FO party, the battle seemed to be going well when Plummer called me on the telephone and said that a tank shell had just hit alongside of the window from which Canham was observing and that Canham had been hit. I grabbed the platoon aid man and went upstairs. He said that Canham was dead. I reported this to our FDC which urged Plummer and me to remain in Noville. We, of course, had no intention of doing other than that and were a bit put off by the urging from FDC. Plummer took over from Canham and we continued to direct the fires of the 321st. By 1:00 P.M. the 1st Battalion had lost contact with the headquarters of the 506th and our FO party's radio was the only means of communication be-tween the two. The liaison officer from the 321st at the headquarters of the 506th had a radio in the FDC net and he relayed messages from the 506th headquarters to our FO party. We then gave them to the commander of the 1st Battalion. It be-came obvious to the division commander, Brigadier General Anthony McAullife, that the 1st Battalion and TEAM Desobry, while they were holding, would soon be surrounded, and so he ordered Colonel Robert Sink, the commander of the 506th to withdraw them. At 1:15 P.M. the order for the withdrawal came down to us on the artillery radio and we relayed it to the commander of the 1st Battalion.

The German attack around the southern side of Noville was rapidly becoming more successful. Because of this, the Noville force was in danger of being cut off from the rest of the 506th and so there was little time to plan the withdrawal. Shortly after it began, we came under observation and direct artillery fire by the Germans on the high ground to the east. By this time we were traveling with the battalion commander. We told him that we could get artillery fire from the 321st on the enemy position. He told us to do it. (Note: I know that other measures were being taken at this time but I did not know of them and cannot describe them here.) We sent the fire mission down and while the fire was on the way, the battalion commander ordered the battalion to leave the road and continue the withdrawal on the western side of the road which was low ground – so low that it was not vis-ible to the enemy. The combination of fire from the 321st and the low ground en-abled the 1st Battalion and TEAM Desobry to continue their withdrawal in order to fight another day. There was considerable confusion once we moved off the road and control was lost. This was certainly undesirable but was not as bad as it might be inasmuch as we were no longer in contact with the enemy. Low ground is often wet and this our route was. By this time I was riding on a half-track of TEAM Desobry. The tracks on the rear of the vehicle drove the wheels in the front into the wet ground and we came to a halt. After we freed the vehicle, I decided that it would be better to proceed on foot and ended up south of Foy back on the road.

There was no clearly defined German front line and as I looked at the high ground to the east of the road, three German soldiers emerged from the woods 100 yards away. When they saw me they immediately surrendered. I searched them and took from them their military papers. I later gave these to Captain Joe Perkins, the S2 of the 321st. It took some time, but I finally found someone in the 506th who would take the prisoners from me.

The troops of the 506th were busy people just then and few of them wanted to have prisoners on their hands. As soon as I got rid of the prisoners I looked for our liaison officer from the 321st. I located Captain Sam Skinner, who had been

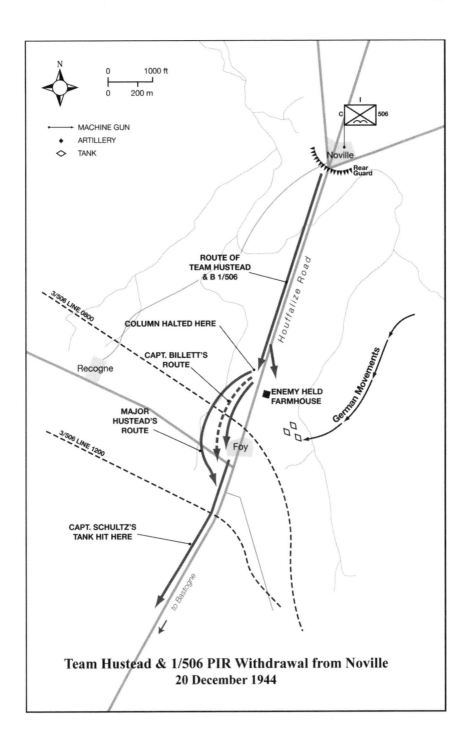

Team Hustead & 1/506 PIR Withdrawal from Noville
20 December 1944

our battery commander in England and Normandy. I told him what had hap-
pened and he told me to come with him while he spoke with the commander of the
battalion of the 506th with which he was working. When he met the battalion
commander Skinner asked him if it would be alright if Lieutenant Eugene Brooks
of Battery A worked as an FO with the battalion. (Brooks, who had joined the
battalion with Canham, would be wounded badly on the next day.) The battalion
commander replied, "Sure. Brooks, Canham or any FO from the 321st is OK."
Skinner told the battalion commander that Canham had been killed in Noville.
He replied, "I knew he'd get it. He took too many chances."

I doubt that Canham would have agreed with that battalion commander's
assessment. Canham did not take "too many chances." He was a skillful, well-
trained officer who pushed the fight to the enemy at every opportunity. He never
let up. His skill, his attitude toward his duty, and his ability to get along with
others probably brought him to the attention of the commanders in the 506th and
they saw this man, who performed his duty to the utmost, as one who, "took too
many chances."

Plummer and I had not seen the last of Noville. The 321st continued in direct
support of the 506th and we—each with different FO parties—were with the
2nd Battalion of that regiment when Noville was retaken several weeks later.
Our artillery fire and the bombs of close air support aircraft had finished the job
that the Germans had begun and not a building was left standing. Noville held
bitter memories for me, and so on the following day I was happy to leave as the
506th continued its advance supported by the 321st and took Rachamps north of
Noville. [106]

Corporal Antonio Gonzales 3rd tank Battalion, Bronze Star citation:
On December 20, 1944, at Foy, Belgium, Corporal Gonzales, tank
gunner, braving hostile fire displayed unusual leadership and courage
in successfully leading an outnumbered group of men to the safety
of friendly lines.[107]

Major Charles L. Hustead Jr., 20th Armored Infantry Battalion,
Silver Star citation:
On 20 December 1944, the enemy launched three exceedingly
strong attacks on friendly forces defending the town of Noville, Belgium. Although the attacking enemy forces represented an overwhelming numerical superiority, Major Hustead so expertly deployed and directed his men that they accounted for twenty-two

Above: The crossroads town of Bastogne is pictured here with halftracks and other vehicles of the 10th Armored Division as its Combat Command B arrived to stop the German advance. The streets look calm enough, but soon, with German artillery and tanks approaching, Bastogne would become a war zone.—*courtesy National Archives*

Below: A group of German POWs are led through the streets of Bastogne in front of the ruins of Colonel Cherry's CP. Early in the morning on 30 December 1944, a lone German plane bombed Cherry's CP which resulted in the death of five officers. Sigmund Faye wrote on the back that the POWs helped clean up the wreckage.—*courtesy of Norman Faye*

With the howitzers of the 101st Airborne artillerymen running low on ammunition, and the 420th AFAB down to only five rounds each for its M7 self-propelled howitzers, the 23 December air drop allowed protection of the city, by the artillerymen, to continue. Along with ammunition, food and medical supplies, also dropped over Bastogne were soldiers who survived on cheese and crackers, and medical staff who used drinking alcohol to dull the pain of their wounded comrades.—*courtesy Richard Barrett*

Medical officer Sigmund Faye is pictured here in front of the many gliders that landed outside of Bastogne during one of the air drops. The gliders helped provide medical supplies, food, ammunition; even surgical teams arrived in gliders after the siege was broken on 26 December.—*courtesy of Norman Faye*

Medical officer Sigmund Faye poses inside one of the many gliders that were towed into Bastogne after the siege was lifted on 26 December.—*courtesy Norman Faye*

The M7 Priest was one the most important weapons during the Siege of Bastogne. The 420th Armored Field Artillery Battalion used these self-propelled 105mm howitzers to defend the circular perimeter of Bastogne. Although the artillerymen did not get the same protection from the icy wind that the tankers got in Sherman tanks, the M7 Priests and their crews proved to be tough enough to fight off infantry and German tanks.—*courtesy National Archives*

Tankers and paratroopers work together to extinguish a fire in a Bastogne house during the battle.—*courtesy National Archives*

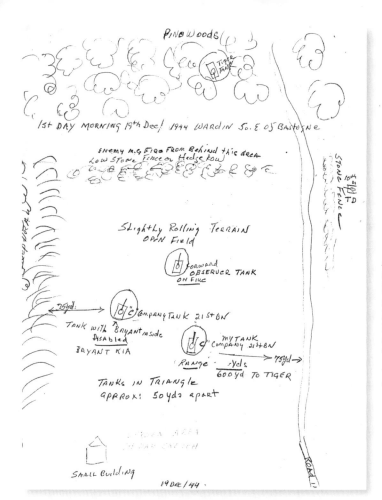

PINE WOODS

TIGER TANK

1st DAY MORNING 19th Dec/ 1944 WARDIN So. E OS BASTOGNE

ENEMY M.G FIRE FROM BEHIND THIS AREA
LOW STONE FENCE OR HEDGE ROW

STONE FENCE
10th
⊟
TD

Slightly Rolling TERRAIN
OPEN FIELD

⊟ FORWARD
OBSERVER TANK
ON FIRE

25 yd →

⊡ COMPANY TANK 21st BN
TANK WITH BRYANT INSIDE
DISABLED
BRYANT KIA

⊡ MY TANK
COMPANY 21st BN
RANGE   Yds → 75 yd →
600 yd TO TIGER

TANKS IN TRIANGLE
APPROX: 50 yds apart

SMALL Building

19 Dec / 44 .

A hand-drawn map by tanker Don Nichols shows the situation on 19 December when he knocked out a Tiger tank outside of Wardin, Belgium. —*courtesy Donald Nichols*

After being searched and processed, German POWs are being loaded into trucks to be taken out of Bastogne to prisoner of war camps. Despite the German retreat after the breakthrough to Bastogne of the 4th Armored Division, there were numerous Germans taken prisoner during the siege.—*courtesy Norman Faye*

Above: After the 9th Armored and 28th divisions retreated from their initial positions east and north of Bastogne, many of the stragglers were integrated into other units of Combat Command B, which became known as Team SNAFU. Team SNAFU became a fire brigade that was available at a moment's notice and served to plug gaps in the defensive lines around Bastogne.—*courtesy National Archives*

Right: Medical officer Sigmund Faye is pictured in front of Combat Command B's headquarters at The Hotel LeBrun in Bastogne. The Hotel LeBrun served as Col. William Roberts' headquarters during the first few days of the battle while Combat Command B was on its own in Bastogne. Roberts eventually moved to the Heinz Barracks when CCB was placed under the operational control of the 101st Airborne Division.—*courtesy Norman Faye*

Above: Sherman tanks being hauled off the battlefield unfortunately became a commonplace occurrence during the battle of Bastogne. The 3rd Tank Battalion in Noville lost over half of their tanks in just two days of fighting. The weakness of Sherman tank armor became all too real for the 10th Armored tankers in the Battle of the Bulge.—*courtesy National Archives*

Below: This knocked-out Sherman tank lost both tracks during the first few days of battle outside of Bastogne. This tank illustrated the difficulty American tankers dealt with throughout World War II in Europe, and was not just a 10th Armored Division problem. The 105mm howitzer tank and the 76mm Tank Destroyers were the only tanks that could go head to head against German Panthers and on occasion even Tiger tanks.—*courtesy National Archives*

Medical Officer Sigmund Faye is pictured on the main street in Bastogne during the battle. There is snow on the ground and civilians in the street which indicates it may have been taken after the siege was lifted. There was not a date written on the back of the photograph so the exact date is unknown.
—*courtesy Norman Faye*

As shown by the large hole right above the "4" in the middle of the tank this 10th Armored Division Sherman lost against a German 88. This photograph was taken in the Neffe and Mageret area just east of Bastogne. This 3rd Tank Battalion Sherman would not be the last 10th Armored Divison tank to be knocked out by an 88 during the Battle for Bastogne.
—*courtesy National Archives*

The village of Noville was the deadliest battle of the Siege of Bastogne. The soldiers of Team Desobry held the town alone until the 101st Airborne Division arrived on 19 December. The tankers and paratroopers finally retreated back to Bastogne after the village became encircled on 20 December. Noville was not taken back from the Germans until early January 1945.—*courtesy National Archives*

This photo of the church in Noville is a testament to the destruction that occurred in the village. It was an easy target for artillery and mortars since it was the tallest building in the village. The church's interior was just as destroyed as the exterior and after the war it eventually was torn down.—*courtesy National Archives*

Three unidentified members of the 21st Tank Battalion pose for a picture next to a Sherman tank while they get ready to get a quick shave in between fighting. Notice the white sheet placed over part of tank that was used as a make-shift camouflage.
—*courtesy Howard Liddic*

Members of Section 6, Battery B, 420th Armored Field Artillery Battalion, pose for a picture outside of Lonnstroff, Germany, during rest and recuperation before the Battle of the Bulge. Standing: Kiwosl, Sprouse, Hetrick, Torres. Sitting: Barrett, White, Migilore, and Stidam.
—*courtesy of Richard Barrett*

Carl Moot, a forward observer for the 420th Armored Field Artillery Battalion, and his tank crew. He was attached to Team Cherry near Longvilly, Belgium. Moot successfully called in artillery fire throughout the first days of Team Cherry's stand in Longvilly, helping slow the German advance towards Bastogne. Moot was seriously wounded on 19 December and evacuated the following day.
—*courtesy Thad Krasnoborski*

Two unidentified 10th Armored Division tankers still want to be clean-shaven despite the bitter cold and fighting around them. Most of the time the soldiers used cold water or melted down snow to shave with as there was not any warm water handy. For some tankers and paratroopers a good shave brought some normalcy in the face of constant shelling, lack of food, and frostbite.—*courtesy Howard Liddic*

Medical officer Sigmund Faye and another unidentified American soldier search German POWs in Bastogne for any weapons before they are sent out of the town.—*courtesy Norman Faye*

Irving Lee Naftulin wrote on this photograph of the bombed out battalion aid station, "Bastogne, Where I Got." The bombing of the aid station killed numerous wounded soldiers. It also killed Belgian Nurse Renée Lemaire and wounded Naftulin, Jack Prior, and Belgian-Congolese Nurse Augusta Chiwy.—*courtesy Donald Naftulin*

Above: Before the 10th Armored Division moved up to Bastogne, many elements of the division were scattered around Metz, France, southern Luxembourg, and even parts of Germany, resting and recuperating following the fiercely-fought battle for Metz. Sigmund Faye posed in this photo with 10th Armored chaplain Captain David Shepherd, PFC Sturm, and the Schneider family.—*courtesy Norman Faye*

Below: This prewar photo shows the Neffe Chateau where Lt. Col. Henry Cherry had his headquarters during the first days of the Siege of Bastogne. The building became surrounded on 19 December and was burned down by the Germans as Cherry and his men retreated back towards Bastogne.—*courtesy Christian Pettinger*

Above: The roads in and around Bastogne were not snow-covered until later on in the siege. These Sherman tanks illustrate the difficulty that 10th Armored tankers faced with snow and frigid temperatures. A tank did not guarantee warmth for its occupants. With cold steel all around them the threat of frostbite was still a major problem, as many tankers kept their boots on the cold steel floor for hours at a time.—*courtesy National Archives*

Below: The lack of traction on snow and ice was just as much of a threat as German 88s and panzerfausts were to American tanks during the Battle of the Bulge. The 10th Armored Division tankers had to use extreme caution when driving around the snow-packed roads in and around Bastogne. Some tanks had to be towed out of not only snow but also the mud that the snow left behind.—*courtesy National Archives*

Above: For members of the armored infantry, the snow also posed a difficulty in transporting supplies and troops to the front line. With trench foot and frostbite accounting for more medical evacuations than combat wounds, the men of 20th and 54th armored infantry battalions needed to be mindful of keeping themselves warm. This was difficult in and around Bastogne due to the lack of supplies and food. Many soldiers went days without food while shivering in fox holes or in basements of bombed-out buildings in Bastogne.—*courtesy National Archives*

Below: When General Eisenhower ordered that General Patton send one of Third Army's tank divisions to hold the town of Bastogne, secrecy was of the utmost importance. Many tanks of 10th Armored Division took off their insignia and covered up any markings that would tip the Germans off that a unit from Patton's army had been sent to stop their advance. This was one of the main reasons that the 10th Armored Division's role in the battle of Bastogne remains little known.—*courtesy National Archives*

Above: The German Panther was a formidable foe for the outgunned American Sherman tanks during the Battle of Bastogne. The Panther tank had stronger armor plating, but it was armed with a 75mm gun which was the same as many Sherman tanks in Bastogne. Don Nichols, C Company 21st Tank Battalion, was able to knock out a Panther with his Sherman 105mm howitzer, but his tank was also damaged in the tank duel.—*courtesy National Archives*

Below: For many 10th Armored Division Tigers, Christmas was just another day. For some it meant huddling together in the basement of a building, and for others it meant fighting a German counterattack. Even the little joys of eating a hot meal or decorating a small Christmas tree could help lift the spirits of surrounded defenders of Bastogne.—*courtesy National Archives*

enemy tanks and innumerable enemy casualties. When ordered to disengage his forces from the surrounded town, Major Hustead skillfully directed the action in a superior manner. He personally organized a group of Headquarters personnel to outflank the enemy who were hindering the withdrawal in the town of Foy, Belgium. Throughout the entire engagement, Major Hustead displayed unusual courage, skill, and superior leadership, inspiring the men in his command, causing heavy losses among the enemy troops, and contributing greatly to the defense of the key town of Bastogne. His actions were in accordance with the highest standards of the military service. Entered military service from Nebraska.[108]

Despite the overwhelming odds Team Desobry had stopped the whole Second German Panzer Division, which had assumed it was opposing a much stronger force. With the odds around ten to one, Team Desobry had knocked out thirty-one enemy tanks in two days. Captain Jack Prior, a doctor assigned to the 20th AIB courageously volunteered to stay behind with some of the wounded, fully aware that he would probably be taken prisoner along with his wounded patients. At the last minute as German armor was entering the village and only yards away from his aid station, he managed to load the remainder of his wounded soldiers on a halftrack and leave the devastated village.

SERGEANT WARREN SWANQUIST, HEADQUARTERS, 3RD TANK BATTALION

We were able to get back to Bastogne mostly unscathed, but on our way back, we almost got shot by the 101st Airborne, they started firing at us. We had to wave our banner to let them know we were Americans.[109]

Bastogne at this time was intact, but due to the current semi-troglodyte existence of its inhabitants it appeared to be a somewhat deserted city. The sight of abandoned streets still festooned with Christmas decorations must have been generally regarded as an ominous sign for the survivors of Team Desobry as they entered the city.

TECH SERGEANT THADDEUS KRASNOBORSKI, HEADQUARTERS, 420TH ARMORED FIELD ARTILLERY BATTALION

The 420th moved 2.3 miles west of Bastogne to the small town of Senonchamps,

Belgium to set up a 360 degree firing range to support both Combat Command B and the newly arrived 101st Airborne Division.

The move on the 20th gave us breathing room. The battalion headquarters was set up in a little one-room school house which was used by the local children just a day or two before.

On the black board, chalked in French, was the story of St. Nicholas. The Christmas story under these harsh conditions was strangely moving. Looking down, while we were here, St. Nick would see how brave men died. Perhaps setting down his sack of gifts to welcome them with open arms and bestow on them the ultimate and eternal gift.

It was here that Lt. Col. Browne and I, I on the radio, were burning the midnight oil. I don't remember if there was any one else there. Probably so, but because I had to relay a message that would surely send men to their death, it was just he and I in my memory. The fine details have eroded over half a century. I remember I received a message from the commander of a half-track from one of our batteries, he wanted to know what he should do. His intention was to get back to his battery but the road ahead was littered with burning vehicles. Small arms and heavy ordnance fire indicated that the enemy was in control of the road.

The young GI's voice betrayed a terror that I've never encountered before. Almost pleading not to be sent forward, but determined to do his duty, he put his fate in the hands of Headquarters. After the transmission I asked, "Colonel?" The lives of several good men were wrapped up in that single word question. Colonel Browne heard the whole thing. I vividly remember his despair; he held his head in his hands with elbows on the teacher's desk for quite some time. He finally, softly said, "Tell him to break through." On relaying the message, the last words I heard from this poor guy were, "Roger Out" in a voice that sounded like the gates of hell just clanged shut behind him. I never heard what happened, but I feel these GIs gave their lives for their country.[110]

Meanwhile Team Desobry had retreated from Noville only to discover that the German's had occupied the village of Foy. This subjected the fragile convoy to an even further running battle as they attempted to reach the relative safety of Bastogne. Out in Longvilly Team Cherry was faltering and Team O'Hara had so far failed to stop the flow of German troops and vehicles heading toward Bastogne. Due to various misadventures, Team Cherry could no longer tackle the approaching enemy. They now had to focus their energies on saving its remaining elements, and covering its flanks and the rear. Whether the German advance into Bastogne from the east could be checked and thrown into recoil now remained to be seen, but as each hour passed it became increasingly unlikely.

Troop D, 90th Cavalry Reconnaissance Squadron (Mechanized) after action report:

20 December

1ST PLATOON:

At 0730 there was considerable small arms fire from an enemy attack from the north, north-east, and west, on the town of Noville. At 0830 three enemy tanks broke into town. One tank was stopped by a land mine and the other two proceeded to escape along a trail leading to the north-west. Both of these tanks were stopped by fire from an 37mm in an M8 armored car which gun was manned by Tech 5 Coward. After they were stopped they were destroyed by fire from friendly tanks and TDs. During this action the town was under constant fire from artillery and from tanks placed upon the ridges surrounding the town. One of the friendly TD units near Tech 5 Coward's armored car received a direct hit. After the armored car had fired its last round of ammunition Tech 4 Harold C. Knuppenburg and Tech 5 Coward checked two men lying near the TD and finding one still alive carried him to the aid station. This was done while under continual direct fire.

The platoon then sent a six man patrol consisting of Tech 5 Coward, PFCs Mike R. DeMaria and Eligah L Willams, and PVTS Way O. Bruce, Aneil G. Cress, and Charles W. Meyers, to the town of Foy to see if the road to the rear was still open. When about 500 yards north of Foy, they discovered the enemy occupying a house near the road and covering the road with fire. The patrol turned around and returned to Noville to report to the CO. The order was given to evacuate the town and withdraw to the town of Foy where the 101st Airborne had established their lines. The platoon moved out with the column withdrawing to Foy. The column proceeded until it was within the immediate vicinity of the house reported by the patrol and the lead tank was knocked out. The platoon leader then dismounted all men except the drivers of the vehicles and assisted in the dismounted assault on the enemy positions blocking the approach to Foy.

The action stated in this paragraph is one of the most outstanding accomplishments by men of this platoon performed during this operation. While the town of Noville was still under heavy enemy attack, artillery and direct fire from tanks, Tech 4 Knuppenburg returned to his armored car by the destroyed TD mentioned above, and gained contact with Troop Headquarters in Bastogne. With the enemy firing at his vehicle with heavy weapons, he remained at his radio and maintained the only direct radio contact between the Headquarters in Bastogne and the action proceeding in Noville. When the order was received for withdrawal from the town Tech 4 Knuppenburg was joined by his driver, Tech 5 Julius Orsak. They joined the column and rode the vehicle back to Bastogne where the platoon was reassembled.

2ND PLATOON:

At 0900 Tech Linley, PFC Lynn, and PVT Rosocha came into Bastogne in a halftrack with wounded from Mageret. Among the wounded were Brooks, and Kempler of this platoon. At 1500 Cpl. Malone, Tech 5s Balestra, Draw, Jennings, Kraft and McCann, PFCs Brown, Stehle and Kleineweber entered Bastogne.

Enemy artillery fire was very heavy in Bastogne. Concentrations were fire into the city daily, seemingly on a time schedule. With the end of the day the platoon had accounted for its personnel thusly:

Present 22 Killed 1 Wounded 3 Missing 4

3RD PLATOON:

Remained in Mobile Reserve for Team O'Hara. Manned an outpost during the day and no activity reported.

TROOP HEADQUARTERS:

At 1330 Tech Sgt. Solomon A. Osborne was placed in charge of the Troop maintenance, supply and kitchen, and order to take them to the town of Morhet. At Morhet he was to contact the trains of CCB. When his contact was established he was order to remain in Morhet and outpost the town.[111]

General Anthony McAuliffe had his final meeting with General Troy Middleton on the 20 December at his HQ in Neufchateau. They discussed the current situation at some length and as Middleton left his parting, but in retrospect rather ominous remark to General McAuliffe was "Don't get yourself surrounded Tony."

After discovering that Team Cherry had passed through the village of Mageret, the Germans decided to set up their own roadblock and determined the best thing to do was to wait for the Panzer grenadiers to catch up before attempting to capture Bastogne. Cherry soon established that elements of the Panzer Lehr were now getting behind their position. Longvilly was now completely isolated and it became vital for Team Cherry to attempt a breakthrough and reopen the road to Bastogne. By 2330 hours 20 December 1944, the enemy had succeeded in completely severing the Bastogne-Neufchateau road, which had been the last route of evacuation to the rear. Bastogne was now effectively surrounded at all points of the compass. At the HQ in the Heintz Barracks, Brig. Gen. Anthony McAuliffe realized that he was dealing with an increasingly tenuous situation exacerbated by a dearth of medical personnel and supplies. The news that they were surrounded also had a curious effect upon the men. Remarks of the dire situation were rampant like: "They've got us surrounded, the poor bastards." or "Surrounded, good, now we can attack on all sides." German artillery fired propaganda leaflets into the town, urging the defenders to surrender. These were regarded by the GIs as humorous and were collected and swapped like baseball cards. One of these had a photograph of a little girl and her letter to her daddy:

Dear Daddy,
Today I went to the birthday party of Jean, but I didn't have a good time because I was worrying so about you. Last night Mummy cried and cried because we haven't heard from you for so long. Jean got a letter from her Daddy. He is a prisoner of war. Jean says he will be sure to come back home now. Oh, Daddy, you just got to come home. We miss you so.
Loads of kisses,
Winnie

Such things were supposed to break the resolve of the American soldiers in Bastogne. The GIs in the city and out in the foxholes on the perimeter were dealing with a number of problems apart from holding back the German attempts to take the place. The main consideration was keeping warm; this had already proved almost impossible so as a compromise they opted for being rather less cold than usual. Many GIs had never even seen snow in such quantities let alone having to survive in it. The second problem was the lack of hot food. Only some of the lucky ones in town were getting that. When temperatures fell dramatically many soldiers simply froze to death.

Some of their attackers had experienced harsher situations on the Eastern Front and were well prepared to deal with the present conditions. Statistically only one in nine German soldiers died in the western theater of operations. They had winter smocks and other appropriate clothing to deal with the weather. American troops in and around Bastogne didn't have this luxury so they did what all good American soldiers frequently did in World War II: They improvised! Many began to resemble someone who'd just run through a clothing department store during a hurricane.

LIEUTENANT CARL W. MOOT JR., HEADQUARTERS, 420TH ARMORED FIELD ARTILLERY BATTALION

Shortly after daylight the column was some distance from any town, it was slightly foggy when suddenly soldiers from the 101st Airborne Division cane toward us out of the mist. They had opened up a road back to Bastogne. There was not much gun fire they were on foot, carrying only rifles and went on past us toward the German positions.

We proceeded back into Bastogne and all of the wounded were put in a building that was being used for a First Aid Station. Ambulances were loading up to evacuate them to the rear. They were loaded according to the severity of the wounds. I was not badly hurt, so there were only 2 or 3 wounded left when I was loaded into the last ambulance that was there. We were taken to a hospital in Liege, Belgium for a short time, and then that night, that hospital was evacuated to Paris by train because of the danger that it might be overrun by the Germans.

After several days in the Paris hospital I was sent to a hospital in Normandy (do not remember the town) and spent about two months recovering, I returned to duty with the 420th AFA Bn. in Metz. France sometime in February 1945. I found out that my tank crew (except for the assistant driver who was with me) had gotten out without injury. They had gone through some woods off the road and that was the reason I did not see any of them as we drove back down the road in the jeep. My assistant driver was injured severely enough that he was sent back to the U.S.A. and did not return to combat. The tank crew that was trying to get out, and the lieutenant in command, who was left lying in the water hole, did not get out and were listed as missing in action.[112]

———

Nurse Augusta Chiwy was in Bastogne. She had been there since 16 December at the invitation of her father. On that fateful date she had travelled down to Bastogne from Louvain where she worked as a nurse in the Saint

Elizabeth general hospital. Despite ample rations being available she hadn't eaten properly for a few days and the almost constant racket of artillery exchanges had deprived her and all the other inhabitants of Bastogne of much needed sleep. Despite all the adversity she labored on tending civilians in the cellars beneath her old school. Wearing two thick overcoats above her own nurse's gabardine she darted from one patient to the next checking temperatures and administering what medication she had. Outside the fog still hadn't cleared, and Bastogne was beginning to resemble a forsaken ruin.

When Team Desobry had entered Noville they had fifteen tanks. As they returned to Bastogne only four of these tanks were still operational, and one of those looked like it had escaped from a junk yard. Furthermore, the 1st Battalion/506th PIR was a full strength unit when it marched out to assist Team Desobry. Throughout the course of the fighting at Noville it had lost 13 officers and 199 enlisted men. By their combined efforts they had destroyed or immobilized somewhere between twenty and thirty enemy tanks of all types, including three Mark V Panthers. There's every possibility that they probably damaged or destroyed many more. Headquarters of the 506th estimated that the assaults of the German infantry had cost the enemy the equivalent of half a regiment. The men who had fought in Noville had held their ground for a decisive forty-eight hours. This proved to be sufficient time in which to organize the defense of Bastogne.

LIEUTENANT COLON EL JAMES O'HARA, 54TH ARMORED INFANTRY BATTALION

To reinforce the 327th Glider Regiment of the 101st Airborne Division, five light tanks from Team O'Hara were placed on their right flank in the town of Marvie. At approximately 1115 these light tanks engaged enemy armor at extreme range. Twenty minutes after the shelling commenced, four Mark IV tanks, a self-propelled 75 gun, and six infantry-carrying half-tracks moved out of the woods east of the town. Apparently they had seen the light tanks because they concentrated their fire and rained shells in the direction of the troops who were protecting them. The light tank platoon leader withdrew his forces further into the town as enemy armor continued to move forward continuously firing at the light tanks. Since O Hara's tanks were having no effect on the enemy armor and his presence in the town was only exacerbating the situation by drawing fire on the friendly infantry, the light tank commander realized that he wasn't helping the infantry and requested permission to withdraw to the high ground north and west of Marvie. This permis-

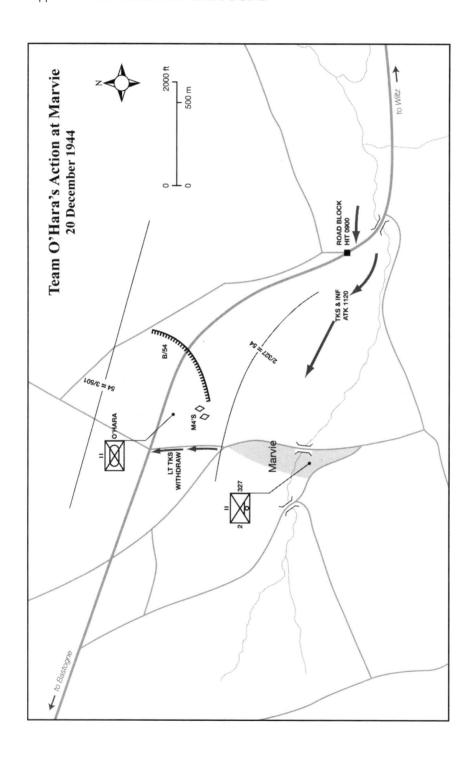

Team O'Hara's Action at Marvie
20 December 1944

sion was granted. During this interim one light tank was hit and set afire but continued to withdraw. The attacking enemy armor now consisted of a self-propelled gun, three Mark IV tanks, and a half-track personnel carrier. 75mm guns from O Hara's medium tanks now engaged the enemy. Two rounds accounted for two Mark IV tanks. The enemy realizing they were vulnerable to flanking fire, scattered in an attempt to escape. The self-propelled gun struggled to retreat back down the road but was disabled by the tankers. The personnel carrier was next. One Mark IV tank headed into Marvie but a bazooka team of the 327th accounted for him. At 1325 a half-track personnel carrier was found to be stuck off the road east of Marvie.

This vehicle became a target for one of O Hara's tanks which scored a direct hit and caused him to burn. At 1420 an armored car was found in the same predicament as the half-track. *He, too, was disposed of in a like manner.*[113]

At daylight on 20 December German artillery began to shower O'Hara's position approximately a thousand yards southeast of his infantry positions. The fog effectively masked all observation, but by 0800 Team O'Hara could effectively discern the sound of armor moving toward their barricade. About an hour later the fog gradually began to lift revealing a dozen industrious German soldiers attempting to fell trees. A request was made for artillery support from the 420th AFA, which promptly responded. As a result of this concentrated barrage some of the Germans were killed while the rest beat a hasty retreat. The enemy made a further attempt to breach the roadblock, this time using a smokescreen. Fearing that an infantry assault was imminent O'Hara's men raked the smoke with every gun and mortar that they could bring to bear on the position. The German infantry attack never materialized and after they had been thwarted by the tankers guns the enemy decided to bypass the roadblock and head west through the tiny village of Marvie. At 1100 the 2nd Battalion, 327th GIR, in the process of relieving elements of the 326th Engineers in Marvie, began to receive artillery fire. The five light tanks sent to the village the night before remained in position to support the newly arrived glider men. Twenty minutes after the shelling commenced, four Mark VI tanks, a self-propelled 75mm gun, and six half-tracks carrying infantry moved out of the woods east of the town. They had apparently seen the light tanks as they concentrated their fire against the armor. The M5s replied with their 37mm, but these guns lacked the range to inflict any serious damage. This bolstered the Germans and caused them to intensify their firing. The light tank commander realized that he was not

really helping the situation by drawing even more fire onto the infantry position so he requested permission to withdraw. The M5's attempted evasive
maneuvers by darting from one place of cover to the next on the northern
edge of the village, hoping to avoid drawing fire from the Germans. This
tactic did not prove wholly successful because one of M5s was set ablaze
and the other was immobilized by a damaged drivetrain. The extent of the
damaged became apparent when the light tank had to travel in reverse gear
all the way back to Team O'Hara's position. Throughout the engagement
O'Hara's medium tanks that were positioned on the hillside refrained from
firing in an attempt to get the enemy to reveal his flank. When the German's
saw the light tanks retreating they moved in for what was supposed to be an
easy kill. This gave the medium tanks an opportunity to hit them with a
broadside at around 700 yards range. One Sherman immobilized a Mark
IV while the second Sherman effectively damaged another Mark IV and a
half-track. A third Mark IV attempted to extricate itself from the situation
and make it back to the cover of the woods, but it was promptly destroyed
by a bazooka man from the 327th GIR.

While O'Hara's tanks were taking out the Mark IV's piecemeal, German
half-tracks made a dash for the outer perimeter of the village. One they had
reached their destination the infantrymen they were carrying immediately
disembarked and sought refuge in the houses. A house to house battle ensued
with the men of 2nd Battalion, 327th GIR, that culminated in thirty Germans being killed with the rest taken POW.

STAFF SERGEANT STANLEY E. DAVIS, COMPANY C, 21ST TANK BATTALION

*The Germans tried to get past the road block established by Team O'Hara on the
morning of the 20th but it was well covered by the 420th Field Artillery Battalion. When the Germans could not make progress here they pulled and headed across
an open field towards Marvie.*[114]

Team O'Hara after action report:

> December 20
> Starting at 0645 enemy artillery was active. Under this cover they
> tried to remove our roadblocks but were driven off with two killed
> [0900]. At 1132 a German armored column hit our right flank. They
> were repulsed. Active patrolling to our front and flanks during the
> night and early hours of the morning kept the enemy off balance.

We established contact with the unit on our right, withdrew patrols from Marvie.[115]

Team Cherry after action report:
December 20
Weather and visibility—Fair, Cloud
Team Cherry received orders from CCB at 0030 Hrs. to withdraw Team Ryerson prior to dawn. Team Ryerson was ordered to withdraw from Mageret at 0630 by way of Bizory with contact point at Bizory, through lines held by the 501st Parachute Inf at Bizory and reinforce their lines. Team Ryerson started from Mageret at 0730 and move was completed by 0810 Hrs. Team Ryerson was compelled to fight his way out of Mageret toward Bizory because he was under constant attack from enemy tanks and infantry. Team Ryerson reinforced the lines of the 501st Inf for the remainder of the day.

Bn Trains moved from Magerotte to Rossignol at 1000 Hrs.[116]

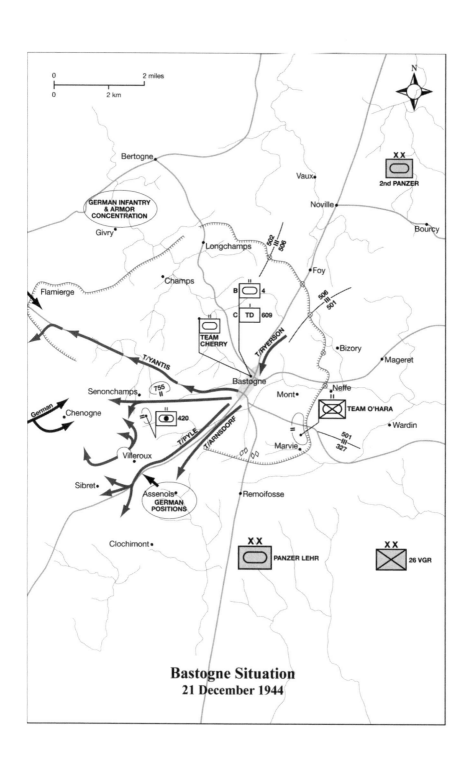

Bastogne Situation
21 December 1944

CHAPTER SEVEN
THURSDAY 21 DECEMBER

Weather report for south Belgium, London
Meteorological Office, Thursday 21 December, 1944:
*Persistent low lying dense fog, heavy snow showers
expected all areas. Remaining overcast, mild north
easterly wind. Temperature: −18°C.*

It was on the morning of the 21st that the Germans effectively
completed the encirclement of Bastogne by severing the last road
out of the city, the road to Neufchateau. Shortly before 1000 hours Capt.
Keith J. Anderson, D Troop, 90th CRS, conducted reconnaissance with two
assault guns and a tank destroyer. He reported that he had observed enemy
troops wearing American uniforms and driving U.S. Army vehicles somewhere near the village of Clochimont. A little later another patrol returned
from the village of Assenois and reported that the Germans were well en-
trenched there. The ensuing culmination of various reports of enemy activity
in Villeroux, Sibret, and Chenogne induced the defenders of Bastogne to
conclude that they were effectively surrounded.

Germans now maintained continuous shelling of the city in an attempt
to break the resolve of its population and its defenders. The artillery fire didn't
always have the same intensity and could be quite sporadic at times because
the Germans were also experiencing supply problems. Debris from the
shelling was everywhere and bodies lay where they had fallen, frozen into
grotesque shapes in the snow more reminiscent of the Russian front rather
than the western theater.

During the night of 20–21 December the Germans had successfully isolated Bastogne to the north and south. When their columns arrived from the
east and west the city was effectively under siege. The 5th Parachute Division,

which had an estimated strength of around eight thousand, maintained the German lines south of Bastogne. On 21 December the overall situation concerning German forces in the area still lacked clarity. Weather-beaten remnants of the 28th Division and the 9th Armored Division along with engineers and corps artillerymen were still stumbling into the city in dribs and drabs. The general situation was still vague. [117]

WILLIAM KERBY, 20TH ARMORED INFANTRY BATTALION

When we pulled back from Noville to Bastogne, Captain Geiger informed me that we were now attached to the airborne division. He stated that we were going into reserve and would be used when needed. He said to look for a billet for your men and to notify him of our whereabouts. I found a nice three-story building with a big basement. The first floor was a 5 and 10 cent store with a large kitchen at the rear. The second and third floors were living quarters. While in the basement, we started a small fire with what we thought was play money that we found in the corner of the basement along with a broken chair. (About a month later, we found out that it was real money). Down the stairs came Dr. Naftulin and Nurse Renée Lemaire. He introduced her to me and said they were looking for a building that would serve as an aid station. They left for about fifteen minutes. When they returned, Dr. Naftulin said, "Sergeant, this basement would make an excellent aid station." I told him that was fine, and he could have it. I stated that I would take my men elsewhere to find another billet. We moved down and across the street about forty yards. The house was on the side of a hill. You could walk in the door from the roadside and go down a flight of stairs, walk in and out into the backyard. There we dug foxholes and a latrine.[118]

420th Armored Field Artillery Battalion after action report:

December 21

Enemy ring complete. Bastogne garrison encircled and cut off from supply routes. Battalion acted as dismounted infantry and protected Senonchamps from infantry and small arms fire. Battalion supplied infantry and tankers with machine guns, shovels, blankets, small arms, ammunition, and rations. Service Battery avoided trap and arrived safely at Rossignol. CO half track and crew of four men left to look for 73rd Armored Field Artillery Battalion. Casualties: 4 EM-MIA.[119]

Dentist Lee Naftulin had made his way to a local communal cellar and asked some of the locals if there were any medical personnel in Bastogne. A little while later he was knocking at the door of Gustave Lemaire's haberdashery store on the main square. His daughter Renée answered the door and within moments she had her coat and bag and was following Naftulin to the new aid station around the corner on the Rue Neufchateau. On the way there Renée mentioned another nurse who also lived in Bastogne.

OTTO C. NERAD, COMPANY B AND SERVICE COMPANY, 20TH ARMORED INFANTRY BATTALION

In Tellet, Belgium it was cold but bright that early morning as we lined up for roll call of the Service Company Supply Trains personnel. I really was on the official roster of Company "B" of the 20th Armored Infantry as Mail/Supply Clerk. In order to carry out my multi duties I was attached to Service Company and that was why I had to stand for Service Company roll call that morning. After roll call, the commander of the Supply Trains informed us that there was a rumor a stray German tank was operating in the area and in order to protect our supply trains he was setting up a roadblock/outpost. He asked if any of the men standing before him had been trained in the use of a bazooka. Typically no on volunteered any knowledge of the weapon but I did offer the fact that I seen one once.

I was "volunteered," given a bazooka and two permanent KP's were given the rocket ammunition. We were loaded into the back of a jeep driven by Dwight Walker and a lieutenant occupied the seat alongside Dwight. We left the security of the Supply Trains and followed an armored car out into the snow covered countryside ready to protect our Supply Train against the stray German tank.

The armored car was about 100 yards ahead of us as our little convoy rounded a bend to the right of the road as we headed for our outpost location. The armored car made the turn and started down the straight road ahead with our jeep following close, something four or five hundred yards ahead fired a shot toward us. The armored car crew threw the car into reverse and headed back from whence it came at top speed reverse. Along the right side of the road was an earth bank about 3 or 4 feet above the level of the roadway. Dwight quickly pulled to the right side of the road and before the vehicle stopped and the lieutenant took off up the bank and disappeared into the pine trees beyond the road. The lieutenant was quickly followed by the two permanent KP's with their bags of rocket ammunition flying out behind them like the white bag of the Saturday Evening Post delivery boy being chase by a mad dog.

In my over excited hasted to set up the bazooka I jammed my knee as I jumped off the side of the jeep before it came to a complete stop against the bank. Dwight came around the right side of the jeep and we held a high level conference to decide our next move. Our outpost commander (the lieutenant) had disappeared into the trees at full gallop along with the KP's and the bazooka ammunition right behind him and I was left stuck with a five foot long piece of useless stove pipe. This high level conference lasted about 15 or so seconds and we decided right there, on our own, that the better part of valor was to get the hell away from the jeep and head back to our Supply Trains across country as quickly as possible. Meanwhile the unseen enemy fired another round at the armored car during our hastily held conference missing it and us, but it sure helped us to come to a quick accord.

My jammed knee was really hurting as we climbed the steep bank and I told Dwight to go ahead and I would follow as quickly as I could. I went as far as a row of pine trees about twenty yards from the road. I climbed under the ground hugging branches of one of the pine trees to rest because my knee hurt so very much. It was still early in the morn as I remember about 9 a.m. I laid hidden expecting some further action by our enemy but none came until about 11 o'clock when down that same road where we were to set up an outpost came an armored column that took forever to pass by my hiding place. Somehow a four hour time frame for its passing is still in my mind.

Then there was silence, only sound was that of the wind blowing through the pines around me and the occasional burp noise of a distant automatic weapon. I waited until it got dark, it got dark about four thirty p.m. I hatched a plan. I was equipped with a wrist compass and a pocket full of English chocolate bars I had liberated in Bastogne the day before. I would head west because that was where our troops were supposed to be. I started moving as quickly as my injured knee would allow me to traverse the pinewoods and open snow covered firebreaks between the pine groves. The moon was bright that night and crossing a snow covered fire break of about 100 yards in a dark colored uniform made me a real target but my desire to see friendly faces overcame that fear.[120]

TECH SERGEANT THADDEUS KRASNOBORSKI, HEADQUARTERS, 420TH ARMORED FIELD ARTILLERY BATTALION

The next day Sgt. Guyer, a corporal whose name I can't recall, and I were standing near a hedge that neatly led the children to the front door of the school house, when a mortar round came whistling in. It exploded in the middle of the hedge about eight feet away from us. Sgt Guyer was mortally wounded when shrapnel cut the artery in his neck, the corporal took shrapnel in his heel and I, miraculously, just stood there without a scratch!

This should have told us something. Why were we under [obviously observed] mortar fire when we just moved back 2.3 miles from the front? The answer would soon come from my plotting board. We were firing steadily and coordinates from the FOs were pouring in. Then the coordinates for a target came in that made me wonder. Did I make a mistake? I checked my plot, it was correct. I asked the FO to repeat the coordinates; everything checked out except that the target was in our rear! Several more of these came in and enemy infantry were spotted in our back-yard. That was the first indication I had that the Germans had us completely surrounded. The school house serving as the Fire Direction Center was hit by an enemy shell and set ablaze. We had to evacuate once more.[121]

ROBERT PARKER, COMPANY C, 21ST TANK BATTALION
We were sent out to help the 420th Armored Field Artillery. One of their artillery tanks had been hit by a phosphorous round and we had to get out of our tank to put it out. We were illuminated to the enemy and they were about 1000 yards around us. We did all kinds of things. We were a fire brigade.[122]

THOMAS HOLMES, INTELLIGENCE AND RECONNAISSANCE PLATOON, 54TH ARMORED INFANTRY BATTALION
Our mounted patrols were down, I only went on one down the Arlon Road and I also went on one down the Neufchateau Road as well. We were so damn busy, we had reached a point where we were so damn hungry. There just was never any warm food, ever. We didn't have a house to go into and we only had a hole to jump into for a break. [123]

———

The order for Combat Command B on December 21 was clear and precise: "Hold Bastogne at all costs." During the previous evening Corps Commander Troy Middleton had talked with McAuliffe and expressed serious doubts on the American military forces at Bastogne were sufficient for the task. All along Middleton had been willing to take the gamble of an encircled force at Bastogne, and for a few hours he may have wavered in his conviction. Now, after meeting with McAuliffe, his resolve to hold the city strengthened. McAuliffe now had the answer to all of his questions; no situation could have been more clearly defined. During the first two days he had entertained many doubts and had continued to wonder just what the situation was. He had heard about the 28th Division, the remnants of which were still out fighting somewhere to the east and might fall back upon the city. He had also had to worry about the organization of stragglers, but Colonel Roberts had dealt adequately with that problem. Major General Norman D. Cota of the 28th Division had called McAuliffe on the morning of December 20 and said, "I'd like to see you," and McAuliffe had replied, "I'm too damned busy." Cota replied, "I'll come up to see you." Cota never made it to Bastogne.

Battery B, 796th Antiaircraft Artillery Battalion, after action report:
December 21
At dawn, the enemy attacked both Foy and Recogne with infantry and tanks. Foy was taken fairly easily because the defense of the town had been set up on the South side due to enemy artillery shelling Foy during the night. Around 0930, Lt. Palmaccio and the 3 M-15s abandoning their ammo trailers withdrew with the Tank Destroyers to the Battery CP, where they were used in the defense (AA) of the artillery. One M-16 in Recogne had been damaged by tank fire and the squad leader was wounded, so the crew returned with the half-track to Senonchamps. This squad had held an outpost and road in Recogne all night against enemy patrols and slowed up the attack enabling the infantry to withdraw in an orderly manner to stronger positions. Another of the M-16s burned out a coil and had to be abandoned and destroyed. The crew returned on foot to the Battery CP. The third M-16 and Lt. Nell remained with the infantry securing the right flank of the 502nd AB as the 506th withdrew, until the 502nd could reform their lines. This vehicle, armed only with four .50 cal MGs turned a Tiger Royal tank from advancing on the CP of the CO of the 502nd. At Senonchamps, we used four halftracks to repulse an infantry and tank attack from the west. After the attack had been quieted, three tanks with infantry went on and drove the enemy back about 500 yards. We held four vehicles with crews alerted to operate in a ground role in any direction.[124]

JERRY GOOLKASIAN, COMPANY B, 3RD TANK BATTALION
So I fell asleep, at midnight she came by with a flashlight, she went by me, then she came back and said "you're the one that's hard to get," they grabbed in the neck with the needle and gave me two more pints of blood there. Fortunately, this was before Bastogne was surrounded, they put me on a train to Paris for Christmas, they had some more surgery in Paris, after a week in Paris I went to England for more surgery.[125]

With the siege came a siege mentality. The people of Bastogne developed even more resilience and fortitude to combat the ensuing battle and terrible conditions that now prevailed. As the deep snow fell unabated and temperatures dropped to record levels they remained resolute and more determined than ever to see this through with their erstwhile companions from the U.S. Army. The conditions affected everyone and no one was immune to the soul crushing cold that sapped the spirit and blunted the mind. Despite this they gritted their teeth and fought on through. German artillery shells fell indiscriminately all over town killing civilians and soldiers alike. In between each barrage civilians and soldiers worked furiously dousing fires as best they could and pulling wounded and dead bodies from the rubble. It was a heartbreaking and arduous task exacerbated by the freezing conditions and lack of supplies.

Paratroopers from the 101st Airborne were charged with holding the perimeter around Bastogne and preventing the Germans from gaining access. Consequently, being in the front line they were notching up the lion's share of the casualties. Back at the aid station in Bastogne conditions were deteriorating from untenable to downright squalid. Sleep deprivation and fatigue were taking a heavy toll, but the team carried on regardless. All the serious cases had been assembled on the first floor while the rest were dispersed around the cellar directly below. There were well over a hundred patients by that time.

Bastogne was a city completely encircled and held under siege by around twenty-five thousand German troops. Only a few thousand more than the defenders but that wasn't known at the time. In some places the German forces were as close three kilometers from the city center. During the previous day the 26th Volksgrenadier had succeeded in taking the nearby villages of Assenois and Sibret, and in doing so they had severed the last two roads into Bastogne.

Team O'Hara after action report:
December 21
Enemy continued to probe our lines, feeling for a soft spot. Machine gun fire forced their withdrawal. A combat patrol during the day was forced to withdraw because of enemy machine gun fire. Mortar fire was brought to bear on these reported points. Harassing artillery fire continued throughout the day on all targets of opportunity. Our night patrols to the front continued.[126]

Team Cherry after action report:

December 21

Weather and visibility—Fair, Cloudy

Team Ryerson ordered back to vicinity of Bn CP (Bastogne) at 1500 Hrs. Team Hustead was attached to Team Cherry and the Team placed in Division Mobile Reserve (101st AB Div). Team was placed on a thirty (30) minute alert status, to be prepared to counterattack the enemy in any direction. Bastogne under constant shelling at this time. During the night of the 21st December the Germans cut the Bastogne-Neufchateau Highway and completely surrounded Bastogne. One (1) Tk (M) from A/3 and two (2) squads of infantry from C/20 under command of Lt. Yantis, reported to CP, CCB for instructions at 1900. Mission of this force; To fight way through to and bring back ammunition trains for 420 FA Bn. [that] were cut off by enemy.[127]

CHAPTER EIGHT

FRIDAY 22 DECEMBER

Weather report for south Belgium, London
Meteorological Office, Friday 22 December, 1944:
*Fog in low lying areas. Winds light and variable,
more snow showers expected. Remaining overcast.
Temperature: −12°C.*

The 22nd of December began as a day of relative relief from the constant German bombardments. A heavy snowfall the previous night had blanketed the whole area and covered most of the scars from the recent combat. In the center of Bastogne supply officers began searching for white paint and white bed sheets to use as camouflage for both vehicles and men. Out in the foxholes battle-weary GIs crept tenuously out toward straddle trenches to treat themselves to a wash and shave, the first in days.

Nevertheless, there would be little respite for these U.S. troops in the field. Nerves were frayed and shattered as freezing, hungry soldiers strained their eyes and glared into the fog, flinching at every approaching shadow, cringing at every unfamiliar noise that emanated from the gloom around them. The instruction to "Hang tough" from General McAuliffe was testing even the most resilient of constitutions as GIs shivered and huddled together in a vain attempt to stave of debilitating cold in foxholes out on the city's perimeter. The place was still shrouded in dense fog and over a foot of snow had accumulated over the past few days exacerbating an already bad situation. Artillery units were down to their last few shells and all stocks of ammunition were now seriously depleted.

420th Armored Field Artillery Battalion after action report:

December 22

Lt. Col. Browne and Major Crittenberger direct tanks in direct fire on enemy tanks. Enemy uses white snow suits and white tanks for camouflage in snow. The enemy made a breakthrough in sector of Headquarters Battery. Capt. McCloskey, Battery Commander, organized the defense of his area and formed a perimeter defense which repulsed the attack. On the night of December 22, Capt. McCloskey attempted to lead a small armored party back through the enemy lines to bring up much needed ammunition. Capt. McCloskey's half-track was knocked out, but he and two of his crew escaped. Lt. Crouch, Battalion Surgeon, cleared 76 casualties through Battalion receiving station on December 22. Lt. Col [*sic*] Roberts, CCB Executive Officer, takes over command of entire sector. Capt. Kite, Battery Commander of Battery "C" was wounded. Capt Oleson, Bn S-2 assumes command of Battery "C". Casualties: 1 Officer and 2 EM wounded.[128]

In an attempt to effectively gage the size of the German forces in the vicinity Troop D, 90th CRS, sent out a patrol in the direction on Givry. Once there they observed substantial numbers of German infantry and armor. Out at Senonchamps three separate attempts were made to breach Lieutenant Colonel Browne's forces there, but each attempt was vigorously fought off. Colonel Roberts was now instructed to take charge of all miscellaneous U.S. forces while Browne focused on his artillery duties.

Battery B, 796th Antiaircraft Artillery after action report:

December 22

The morning of the 22nd was bright and clear. The Americans had lots of air support. Things were getting hot in Senonchamps. Mortar and artillery shells were coming in regularly. Four halftracks were kept out in position with the F.A. and these had to change position quite often because of enemy fire. Six of the First Platoon halftracks had now rejoined the Battery. These halftracks were held in reserve at the C.P. with the others.

Because of the low temperature and fog of those days in Senonchamps, the artillery men found solenoids would freeze, as would .50 caliber machine gun trigger linkages of the M-15's and the carburetors and gas lines of most of the halftracks. At first the answer to the problem was a couple of blow torches. But it was too much work for the torches available.

One of the boys on an M-16 hooked up a rubber hose from the exhaust outlet of the generator motor to the solenoid. That was the answer to that problem. All oil was removed from the .50 caliber machine guns and they were wiped dry. After that, they gave us no more trouble other than a slight stiffness that was easily worked out.

The frozen gas lines and carburetors were taken care of by shutting off both gas tanks and running the motor until all the gas drained out of the lines.

They never did resolve the problem of the frozen linkages of the M-15, except by thawing them out and cleaning them thoroughly. That and constant checking helped a lot.

During the day of the 22nd, two more attacks were beaten off. 37mm H.E. bursting in trees about head-high off the ground was very effective. That evening, Lt. Nell reported back from Recogne with one M-16.[129]

The Germans had already identified Bastogne as a major hazard to their progress. This fact was aggravated by newspaper headlines in the west beginning to report about the "Brave defenders of Bastogne" and comparing the siege to Verdun and the Alamo. These reports had come to the attention of Adolph Hitler who was more than acquainted with the power of propaganda. He explicitly ordered that Bastogne should be captured. This mission was given to the German 5th Army commanded by General Hasso von Manteuffel. General Baron Heinrich von Luettwitz, a corps commander, had specifically asked about Bastogne at a conference prior to the offensive. In the presence of General von Manteuffel, the Fifth Army commander, von Luettwitz was told that Bastogne would definitely have to be taken. Accordingly, in instructions to his subordinates, he stated: "Bastogne must be captured otherwise it will be an abscess in the route of our advance and will tie up too many forces. Bastogne is to be eradicated first, and then the bulk of the corps can continue its advance."

Troop D, 90th Cavalry Reconnaissance Squadron (Mechanized) after action report:

22 December

1ST PLATOON:

Remained in Bastogne. Elements went on reconnaissance patrol with Captain Anderson.

2ND PLATOON:

Remained in Bastogne. Elements went on reconnaissance patrol with Captain Anderson.

3RD PLATOON:

Remained in mobile reserve for Team O'Hara and maintained outpost during the day.

TROOP HEADQUARTERS:

On orders of higher headquarters the Troop was given the mission of reconnoitering Route N15 between Bastogne and Neufchateau. Captain Anderson organized a patrol consisting of two 1/4 tons, two armored cars and two tank destroyers. The column proceeded down highway N15 until it reached the vicinity of Vileroux where in contacted a friendly American column. As it proceeded west from this point one of the TD units was hit and destroyed by enemy fire. The destruction of this vehicle on the highway split the column into two. Nevertheless the two 1/4 tons and Captain Anderson's armored car proceeded on its mission until it came to the cut 800 yards east of Sibret. Here the three vehicles halted while Captain Anderson and Tech 5 W. T. Kraft covered his advance, the two proceeded on foot to reconnoiter the town of Sibret. When they reached the outskirt of town Captain Anderson stopped to observe the activities within the town. The town was filled with men in both American German uniforms as well as American and German vehicles. While observing this, a German soldier in a complete American uniform stepped from the doorway of a house in back of Captain Anderson and fired an M1 rifle at him. Captain Anderson and Tech 5 Kraft withdrew, returned to their vehicles, and all returned to Bastogne.

At 1400 Captain Anderson received orders to establish an OP in vicinity of Vileroux overlooking the Neufchateau road. He placed Staff Sgt. Curran in charge of the patrol with one armored car, one 1/4 ton crew from the 2nd platoon, and one 1/4 ton crew from the first platoon. When the patrol reached Senonchamps Staff Sgt. Curran was informed the enemy had taken Vileroux and the high ground surrounding it. Staff Sgt. Curran returned with his patrol and reported to higher headquarters.[130]

On the morning of 22 December, a German surrender party, consisting of two officers and two NCOs, approached the perimeter of the 327th Glider Regiment, carrying a white flag. The party was taken to a nearby platoon command post. While the enlisted men were detained the officers were blindfolded and taken to the command post of the 327th where they presented their surrender ultimatum. The ultimatum said in essence that the position held by the 101st was hopeless and that if they refused to surrender they would inevitably suffer the terrible consequences.

HARRY H. KINNARD, HEADQUARTERS, 101ST AIRBORNE DIVISION

While we were still surrounded, on the morning of December 22, a German surrender party, consisting of two officers and two NCOs, and carrying a white flag, approached our perimeter in the area of our Glider Regiment, the 327th. The party was taken to a nearby platoon command post. While the enlisted men were detained the officers were blindfolded and taken to the command post of the 327th where they presented their surrender ultimatum. The ultimatum in essence said the 101st's position was hopeless and that if we elected not to surrender a lot of bad things would happen. . . .

The message was brought in to the Division Headquarters by Major Alvin Jones, the S-3, and Colonel Harper, the Regimental Commander. They brought the message to me, the G-3, and Paul Danahy, the G-2. My first reaction was that this was a German ruse, designed to get our men out of their fox holes. But be that as it might, we agreed that we needed to take the message up the line. We took it first to the acting Chief of Staff of the Division, Lt. Col. Ned Moore. With him, we took the message to the acting Division Commander General Tony McAuliffe. Moore told General McAuliffe that we had a German surrender ultimatum. The General's first reaction was that the Germans wanted to surrender to us. Col. Moore quickly disabused him of that notion and explained that the German's demanded our surrender. When McAuliffe heard that he laughed and said: "Us surrender? Aw, nuts!" . . .

To the U.S.A. Commander of the encircled town of Bastogne.

The fortune of war is changing. This time the U.S.A. forces in and near Bastogne have been encircled by strong German armored units. More German armored units have crossed the river Our near Ortheuville, have taken Marche and reached St. Hubert by passing through Hompre-Sibret-Tillet. Libramont is in German hands.

There is only one possibility to save the encircled U.S.A. troops from total annihilation: that is the honorable surrender of the en-circled town. In order to think it over a term of two hours will be granted beginning with the presentation of this note.

If this proposal should be rejected one German Artillery Corps and six heavy A. A. Battalions are ready to annihilate the U.S.A. troops in and near Bastogne. The order for firing will be given im-mediately after this two hours' term.

All the serious civilian losses caused by this artillery fire would not correspond with the well-known American humanity.

But then McAuliffe realized that some sort of reply was in order. He pondered for a few minutes and then told the staff, "Well I don't know what to tell them." He then asked the staff what they thought, and I spoke up, saying, "That first re-mark of yours would be hard to beat." McAuliffe said, "What do you mean?" I an-swered, "Sir, you said 'Nuts'." All members of the staff enthusiastically agreed, and McAuliffe decided to send that one word, "Nuts!" back to the Germans. McAuliffe then wrote down:

To the German Commander,
Nuts!
The American Commander.

McAuliffe then asked Col. Harper to deliver the message to the Germans. Harper took the typed message back to the company command post where the two German officers were detained. Harper then told the Germans that he had the American commander's reply. The German captain then asked, "Is it written or ver-bal?" Harper responded that it was written and added, "I will place it in your hand."

The German major then asked, "Is the reply negative or affirmative? If it is the latter I will negotiate further."

At this time the Germans were acting in an arrogant and patronizing man-ner and Harper, who was starting to lose his temper, responded, "The reply is de-cidedly not affirmative." He then added that, "If you continue your foolish attack your losses will be tremendous."

Harper then put the German officers in a jeep and took them back to where the German enlisted men were detained. He then said to the German captain, "If you don't know what 'Nuts' means, in plain English it is the same as 'Go to Hell'. And I'll tell you something else, if you continue to attack we will kill every goddam German that tries to break into this city."

The German major and captain saluted very stiffly. The captain said, "We will kill many Americans. This is war." Harper then responded, "On your way Bud," he then said, "and good luck to you." Harper later told me he always regretted wishing them good luck.[131]

(There are many versions of this story, but the authors believe this to be the most accurate account. Some historians even proposed, somewhat audaciously, that McAuliffe gave a more profane response to the German ultimatum, but we don't believe that. Moreover, we don't think that the word "nuts" was intended as a profanity at all? It was used a mild imprecation like "damn." The Oxford English Dictionary traces the usage "Nuts" to 1931. Used as a derisive retort: nonsense, rubbish; I defy you. Another thesaurus refers to it as an "Interjection, expression of annoyance, disbelief or contempt." According to Kinnard's account and other sources McAuliffe initially assumed that it was the Germans who wanted to surrender, but this is probably historical conjecture contrived to bolster the reputation of the illustrious Screaming Eagles. As if it needed that?)

THOMAS HOLMES, INTELLIGENCE AND RECONNAISSANCE PLATOON, 54TH ARMORED INFANTRY BATTALION

I allowed my men to go to the basement of the CP to get warm, and there was a BAR man, H. T. Williams who was about thirty-two years old. I discovered that he did not come back after some time. I told him, "we have got guys who are colder than hell, who need to get warm" He told me "I am thirty-two years old. I'm old, I'm too old for this." Finally I said, "If you don't get your fanny out there I will shoot you myself. These guys, your buddies are out there and they're cold, and they want to get in there too." Needless to say he got out of there. He took a little abuse from the other guys, but he settled into it.[132]

OTTO C. NERAD, COMPANY B AND SERVICE COMPANY, 20TH ARMORED INFANTRY BATTALION

About 2 a.m. I got really tired and climbed under more ground hugging branches of another pine tree, took off my shoes to rest my feet and feel asleep. I sleep very soundly, to let you know how soundly I sleep one night while I was asleep in my truck a self-propelled 105 howitzer moved very near to my parked truck complete with their AA supporting unit and started to fire at the unseen enemy. The AA's supporting unit's fire shot down a friendly plane that crashed landed about 300 yards from where I was sleeping. When morning came I was surprised to find what had gone on so close to me during the night, however, I did have a good night sleep, but back to my story.

I woke in the morning, December 22, 1944, to the familiar friendly sound of our halftracks and M-1 armored cars. The sound was coming from the other side of a wall of thick pine trees about 25 feet away. All my earlier Boy Scout training did well by me for my Scouting compass training had paid off. I had found my boys. I quickly put on my shoes, picked up my carbine and ran to wall of pine trees. As I burst through the trees to the friendly column of American halftracks and tanks I happily yelled, "Hi Ya Fellows!"

The canvas top of the closest halftrack was quickly folded back at sound of my yell and two heads popped up to see what caused that noise. Then in an instant one head said in a loud voice to the other "Johann, Das ist eine Amerikaner!" Yep, you are right. Right vehicles—Wrong army. I spent the next four months or so touring western Germany along with a large group of other Americans all at the courtesy of the Third Reich.[133]

Team O'Hara after action report:
December 22

Commencing at daylight the enemy shelled our positions with mortar and artillery. This was answered by counter-battery silencing two known positions. Artillery fire was brought to bear on enemy infantry concentrating in area west of our front lines. Enemy once again felt out left flank but were forced to withdraw after small arms fight. A combat patrol reported movement of cargo vehicles on the Wiltz-Bastogne highway to our front. Harassing artillery fire was brought to bear on this highway. [134]

Team Cherry after action report:
December 22

Weather and visibility—Snow and limited
At 0450 Hrs., Team put on a ten (10) minute alert status to attack in any direction. Two (2) squads of infantry transferred from Team Hustead to Team Ryerson because of depleted state of Team Ryerson. Transfer complete at 1000 Hrs. Team alerted for counter-attack to Southwest and stayed on alert throughout the day.[135]

CHAPTER NINE

SATURDAY 23 DECEMBER

Weather report for south Belgium, London
Meteorological Office, Saturday 23 December, 1944:
*Heavy frost all areas. Light mist in low lying areas
clearing before noon. Clear skies. Winds N/E 6 miles
per hour. Temperature: −25° C.*

As the freezing dawn broke on 23 December immaculate clear skies greeted the weary defenders of Bastogne and before long streaming vapor trails began to appear above. All along the battlefront a milky sun cracked thin shards of spectral light through the freezing haze on that bitterly cold winter's morning. As hard as it was for all to believe the skies appeared to be clearing and an azure blue sky was already greeting the day. This was going to be a "special" day for the besieged inhabitants of Bastogne.

420th Armored Field Artillery Battalion after action report:
December 23
Major Crittenberger was put in charge of defending our western sector and Capt. Lane, the southern sector. Great drive and initiative were displayed by both in rounding up stragglers from other units and organizing defense of the area. One tank attack and two infantry attacks repulsed in western sector. Staff Sgt. Jarrell, "C" Battery Rear Observer was commended for superior manner of directing artillery fire. Battery "B" of 796th AAA Battalion, attached, was successfully employed in sweeping the woods with their AA guns, helping clear sector of enemy infantry. Small arms battle 300 yards west of CP.

Battery "A" took up direct fire positions and engaged four tanks. M-7 of Battery "A" received a direct hit and burned with part of crew

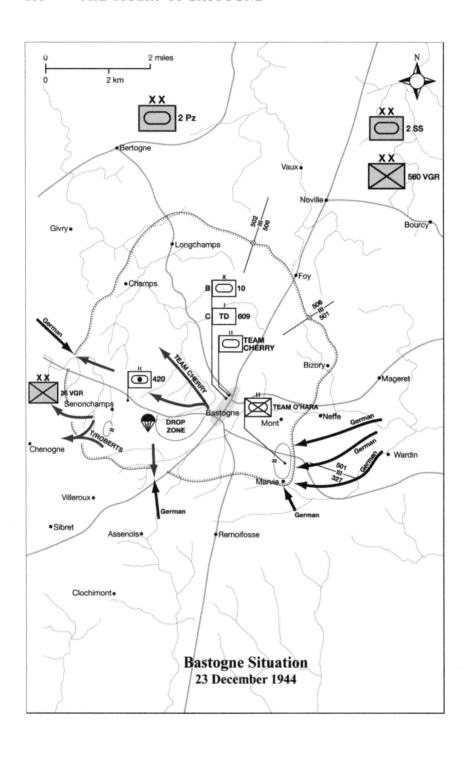

Bastogne Situation
23 December 1944

inside. Capt Oleson, seeing this, mounted the piece and attempted to put out the fire and evacuate the wounded personnel. Although exploding ammunition blew him from the tank and burned him and heavy enemy mortar and artillery fire was landing all around, Capt. Oleson returned to the tank and continued his efforts to save the gun and crew. Casualties: 7 EM wounded, 1 EM killed, 4 EM- MIA.[136]

Eyes filled with quiet expectation gazed hopefully skyward as the day began. On that day in Bastogne the skies above filled with squadrons of C-47s roaring into view and dropping different colored parachutes. The chutes were color coded to indicate their contents such as medical supplies, ammunition, food, etc. The first of the carriers dropped its six Para packs at 1150, and in little more than four hours 241 planes had reached Bastogne. Escorting the cargo airplanes were waves of P-47 fighters, which cavorted unopposed up and down the perimeter, raking the Germans wherever they were exposed. The air force could now unleash its wrath with a vengeance and as the day progressed they dominated the skies above Bastogne causing the Germans to scurry for cover wherever they struck.

Battery B, 796th Antiaircraft Artillery Battalion after action report:
23 December
Infantry attacks were repulsed at 1000 and again at 1430. The Battery Commander's 1/4 ton was hit and destroyed by artillery fire and eight men were wounded. [137]

Each C-47 carried some twelve hundred pounds of supplies, but not all reached the drop zone nor did all the Para packs fall where the Americans could recover them. Despite this it was widely considered as being the most accurate supply drop of the war.

A German attack led by the 26th Volksgrenadier Division and the attached regiment left behind by Panzer Lehr was about to commence. Extensive preparatory salvos by German artillery and *Nebelwerfers* (screaming meemies) would open the proceedings and fly into the U.S. lines like banshees while the infantry crept in as close as possible to the American foxhole line. By this time the new fallen snow had put every dark object in full relief; the German grenadiers had donned white snow capes, their mobile artillery and tanks whitewashed to provide additional camouflage. The Americans compensated by requisitioning what Belgian bed linen hadn't already been procured to use as bandages and used it as impromptu ponchos and helmet covers. They were also able to find whitewash for some of their tanks and other vehicles.

SERGEANT WARREN SWANQUIST, HEADQUARTERS, 3RD TANK BATTALION

While I stayed in a house we had a stove in the basement, which fell over, and thankfully I did not get burned. The air drop was quite a scene; the C-47s were towing in gliders in a field behind our house. We saw a few planes crash into the stone fences there and the gliders were cartwheeling through the field. We got some medical supplies and ammo, but no food: we were starving.... We went hunting in every house for food. We did find a crock. We thought it had water in it, but when we tipped it over there were eggs in it. They were good and hard-boiled. We did not have any K-rations.[138]

The real strength of the U.S. Army was in its soldiers' ability to improvise, which was the antithesis of the Germans who were not renowned for their flexibility. The German assault would be led by a tank platoon—normally four or five panzers—followed by fifty to a hundred infantry. If this first wave failed, a second or third—seldom larger than the initial wave—would be thrown into the fray. It is clear, however, that due to a lack of resources the German commander and his troops were cautious about employing massed tactics at this stage of the game.

WALTER LEPINSKI, HEADQUARTERS COMPANY, 20TH ARMORED INFANTRY BATTALION

I heard there was going to be an air drop, but no one pulled me away to get any of the supplies. Captain Geiger didn't tell me and my motor officer didn't either. I was right at the back of the house when the air drop planes came in really low. You could see the side doors open with the guys kicking supplies out with different colored parachutes: green, white, red, and blue on them for different supplies with ammo. I also saw the gliders come in with the medical equipment and stuff. I never got to see any of the dog fights overhead.[139]

EARL VAN GORP, COMPANY D, 3RD TANK BATTALION

It was quite a sight, they dropped parachutes with gas, ammunition, and every-thing.[140]

THOMAS HOLMES, INTELLIGENCE AND RECONNAISSANCE PLATOON, 54TH ARMORED INFANTRY BATTALION

We were sent to the positions of the machine gun platoon near the main road, and we stayed there throughout the next few days until the breakthrough after Christmas. I looked up to see what the hell I could see as the sky cleared in the morning. The planes were making contrails in the sky and we thought they were going to come and get us for sure. The fighter-bombers were flying around the city and I thought it was super. We were told to stay put during the air drop; the main road remained suspect. I wondered why in the hell they did not come down the road. We got some ammunition on the 23rd, but we were mad about it because the people in Bastogne proper were getting more supplies than we were out on the outposts. We wondered if they were getting hot meals and we weren't. The guys were getting a little surly at times wondering if we were going to get any help.[141]

The besieged residents and defenders of Bastogne had almost hit rock bottom. Life in the city had long since lost any semblance of normality; the situation was at its absolute nadir. The local civilians, oblivious to the magnitude of the conflict, had even taken to scraping the wax off U.S. ration tins to make candles. There was no electricity or operable telephones, and due to the ruptured and smashed up pipes, water was now the most sought after commodity. All inhabitants had taken to either domestic or communal cellars, and this also caused problems. Firstly personal hygiene suffered due to poor sanitation, which caused lice and flea infestations, and secondly there was the problem of widespread respiratory illnesses caused by the damp and bitterly cold conditions.

ELTURNIO "LUCKY" LOIACONO, COMPANY B, 54TH ARMORED INFANTRY BATTALION

It was December 23rd, 1944, the day the Air Corps was able to do their thing. I guess we all felt sort of relieved that at last we were getting some of the pressure we were under removed. For the first time since we had occupied our positions on the Wiltz/Bastogne road I wandered more than thirty feet from my foxhole in order to visit with Staff Sergeant Marty Grossman, who had a field phone in his hole that was a direct line to the artillery. While we were making "small talk", about twelve German machine guns opened up on the village about 2000 yards on our right flank. Marty seemed unconcerned. I, being a recently made PFC, had no idea of field phone procedures and blurted out " Marty why don't you tell the artillery that you can spot those machines," to which he answered in his finest Brooklynese "Yeah, yeah, right!"

He pulled the phone out of the case, blew into it and announced, "I can spot some machine guns up here" and hung up. Within seconds three rounds came in, two behind us and one to our front. Marty seemed oblivious that they were hitting in our area. I shouted, "Marty, why don't you tell the artillery that they're shooting short?" He gave two puffs into the phone and said, "you're shooting short, Oh, okay," and hung up. I asked him what they said, he answered, "they said they ain't shooting" which suggested to me that I had better high-tail it back to my own hole because if our guys weren't shooting that mean that the Germans were shooting.

I figured that there was one of three reasons why Marty showed little concern for those three rounds coming in on us. Reason one, Marty did not really call the artillery as he knew that the gunners were short of ammo so he went through the motions to put me at ease. Two, our artillery didn't get the message, but the Germans did. Three, the artillery put Marty's call on hold.

We had been located near two farm houses since December 18th. At sundown on December 23rd a German force attacked a 101st glider unit on our right. At about 7:00 p.m. we heard German tanks and infantry coming up the Bastogne/ Wiltz road. There were four of us next to the road in front of a farm house and the rest of what was left of our company were in a field between that farm house and another house about 200 meters away.

Apparently the Germans were not aware of our location because it was very dark and we were concealed in our foxholes quietly waiting for them. When the soldier on my right side hit the first tank with a bazooka shell the Germans suddenly realized that they had stumbled into us and began shooting. We also began shooting to defend ourselves. Meantime a second tank, a panther I believe, started to shoot his 75mm gun at the house which was about 25 meters behind me. A piece of shrapnel hit me in the right eye and I immediately dropped down in my foxhole and doctored my wound. I thought that I had lost my eye. When I regained my senses several minutes later I realized that the tank that had hit me, which was then 30 meters to my front had moved to within two meters of my hole. Fortunately, the tank did not run over my hole, probably because I had used a white bed sheet from the farm house for camouflage. The tank crew apparently could not see the difference between the sheet and the snow on the ground. The tank driver later drove away without disturbing me. I was concerned, however, that he had run over my other three comrades foxholes, and had buried them.

It was at this time that I realized that I was alone and the Germans were all around me. My thoughts were that I must leave my hole and get back to the

*other farm house 200 meters away and join the rest of my company before it be-
came daylight. The idea of being captured or killed made me nervous and fright-
ened me. Since I was the only child, I wondered how my mother would take the
news of my being killed or captured by the Germans.*

*It was now late at night and my foxhole was approached by two German
soldiers for the second time. One jumped in my hole and placed his knees on my
side and at the same time felt my pulse as the two spoke each other. My guess was
that they were not completely convinced that I was dead. The German in my hole
bounced up and down a bit causing me to breath and I thought surely he must
know I am alive. Following this they started to put dirt in the hole. At this point
I had decided to surrender, but just as I did, the dirt stopped coming and the German got out and they both left.*

*I suddenly felt more relaxed and almost positive that I would make it back to
my comrades and then a strange thing happened, I fell asleep.* [142]

*Private Elturnio L. Loiacono, 54th Armored Infantry Battalion,
Bronze Star citation:*

On 23 December 1944 in the vicinity of Bastogne, Belgium, his unit
was subjected to an attack by a strong force of enemy infantry supported by tanks. When the rest of his unit withdrew, Private Loiacono remained in his foxhole and fired his Browning automatic rifle
at the enemy until he had expended all of his ammunition. Remaining in this sector in full view of the enemy, he feigned death and allowed the enemy to kick him and feel of his pulse, never moving or
giving away the fact that he was alive. Private Loiacono remained in
this position for ten hours and obtained important information regarding enemy movements and dispositions. Returning to friendly
lines, he reported his finding to his headquarters. Through his outstanding courage and high devotion to duty, Private Loiacono obtained the information which greatly assisted the staff in their
estimate of the situation. His actions were in accordance with the
highest standards of the military service. Entered military service
from the District of Columbia.[143]

MAJOR WILLIS D. CRITTENBERGER, HEADQUARTERS BATTERY, 420TH ARMORED FIELD ARTILLERY BATTALION

*Thank God for the airdrop. They dropped it near where we were; the 101st gave
us all their 105mm ammunition. The red parachutes were artillery ammo and*

the green parachutes were gasoline. The 101st was able to distribute the supplies to everyone once we gathered up all that we needed.[144]

ROBERT PARKER, COMPANY C, 21ST TANK BATTALION

I remember we had to get the supplies from where they dropped; a good percentage of them dropped behind the Germans. We got gasoline, [which we especially needed] because a tank did not go very far on a tank of gas. I don't think they sent any 75mm. They sent 105mm for the artillery plus boxes of .30 caliber ammunition. They sent food, too, and we were running out of food, but when you were in combat you did not consume a lot of food, you were too scared to eat. There was a shortage of everything. I can remember the C-47s coming in, and I saw many of them shot down before they got rid of their cargo.

I remembered my driver was named Briggs, the assistant driver was named Fornier and he was killed. The tank commander's name was Lowandowsk; he had to be evacuated because he had gone completely nuts at what had happened and all he did was cry.[145]

STAFF SERGEANT STANLEY E. DAVIS, COMPANY C, 21ST TANK BATTALION

Early evening on the 23rd, tanks and infantry attacked Hill 500 south of Marvie and surrounded the defenders who were a part of the 327th Glider and were not heard from again. Four German tanks from the assault forces on Hill 500 joined in the firing on Marvie along with tanks in the woods southeast of Marvie. Earlier in the day, Col. O'Hara had sent a half-track with a 57mm antitank gun to support the troops on Hill 500 but it arrived when that hill was under heavy attack so it headed back north into Marvie. It looked to the troops defending Marvie that it was part of the attacking forces. So they placed heavy fire on it knocking it out and killing the crew. Two German tanks followed along the same road and as they approached the church they could see the knocked out track blocking the road so they turned around and headed back south. After taking Hill 500 the German infantry and tanks attacked the south end of Marvie while at the same time enemy tanks and infantry were attacking O'Hara's positions north and south of the Wiltz road where my location was at this time. We knocked out and set fire to a SP gun which lit up the area and then enemy direct or artillery rounds set fire to a barn and hay loft which put us in a well-lit position so we pulled back a short distance to gain some protection in the dark and continued the fight to prevent the German advance. The enemy never did advance any further along this road to Bastogne. It was when we were reorganizing from this battle, taking care of our casualties and getting ready for the next attack (which did not come that night) that another tank commander and I reported to Col. O'Hara and were given the mission to take our two tanks into Marvie to prevent any further penetration and to force the German armor out of Marvie in conjunction with the 327th troops still holding the northern part of the town.

The town of Marvie was under heavy attack by German tanks and infantry who had taken about one half of the town. Marvie was defended by troops from the 327th Glider [Regiment] of the 101st Airborne and had no tank support in town. It was now approaching midnight, we had a brief discussion about the inadvisability of moving tanks into unknown areas in total darkness but the situation in Marvie required immediate action so we mounted up our crews and moved to Marvie which was about one half mile away.

We were not familiar with the road network in Marvie but there was a single road from Bastogne going into the north end of town which split giving parallel roads through town and merging into a single road south of Marvie with three or so cross roads connecting the two roads in town.

We moved slowly on the road to Marvie and were met at the split of the road by a member of the 327th who advised us that German tanks and infantry were in the southern part of Marvie just south of the church, he though there were three tanks. The 327th was dug in mostly in the basements and the first floor levels of the homes. He also said that there was an American half-track on the left hand road and that the tanks were giving them a lot of trouble and they needed some help to prevent the Germans tanks and infantry from taking the town and moving into Bastogne.

The Germans tanks would have to attack on the two roads because of the many residential buildings in town so we decided that each tank would advance as far as possible on one of the roads and set up a blocking position to prevent the German tanks from advancing through Marvie. My tank took the left hand road for a few hundred yards to where we could make the church and the knocked out American [half-track]. There was a cross road just north of the church on the left and another cross road just south of the church where the 327th was dug in, there was sporadic firing at this time.

We backed our tank into a small court yard with a building to our rear and to our right, the north south road on our left and the church and knocked out half-track to our immediate front at about 30 yards. Sporadic fire continued for a while but was not in our immediate area then we could hear tank engines and knew that tanks were moving around to our front and we could not see them because of the darkness and building. We were sure that the tanks (at least one of them) was moving slowly along the road toward us but we still could not see them. Visibility was very poor but we could just about make out the shadow of the knocked out half-track so I directed my gunner to aim just to the right of the halftrack were there was a little room for a tank to advance. I told my loader to put an armor piercing round in the chamber and be ready to fire and to be sure his ready racks were filled with both armor piercing and high explosive rounds, we had a 75mm gun. In a short time we knew the German tank was at the knocked out half-track and trying to push the half-track out of the way (from the revving up and straining noises). We opened fire at point blank range with both armor piercing and high explosive ammo and the German tank returned the fire putting rounds into the buildings to our right and to our rear setting them on fire. We continued to fire AP and HE rounds as fast as we could reload with the Germans doing the same, after several shots were exchanged, the German tank stopped firing and we could see shadowy figures bailing out of the tank so we continued with HE fire and machine gun fire until they disappeared.

We had a short period of relative quiet during which we prepared to fire on the other tanks if they appeared. We then heard tank engine noises indicating tanks backing up and moving around and one tank coming towards us, at this time we aimed our gun as well as we could just over the top of the silhouette of the first tank and when it sounded like the second tank was getting close to the first tank we fired a couple of rounds. The road by now was just about completely blocked and the second tank backed up, sounded like they were making a turn around and headed south on the road out of town. We could hear the third tank moving around and it sounded like they came out of the cross road and made a right turn and also headed south out of town.

The smoke from the burning buildings made it necessary for us to move, we were worried that there might be someone left in the tank or that a gun crew could sneak back into the turret and use the tank gun so we kept an AP round in the chamber and our tank gun aimed as we could on the abandoned (apparently) tank and moved forward about 20 feet. I could not make contact with our other tank by radio at this time. We spent the rest of the night in our combat positions.[146]

Staff Sergeant Stanley E Davis, 21st Tank Battalion,
Bronze Star citation:
On 23 December 1944, in the vicinity of Marvie, Belgium, during a vigorous battle against enemy tanks, he remained in town with his tank and fired continually at enemy armor. Since the heavy armor of the enemy tanks prevented his shells from penetrating, Sergeant

Davis, under extremely heavy enemy fire, exposed himself so that he could move to the enemy flank. From this position he was able to destroy one tank and one half-track and force the remaining enemy armor to withdraw. He then exposed himself continually to enemy fire in order to deliver fire on enemy vehicles, gun positions, and enemy personnel since a shortage of ammunition prevented the artillery from accomplishing these tasks. His actions were in accordance with the highest standards of the military service. Entered military service from Massachusetts.[147]

On the evening of 23 December Team O'Hara was comprised of 19 officers and 292 enlisted men, with six medium tanks, one 105mm assault gun, a forward observer's medium tank, four 75mm assault guns, four light tanks, and sundry small arms and vehicular weapons. The team occupied the reverse slope on high ground north of the bend in the Wiltz-Bastogne highway.

Active combat patrols to the front and flanks gave credence to the belief the enemy was preparing for an attack. Using information gained by these patrols harassing artillery fire was brought to bear on enemy concentrations of troops and material.

DONALD NICHOLS, COMPANY C, 21ST TANK BATTALION

I believe it was on the night of 23rd the Germans launched another attack on our position coming down the road we were guarding. This was a night attack. The first I knew was the M.G. fire and a farm house was set afire to provide light. Our tank was rocked with a close explosion. We were ordered to fall back out of the lighted area. We backed up about 50 or 60 yards, however things had quieted down.

The next order was to fire all weapons at 06:00 A.M. at the wooded and illuminated area we had backed up from. My tank commander told me to traverse my turret slightly and level my gun. I was pointing at the road area to my right front. I did not see anything there. At 06:00 A.M. we got the command to fire, which I did. Apparently there was a German Panther tank on that road. He apparently fired at the same time I did. My round knocked his tank out and his AT hit our tank as it was in recoil and gouged some steel out of tank sheering sprocket bolts out of the right side front track area. Their round must have then ricochet off sending a lot of sparks, like an acetylene torch does. The rest of the crew bailed out and I continued to fire my 30 cal. co-ax M.G. until empty. Crawled around the 105 gun, reloaded my 30 M.G. retrieved another 105 round from the ammo pit in the floor, loaded it, went back to the gunner seat, fired it and M.G. empty, again repeated the same as above and at that time the rest of the crew came back and wanted to know if I was OK and I said OK but I could use some help. They came back, I continued firing but very shortly the cease fire command was given. Since resupply of ammo or food was not available as they were rationed items and could not be resupplied at that time.

Before we went north I mentioned we were full of rations and ammo and what I used on the first day was replaced that same day. We had extra food rations enough for 2 weeks. The 101st Airborne, who were with us also, had come into Bastogne with minimum of each. We shared some of our food rations with them and glad to do it.[148]

The principal enemy effort of the day was thrown against Lt. Col. O'Hara's team and the 327th Glider Infantry at Marvie. At 1820 Team Cherry, which at the time was the division reserve, was sent to counter threatened penetrations toward Monty and Champs. Ten minutes later the front of Team O Hara's position was hit hard and then, supported by withering artillery fire, tanks and infantry hit their right flank. This proved to more than the defenders could handle forcing them to call for assistance. As German armor moved on the road followed by infantry, the 420th AFA unleashed all their batteries on them. In light of these developments Team Cherry, which was en route to Champs, was ordered to return to Bastogne. At the same time as the assault on Team O'Hara's front, German tanks and infantry stormed the 2ndBattalion, 327th Glider Infantry Regiment, from the south. Lieutenant Colonel Harper, commanding this battalion, screamed to O'Hara for tanks, not knowing that at that very moment the 54th Armored Infantry Battalion was itself locked in a desperate life or death struggle.

LIEUTENANT COLONEL JAMES O'HARA, 54TH ARMORED INFANTRY BATTALION

During the remaining daylight hours complete plans were laid for communications within the organization and with the units on our flanks. Detailed fire plans were made, the 81mm mortar platoon and assault guns being set in such position so to deliver fire on any section of our lines firing battery. From our depleted forces a reserve was formed and so placed that it had availability of reaching any section of the lines threatened. As complete a briefing of the situation as possible was given to the entire task force. The men were told what they had, what they expect (hollering, noise makers, nebelwefers, tanks, infantry, flame throwers, wilding shooting, enemy in American uniforms and equipment.) and what was expected of them. The attacked was possible from any sector at any time, probably at dawn. Anything moving to the front after dusk was enemy. The men dug deeper, checked their weapons, and prepared to stand.

At 18:30 23 December 1944, with an artillery preparation, the enemy (tanks and infantry) launched an attack on Marvie on our right flank. Communications kept us completely informed of the situation at all times. At 1915 the enemy without preparation attacked our sector. Armored moved on the road with infantry following. The lead vehicle was a self-propelled 75. The crew was dressed in white sheets and suits. The outpost let them through. They were disposed of by the medium tank who held its fire until they had a perfect target. The infantry was fired on and dispersed by the outpost. A Mark IV tank fired five rounds at the flash of our tank while advancing all the time. Enemy foot elements in strength was now advancing through the woods, shooting wilding and hollering insults in English and German. The Mark IV was disposed of by the 105 AG and the 76 mm gun of the forward observer. A strong patrol invaded our left flank over running our machine gun position. A hand grenade destroyed one gun and forced the other to withdraw to a prepared alternate position. At this time our outposts withdrew since their position was made untenable by small arms fire, but before this they knocked out a personnel carrier. During this entire operation not one man, save the machine gun and their protection, had a fire a round. Due to the burning vehicles and a building hit by enemy fire, our entire position was silhouetted. Our line moved to alternate positions in the shadows. At this time the team commander committed his reserve, placing them on the left flank, which he believed his weakest spot. The reconnaissance platoon went as protection for the light tanks whose tremendous fire power was now believed necessary.[149]

Captain Edward Carrigo, 54th Armored Infantry Battalion, Bronze Star citation:

On 23 December 1944 in the vicinity of Marvie, Belgium, he was acting as S-2 for his organization. He was directed to send out a daylight combat patrol to determine the strength of the enemy to the front of his position. Captain Carrigo, on his own initiative, organized a thirty-six man combat patrol and personally led them. The patrol met the enemy, engaged them in a fire fight and withdrew without casualties. This patrol, under the inspiring leadership of

Captain Carrigo, gained valuable information necessary in planning artillery fires which successfully broke up an enemy attack of armor and infantry. On the following day, he again led a combat patrol of twenty men on a reconnaissance mission resulting in locating weak enemy forces immediately to the front of his position and rescuing a wounded soldier who had been lying in an exposed position overnight as a result of the attack by the enemy. Captain Carrigo's outstanding courage, inspirational leadership and extreme devotion to duty exemplify the highest standards of the military service. His actions were in accordance with the highest standards of the military service. Entered military service from Texas.[150]

Troop D, 90th Cavalry Reconnaissance Squadron (Mechanized) after action report:
23 December
1st Platoon in Bastogne until platoon leader 1st Lt. Paul G. Fleming and elements of the platoon moved with Captain Anderson to the town of Champs.

———

2nd Platoon Remained in Bastogne until elements of the platoon moved with Captain Anderson to the town of Champs.

———

3rd Platoon was ordered to take a 36 man patrol on a combat mission to destroy 3 enemy tanks located in a woods 1500 yards each of their position. The patrol consisted of 12 men from third platoon, 12 men from the 501st Airborne [Regiment] and 12 men from the 54th AIB I & R platoon. The patrol started out through a wooded route. When it reached open terrain the patrol started across to the woods containing the enemy tanks, but enemy MG fire and small arms fire was too heavy and the patrol was driven off.

———

Troop Headquarters In the morning, Captain Anderson received an order to take four 1/4 tons, two armored cars, and one TD, attached, and seize and hold the town of Champs at all costs. When they arrived at a Champs they found Company A of the 502nd [Regiment] of the 101st Airborne Division moving in. They set up a defensive position on the high ground to the south and overlooking the cross-roads and the town of Champs. At night the sections moved into defensive positions within the town.[151]

LIEUTENANT COLONEL JAMES O'HARA, 54TH ARMORED INFANTRY BATTALION

The enemy moved a small flat trajectory weapon, probably a 47mm or 50mm anti-tank gun into position firing directly down the road. Infantry disposed of this gun with grenades. They found a tank was in position to fire on any target challenging the smaller weapon. It is believe the smaller gun was bait for American tanks. The enemy infantry had by now advanced into the light. They were found to be taking full advantage of natural camouflage, wearing a white toque or suite in order to blend with the snowy background. American infantry commenced firing. The tremendous fire power at observed targets broke the enemy's morale and they commenced to withdraw. During this withdrawal they were engaged by American mortars and assault guns. Upon the withdrawal of the enemy, artillery was placed upon the entire American position.

Due to the depletion of their forces by this withdrawal of tanks and infantry by higher headquarters, allied capability to counter-attack was weakened. This fact made it impracticable to try and reoccupy the ground lost before morning.

At daylight the positions were reoccupied and combat patrols to the front ascertained the damage done. It was found that the enemy had abandoned very few of their dead or wounded. Also that they had ransacked the pockets of dead American soldiers taking all their possessions. Before it could be salvaged considerable material abandoned by the enemy was brought under mortar fire and this strip of terrain became a virtual no-mans land.[152]

ZEKE PRUST, SERVICE COMPANY, 54TH ARMORED INFANTRY BATTALION

Oh, that was the most beautiful sight in the world, when those clouds opened up [on December 23] and we saw all that materiel coming down. We knew some of it was landing with the Germans, but other than that it was an awesome sight. I was in Bastogne, and I was asked to do something as far as retrieval. We, our crew actually went into one of the homes where the horses were, and there were big troughs made of concrete, and we laid in those troughs until the shelling was light. Then we got out and back to our area. It was our place that we called home.

We were so fortunate to be in a tank. When a tank was running, the trans-

mission gave off heat, and there were so many who got frostbite. We were next to that transmission, and I tell you it kept us warm.[153]

Note: Cases of frostbite were ubiquitous at the time. Frostbite is distinguishable by the hard, pale, and cold quality of skin that has been exposed to the cold for too long. The area is likely to lack sensitivity to touch, although there may be an aching pain. As the area thaws, the flesh becomes red and very painful. Any part of the body may be affected by frostbite, but hands, feet, nose, and ears are the most vulnerable. If only the skin and underlying tissues are damaged, recovery may be complete. However, if blood vessels are affected, the damage is permanent and gangrene can set in. This may require removal (amputation) of the affected part. Upon warming, it is common to experience intense pain and tingling or burning in the affected area.

The condition occurs when the skin and body tissues are exposed to cold temperature for a prolonged period of time. Hands, feet, nose, and ears are most likely to be affected. The first symptoms are a "pins and needles" sensation followed by numbness. Frostbitten skin is hard, pale, cold, and has no feeling. When skin has thawed out, it becomes red and painful (early frostbite). With more severe frostbite, the skin may appear white and numb (tissue has started to freeze). Very severe frostbite may cause blisters, gangrene (blackened, dead tissue), and damage to deep structures such as tendons, muscles, nerves, and bone.

TECH SERGEANT THADDEUS KRASNOBORSKI, HEADQUARTERS, 420TH ARMORED FIELD ARTILLERY BATTALION

Headquarters was set up in a large well-constructed barn just west of Bastogne. I remember steel beams and concrete in some sections. There was a large hayloft overhead. (For the life of me I can't remember sleeping there). This location turned out to be our final move from whence we fought the rest of the battle. We were running out of food and the most foul C-rations I had ever tasted (which I could not eat) was all that was available. Finally the cooks liberated the farmer's entire chicken coop and we had one decent meal. But our most critical concern was that our ammunition had dropped to a dangerous level, which drastically curtailed fire missions. I remember when the Germans appealed to our better nature and magnanimously would allow us to surrender. General McAuliffe's answer was a short, "Nuts!" After being "socked in" for many days the weather cleared and the most beautiful sight appeared. A bright blue sky filled with C-47s all dropping multicolored parachutes carrying food, medicine, gasoline and ammunition. Some of the boys jumped into jeeps and picked up the ammo in preference to the food. For months the guys were sporting colorful scarves made from the parachute silk.[154]

ROBERT KINSER, COMBAT MEDIC, 3RD TANK BATTALION

Finally, when it looked like the end, the transports came by the hundred with gliders, it was the most beautiful thing I have ever seen. Every GI and civilian yelled and danced with relief, we had thought we were forgotten. The chutes were blue, red, yellow, and white, we all ran here and there, everybody trying to be the first one to get one. I saw one land on a barn and I ran to it and climbed up to it. The barn was rotten and I was afraid it would cave in, but I couldn't leave the supplies there. I went on and got it down, the bundle weighed about 500 lb. We opened it and were very disappointed instead of something to eat it was full of mines, tank mines. Well, I got a piece of the chute anyway.[155]

DONALD NICHOLS, COMPANY C, 21ST TANK BATTALION

I believe it was on the night of the 23rd that the Germans launched another attack on our position, coming down the road we were guarding. This was a night attack. The first I knew of it was the MG fire, and a farmhouse was set afire to provide light. Our tank was rocked with a close explosion. We were ordered to fall back out of the lighted area. We backed up about fifty or sixty yards, however, things had quieted down.[156]

Team O'Hara after action report:
>   December 23
>   At 1915 the enemy attacked without artillery preparation but tanks and self- propelled guns in direct support, the enemy infantry man-aged to force our left flank back approximately 100 yards where it reformed and held. After a fierce small arms engagement supported by mortars, assault guns, tanks and artillery, the enemy was forced to withdraw. His artillery and mortars then shelled our positions but were silenced by counter-battery. No patrolling to the front, but stronger outposts were formed for the evening.[157]

Team Cherry after action report:
>   December 23, 1944
>   Weather and Visibility—Clear, cold, Excellent
>   Team Ryerson and Team Hustead moved out to take up defensive positions at 1900 Hrs. to meet enemy threat from the West. Team

Hustead was recalled while moving to position and put on alert in town of Bastogne. Team Ryerson in position at 2130 Hrs. and started contacting friendly units to the right and left. Team Ryerson had a relatively quiet night except for a few rounds of arty and mortar fire. First supplies by air received this date consisting mainly of medical supplies.[158]

CHAPTER TEN
SUNDAY 24 DECEMBER

Weather report for south Belgium, London
Meteorological Office, Sunday 24 December, 1944:
Clear skies. Mild north wind 10 miles per hour
increasing to 20 mph as the day progresses. Snow
showers expected on high ground. Temperature: −12°C.

Team Cherry was ordered to provide armor support for the 327th Glider Infantry in their bitter fight at Marvie. Team O'Hara's two Shermans had greatly assisted the cause in this village by disabling three Mark IV tanks. This had discouraged further armored attacks, but the Germans persisted with infantry and intense artillery fire. It was not felt that Lieutenant Colonel Cherry's armored force could help much in the darkness, but their presence would have a profound effect on morale, and would be quite effective at daylight. Cherry's men and two batteries of the 81st Antiaircraft Battalion formed a second line just above the village. It was never really necessary to commit both the armor and the antiaircraft. The Germans repeated their mistake of attacking on only one front. Company A, 501st PIR, alerted from the now quiet Longvilly road sector, counterattacked through Marvie and restored the 327th's grip on the situation. Cherry's men remained north of Marvie until 1325 that day when it became apparent that the Germans were all but finished in that sector. Five light tanks under Lieutenant Arnsdorf took over and released Team Cherry to move back to Bastogne where it returned to division reserve.

MAJOR WILLIS D. CRITTENBERGER, HEADQUARTERS BATTERY, 420TH ARMORED FIELD ARTILLERY BATTALION

Christmas Eve, this was the worst day. The Germans decided to have a coordi-

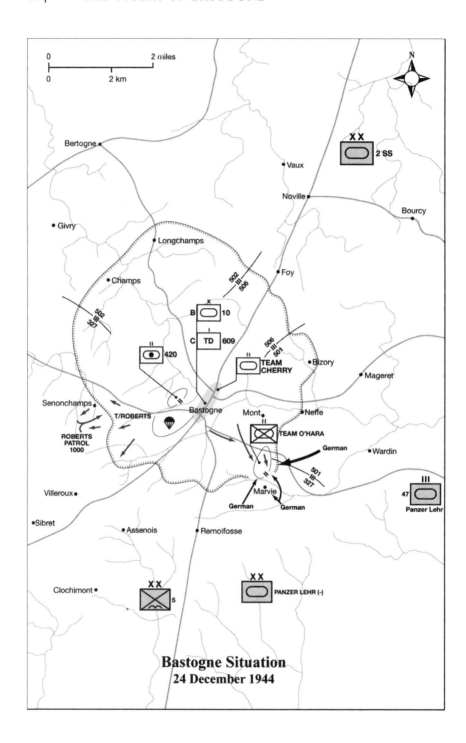

0   2 miles

0   2 km

N

Bertogne

Vaux

XX
2 SS

Noville

Bourcy

Givry

Longchamps

502
III
506

Foy

Champs

502
III
327

x
B | 10

C | TD | 609

506
III
501

Bizory

420

TEAM
CHERRY

Mageret

Senonchamps

T/ROBERTS

Bastogne

Mont

Neffe

TEAM O'HARA

ROBERTS
PATROL
1000

German

Wardin

501
327

III
47
Panzer Lehr

Villeroux

Marvie

German

German

Sibret

Assenois

Remoifosse

Clochimont

XX
5

XX
PANZER LEHR (-)

Bastogne Situation
24 December 1944

nated attack for the first time. We called for help and help came. We were fighting them off. The 101st luckily looked at the situation and reduced the size of the line. They told us to move back closer to Bastogne. That was good because my battalion commander was wounded, fatally, our headquarters was hit and burned, and we were lucky we were able to move out by order and not because we had to. We got mortared by the Germans. That meant two things they knew where we were, and they were getting close to us to mortar us. We beat some more attacks that night.[159]

420th Armored Field Artillery Battalion after action report:
December 24
Lt. Brunson (Forward Observer 3) and crew, attached to Team O'Hara, engaged Tiger Royal tank at 30 yards and destroyed same; also knocked out 2 anti-tank guns. S/Sgt. Jarrell killed while directing artillery fire. Lt. Col. Browne wounded in "B" Battery's position by counter battery fire; Major Crittenberger assumes command. Battalion moved from Senonchamps to 1/2 mile west of Bastogne. Displacement was orderly and conduct of troops superior despite enemy time and direct fire on all batteries. Three enlisted men wounded in HQ Battery just prior to displacement. Bastogne and area heavily bombed by enemy planes about 2000. Capt. Kite, Battery "C" was killed in hospital in Bastogne by concussion from bombs. Frozen ground helps M-7 in making big shifts. Casualties 9 EM wounded; 1 officer and 4 EM killed.[160]

Lieutenant Colonel Barry Duran Browne, Posthumous
Distinguished Service Cross citation:
For extraordinary heroism in connection with military operations against an armed enemy while serving with the 420th Field Artillery Battalion, in action against enemy forces from 20 to 24 December 1944. The skillful, heroic leadership Colonel Browne displayed while leading his men against strong enemy forces near Bastogne, Belgium, during the period 20 December to 24 December 1944, distinguishes him as an outstanding commander. He was continually with the front line troops, inspiring and encouraging them by his courageous personal example. On one occasion Colonel Browne personally led five tanks and two squads of infantry in a bold attack on an enemy column, inflicting heavy losses of men and material. On another occasion he directed the fire of his battalion from an exposed position

in his half-ton truck, completely disregarding his own safety. Lieutenant Colonel Browne's conspicuous heroism, inspiring leadership, and loyal devotion to duty exemplify the highest traditions of the military forces of the United States and reflect great credit upon himself, his unit, and the United States Army.[161]

WILLIAM RICHARD BARRETT, BATTERY B, 420TH ARMORED FIELD ARTILLERY BATTALION

On Christmas Eve the air cleared enough and the air force came in and parachuted supplies to us. Ammunition, food, and gasoline, all that we needed. That gave us another relief and support and let us get back in the action. I got down to two shells on the 105 and they were both smoke. That is not good for fighting armor. The shell that mortally wounded [Lieutenant] Colonel Browne flew right over my head. [162]

Lieutenant Colonel Browne was conscious when he was taken off the battlefield, and his last words to Major Crittenberger were "Hey Crit, take care of our battalion."[163]

Major William D. Crittenberger Jr., Armored Field Artillery, Bronze Star citation:
During the period 19 December to 24 December 1944, he was executive officer of his field artillery battalion which was engaging the enemy in the vicinity of Senonchamps, Belgium. On 21 December 1944 the battalion was attached by strong enemy forces supported by tanks. Commanding the norhern approach in addition to his regular duties, Major Crittenberger exercsied his superior knowledge of infantry tactics and directed his forces in an efficient and effective manner. When the commanding officer of the battalion was mortally wounded on 24 December 1944, Major Crittenberger assumed this command and despite an acute shortage of ammunition, directed fire continuosly at targets of importance with tremendous effect on the enemy. His actions were in accordance with the highest standards of military service. Entered military service from Indiana.[164]

At 1000 hours Colonel Roberts dispatched patrols into the woods adjacent to his position that were unoccupied at that time. When German artillery began to rain down on the exposed 420th positions it became glaringly obvious that the U.S. artillery would have to relocate. At around 1500 the 420th received direct orders to move to a new position northwest of Bastogne. By 2000 it had completed the move which now brought them under the 1st Battalion, 327th GIR, which took over the sector and assumed command of CCB's miscellaneous forces soon after they arrived.

Battery B, 796th Antiaircraft Artillery Battalion after action report:
24 December
At 0930 we were called upon to fire into some enemy Machine Gun nests that had been set up on the west side of the town. On the south side, a half-track in AA positions with the artillery was used to quiet the enemy who on several occasions apparently were preparing to attack on that side. CCB asked for five vehicles to report to Bastogne to form a Reserve unit. We sent 3 M-15s and 2 M-16s. All forces in Senonchamps were withdrawn closed to Bastogne and we were bombed twice this night. We did not fire at the planes because we were under orders to hold fire. One man was wounded.[165]

The air force continued their activity throughout the day. C-47's dropped supplies to the besieged American garrison at 0905 and again at 1505. P-47 Thunderbolts had an absolute field day and struck at the Germans everywhere they could. The most successful sortie was when the P-47s strafed an unsuspecting German column that was tenuously moving tentatively out of Morhet.

Sergeant Angelo Yequierdo, Company B,
80th Medical Battalion, Silver Star citation:
On December 24, 1944, Sergeant Yequierdo was serving inside the besieged city of Bastogne, Belgium as section Sergeant, Collecting Platoon, in an aid station which was suddenly subjected to enemy bombing attack. With utter disregard for his own safety Sergeant Yequierdo immediately raced to the aid of 47 men housed in the upper floor of this building. In the first room entered Sergeant Yequierdo found the stove had exploded. Smothering the flames with blankets he saved 11 men from serious burns. Another bomb explosion caused a large portion of the building to cave in. Although struck by falling debris Sergeant Yequierdo continued going from

room to room extricating litter casualties from great quantities of plaster, brick and heavy debris. Sergeant Yequierdo discovered one casualty pinned under a red-hot stove unable to move. With the aid of a blanket he pulled the stove off the casualty and rendered immediate first-aid. Sergeant Yequierdo then discovered bombs had struck an adjacent building in which casualties were housed. Running into the flaming building, Sergeant Yequierdo passed through intense smoke and flame to the aide of the wounded. He was able to drag four men to a hole in the building from which they were carried to safety. During this time 16 bombs fell in the immediate area demolishing 6 buildings and burying 23 litter casualties. His gallant action saved the lives of many wounded comrades.[166]

ELTURNIO "LUCKY" LOIACONO, COMPANY B, 54TH ARMORED INFANTRY BATTALION

When I woke up it was almost dawn. This worried me because I had wanted to move in the darkness of night but because I had fallen asleep my plans were no longer possible. It was not quite daylight yet and as I looked up to the sky which was dark blue and the stars were still visible against the azure sky. I could hear two Germans approaching my foxhole, but they did not stop. After a while I attempt to try and get to the second house. I got out of my foxhole, not daring to look at my comrades foxholes as they were covered in dirt, since the German tank the night before had turned around on top of them and anyone alive in those holes would have been crushed. The farm house had been completely destroyed by the German cannon fire but the tank that did the damage was in turn destroyed by our tanks and stood about 100 meters from the one time farm house.

As I came closer to the second farm house someone called to me, and I told him who I was and not to shoot. When I arrived at the second farm house the first men to greet me were my three comrades whom I thought had been killed by the German tank. My sergeant, who was very sick with a terrible cold, began to cry, tell me that he thought I had been killed. He said, "If I had known that you were only wounded I would not have left without you." I told him "to forget about the incident because it was all over."

As the sun became brighter my wounded eye began to bother me, so I was taken to Bastogne to a first aid station. Since both of my eyes were covered I could see very little, however, I could see a nun now and then and because it was Christmas Eve I could hear some girls singing carols. It was my guess that I was in some of Catholic school.[167]

First Lieutenant Herman C. Jacobs, Headquarters Company,
20th Armored Infantry Battalion Bronze Star citation:
On December 24, 1944, learning of the necessity of establishing a temporary hospital in the besieged city of Bastogne, Belgium, he afforded invaluable assistance to the battalion surgeon in accomplishing this task. In addition to his regular duties as S-1 of his battalion, he exerted every effort to organize the buildings, secure medical equipment and supplies, and procure the necessary personnel to treat, care and cook for the wounded patients. While assisting a medical officer in one of the buildings, an enemy bomb hit the building, setting it on fire. Although he received wounds from falling bricks and burning rafters, Lt. Jacobs helped to evacuate the patients who were in the building and unable to get out by themselves. He then organized firefighting parties to extinguish the blaze.[168]

Troop D, 90th Cavalry Reconnaissance Squadron (Mechanized), after action report:

24 December

1ST PLATOON:
Remained in Bastogne except for elements with Captain Anderson in Champs

2ND PLATOON:
Remained in Bastogne except for elements with Captain Anderson in Champs

3RD PLATOON:
Remained in mobile reserve for Team O'Hara. Maintained outpost.

TROOP HEADQUARTERS:
The day before Christmas was quiet at Champs. Friendly air was again very active. Friendly OP's on high ground in front of Champs reported enemy movement at Givry and roads to the north. The night in Champs was quiet with enemy activity still being reported to the north by friendly OP's.

At 1830 the town of Bastogne was bombed by enemy air. The attacked lasted approximately 30 minutes. After the attack was over 1st Lt. Eugene Leachman, in charge of the Bastogne detachment, took 1st Sgt. Roy R. Wood and Tech 4 George A. Engle, and set out to find if anyone was injured in the bombing. They discovered a hospital had been hit. First Sergeant Wood returned for the balance of the men in Bastogne. The men formed a bucket brigade directed by Tech 4 Engel. 1st Sergeant Wood continued to round up men to assist with the rescue work. Lt. Leachman worked directly with the rescue crews. After each bombing in Bastogne LT. Leachman and 1st Sgt. Wood went through the town looking for bomb damage where D Troop men could be of assistance.[169]

Captain Irving L. Naftulin, Dental Corps, Bronze Star citation:
During the period of 20 December to 25 December 1944, his battalion aid station was functioning as a hospital since evacuation from the encircled town of Bastogne was impossible. Captain Naftulin was in charge of one of three buildings which comprised the hospital and devoted long hours of the day and night treating and caring for the many wounded patients. On 24 December 1944 the town was attacked by enemy aircraft and two direct hits were made on the hospital, setting the buildings on fire and causing them to collapse. Digging his way out of the debris, Captain Naftulin returned to the burning building and rescued four wounded men. Although injured by falling debris, he continued his valiant rescue work. The outstanding courage and devotion to duty of Captain Naftulin saved the lives of many American soldiers. His actions were in accordance with the highest standards of the military service. Entered military service from Ohio.[170]

Dr. Irving Lee Naftulin, acting as a medical superintendent at the time, was also in charge of rescue efforts and miraculously escaped serious wounds. He said, "We had thirty-four wounded in the building at the time and seven were in the basement. They were screaming with pain as the fire started there. Sergeant Kenneth Souder, an engineer from Michigan, found a tiny hole at the rear of the basement. While the rest of us fought the fire he tied a rope around himself and went in and got out two of the wounded men before he was overcome himself. He was pulled out by Technician Fifth Grade Osborne Wayner of Standardville, Georgia. Another engineer named Riordan got out four more and Corporal Bernard Morrissey of East Providence got out the last man."[171]

STAFF SERGEANT STANLEY E. DAVIS, COMPANY C, 21ST TANK BATTALION

We spent the rest of the night in our combat positions and as soon as we had some visibility the next morning we checked out the German tank and found that we had been fortunate enough to knock off one of their halftracks which immobilized the tank, we disabled the guns and then I went to the right hand road looking for our other tank and learned that it had fired a few rounds the night before, had some gun problems and moved back to the original starting positioning during the night.

The American halftrack and the Germans tank made an effective road block on the left hand road but the right hand road was open so we took up a position to defend against attack along this road. During the day we moved our tank off to the right to have a good field of fire to the south of Marvie and at night we positioned ourselves on the right hand road with an AP round in the chamber aimed at the next intersection south of our position spending the night in the tank with the gunner awake at all times and shifting the crew around, all taking turns as gunner. [172]

ROBERT KINSER, COMBAT MEDIC, 3RD TANK BATTALION

The first German plane came over on Christmas Eve at about 10:00 p.m. It flew around awhile and left at about 11:00 p.m. It came back with a friend and flew over twice, the third time it let go with it's bombs. One hit 300 yards in front of our house, what was left of the glass was blown out. We took the six wounded to the cellar. The next close one was about 200 yards behind our house, it hit about 30 feet from a house and the whole thing caved in. It blew the back door of our house to the front. When you heard the awful whistle of the bomb it seemed to come right at you. You held your breath till it landed.[173]

On Christmas Eve the aid station on Rue Neufchateau took a direct hit from a five hundred pound German bomb. Nurse Renée Lemaire was killed instantly along with thirty wounded GI's. She had spent much of the previous day attempting to procure a parachute from one of the many dropped on that day. The story was that she was planning to make a wedding dress with the silk. Capt. Jack Prior, the 20th AIB surgeon, had gotten one for her and was planning to present it on Christmas day as a present. He used that same parachute to wrap up her remains and return them to her father. She was later buried in the parachute. Nurse Augusta Chiwy miraculously survived the blast. She was blown clear through a kitchen wall but escaped with only minor cuts and bruises.

DONALD NICHOLS, COMPANY C,
21ST TANK BATTALION

Because of the damage to the tank we were limited in our movements, we stayed in that position until Bastogne was relieved with only slight repositioning. We were told to move back to Bastogne. We moved a short distance off the line to the rear and spent the night on our tank. We watched the bombing of Bastogne and were glad we were not there. The next day we traveled into Bastogne and parked behind a building. Most spots were already taken. Apparently assigned to "Team SNAFU," a fire brigade outfit on call for any emergency. That night we experienced the bombing first hand. We stayed there until they brought in a low boy trailer which we loaded the tank on and they drove us back to Metz, France, for 10th AD ordinance to repair our tank. In Bastogne area for 10 days.[174]

After the explosion had occurred Capt. Jack Prior gathered some GIs together and raced to the top of the debris where they began flinging burning timber aside looking for the wounded. At this juncture a low flying German bomber noticed the action, and swooped even lower to strafe them with his machine guns.

Another Luftwaffe bomb from the same sortie fell on CCB head-quarters. Lieutenant John Burke, liaison officer from the 20th AIB, was killed instantly. The Luftwaffe managed to conduct two bombing missions on Christmas Eve. The first went in at 1945 and the second around 2200.

Sergeant Jack C. Reardon, 55th Armored
Engineer Battalion, Bronze Star citation:
On 24 December 1944, in the vicinity of Bastogne, Belgium, during an enemy bombing of the city, a bomb hit the temporary hospital of his organization setting fire to the building and destroying it. An unknown number of wounded had been trapped in the basement of the burning building. Daringly and of his own volition despite the added danger of exploding ammunition, gasoline trucks, and crumbling walls, he entered the debris of the bombed hospital and brought to safety four wounded men. Sergeant Reardon's outstanding heroism, his courageous determination and zealous devotion to duty exemplify the highest standards of the military service. His actions were in accordance with the highest standards of the military service. Entered military service from Michigan.[175]

Technical Sergeant Kenneth I. Sauder, 20th Armored
Infantry Battalion, Bronze Star citation:
On 24 December 1944 in the vicinity of Bastogne, Belgium, his battalion aid station was forced to function as a hospital since the encirclement of the town by the enemy prevented evacuation of casualties. When the enemy bombed the town, the hospital was set afire and demolished. Sergeant Sauder immediately responded to the call for aid, rushed into the burning building and carried out several of the wounded and directed the exit of many others. Although fall debris inflicted burns on his back, Sergeant Sauder continued his work. His actions were in accordance with the highest standards of the military service. Entered military service from Michigan.

WALTER LEPINSKI, HEADQUARTERS COMPANY, 20TH ARMORED INFANTRY BATTALION

I was in the end house at the square at the top of the hill of the main street. Our CP was across the street from there. It was dusk, just getting dark and I was standing at the corner of the building. I heard that goddamn ME109 again and all of the sudden, click, pop, and a flare came again ever so slowly. I ran right down the steps into the cellar of that building. To my surprise, I don't know when, but all these soldiers were down in that cellar and it was standing room only. The ceiling of the building was oval, and made of cobblestones. It had some small windows at the ground level and I heard the heavy planes coming over and you could almost hear the click of the bomb bay doors and I heard swish, swish, swish coming down in a circle and wham, it hit the ground. . . . We were taught in a bombing you open your mouth and holler so that the drums don't get knocked out of your ears. I just opened my mouth and hollered when I heard the swishing coming down. That air displacement coming through those two windows was unbelievable! There were several bombs dropped and luckily the building I was in didn't get hit. The building next to the one next to us was the aid station and that building got a direct hit. I did not leave after the aid station got hit because I didn't know if they were done bombing and the first sighting of the destruction from the vehicles that got a direct hit was not good. It was dark, dark, dark that night and I could not see anything.[176]

Christmas Eve wasn't all doom and gloom in and around Bastogne. The 502nd PIR officers were particularly fortunate to be treated to a Christmas

Eve Mass in the tenth-century chapel of the beautiful Rolle Château, which they were using for a command post. It was by all accounts a happy and peaceful occasion, well attended by the neighboring Belgians who had added to the fair offered by the regimental messes by providing contributions of flour and sides of beef from their own meager provisions. Within a few hours that peaceful scene would be transformed beyond recognition.

GEORGE WATERS, 796TH ANTIAIRCRAFT ARTILLERY BATTALION

We took position across the central squared from a house converted into a makeshift hospital. The aid station housed some 600 wounded under the care of a single field surgeon and two nurses. Not 15 minutes into establishing our position in the cellar of a bar, a shell attack close by rocked the building they were in, leaving them dazed. Soon after, a voice called from the stairs at the rear of the cellar, saying "the hospital has been hit! We need to get the survivors out of the burning building!"

Five of us went up the stairs and out the front door, and saw the carnage across the square. Two of my friends and two guys I didn't know approached the profusely shambles of the former three story building. As we approached it appeared as if a huge cleaver had cut the building in a diagonal swathe from the top corner of the ground level on the opposite side. Part of the second floor dangled over the first and victims were being helped out of a huge hole leading to the basement.

Knowing that we would likely be strafed at any time by the German bomber circling overhead, we surveyed the situation in the bright glow of magnesium flares dropped by the bomber. We knew it would be prime targets for it.

We turned to retreat to the cellar and before I took a couple of steps, I said "Wait a minute, what if we were in there and no one would help us?" We turned back and made our way across the square to help carry out wounded.

The irony of the situation was that this was the hospital that our driver, Pasquale Oritentalle, our gunner, Davis Seigle; and the other cannoneer, Jasper Mauk, were assigned to. Two men of the three survived the inferno.

Note: It's safe to assume that Mr. Waters overestimated the number of wounded at the Aid Station on the Rue Neufchateau. six hundred was the number of patients at the Heintz Barracks 101st Airborne HQ and aid station.[177]

SERGEANT WARREN SWANQUIST,
HEADQUARTERS, 3RD TANK BATTALION

When I came back to Bastogne, we were on a railroad bridge and a bomb hit the bridge. The tank flew over the bridge, it came down, the driver got killed, and I was in the ball-gunners seat and all the shells came from the racks behind me and locked my feet on the seat, and I hung upside and got hit in the chest by the turret as I got out. I hung there for a while and I was knocked out for sure.

I said to myself, "This is a way to feel dead, eh?"

I kept wiggling my feet, and fell on my head upside down to the ground in the snow. The tank commander broke his back but he survived. When I got out of the tank I went looking for help but there was no help. A half hour later a jeep came down and they took the tank commander out on a stretcher on the front of the jeep. They made me sit on the hood of the jeep because my pant leg was full of blood. I sat on the hood and they drove me up to a hospital in town and I could see there was a red cross on top of it. I saw a first aid guy and he wrapped my knee, and he kept wrapping and wrapping it because there was still bombing all around us. He was scared shitless. He kept wrapping until I told him that I wanted to be able to walk. He wanted me to lie down in the hospital on some straw but I said "No way, not in this place. "

I started walking down the street trying to find our headquarters because I was lost completely; it was pitch dark outside. After I was down there a bomb hit the center of that red cross and nearly killed everybody. I found some of our guys and they told me where our headquarters was, and I went in there the Major took me down to the basement; they were all down in the basement. He made me a cup of whiskey coffee, I had never drank whiskey before, and he told me to drink it and lie down on the straw in the corner of the room. It was the best sleep I had during my time in the Army.

I was completely lost mentally; I was still in shock from the tank accident. I thought about my wife and kid. I even wanted to lie in that straw for another hour or so, but the Major told me I had to get going and go to the tank. But when I went to the tank I found out I was not needed so they put me on guard duty on the edge of town right next to an alley.[178]

Team O'Hara after action report:

December 24, 1944

At 0900 a combat patrol to our front recovered wounded men, equipment, and vehicles from positions which had been over run the night before. This patrol also contacted an enemy outpost and drove them back after inflicting casualties. Enemy patrols trying to infiltrate through our lines were repulsed. We continued our harassing fires on enemy positions as much as possible throughout the night, always taking into consideration the shortage of ammunition.[179]

Team Cherry after action report:

December 24

Weather and visibility—Clear, Cold, Good

Team Hustead alerted at 0130 hours for movement to Southeast, moved out 0300 Hrs. Team Ryerson received orders via the Bn S-3 to return to Bastogne. Team Hustead moved into position at 0255 Hrs. Team Ryerson started back to Bastogne at 0226 Hrs. and reverted to mobile reserve upon closing in the town of Bastogne at 0400 Hrs. Team Hustead was recalled to Bastogne at 1410 Hrs. and reverted back to mobile reserve. Bastogne was bombed for a period of 15 minutes at 1930.[180]

CHAPTER ELEVEN
MONDAY 25 DECEMBER

Weather report for south Belgium, London Meteorological Office, Monday 25 December, 1944: Some cloud clearing by early afternoon. Fog overnight and ground frost. Winds from the north at 15–35 km/h. Chance of snowfall amounts near 0.8 mm possible. Temperature: −8° C.

There would be no Christmas truce in Bastogne, on the contrary in fact. At 0350 the Germans seized the initiative to employ their armor over the frost-hardened ground, free from aerial harassment, and launched a coordinated attack on the village of Champs, northwest of Bastogne. At that time this sector was being defended by the 502nd PIR, supported by Troop D, 90th CRS, and elements of the 705th Tank Destroyer Battalion. Due to the overwhelming onslaught of eighteen hostile tanks at around 0700 American troops had been effectively pushed back east of the village. Confusion reigned for over an hour, but eventually all eighteen German tanks were destroyed and most of the supporting infantry was killed or captured. The coordinated action of the paratroopers supported by the 705th's tank destroyers had proven to be more than a match for the attacking Germans. Team Cherry was ordered up to the line to provide additional support but by 0800, the time they arrived, the fight was pretty much over. Team Cherry remained in position and kept a watchful eye on the situation for the rest of the day, returning to Bastogne at 1725.

420th Armored Field Artillery Battalion after action report:
December 25
Lt. Col. Browne, Battalion Commander, dies in hospital in Bastogne

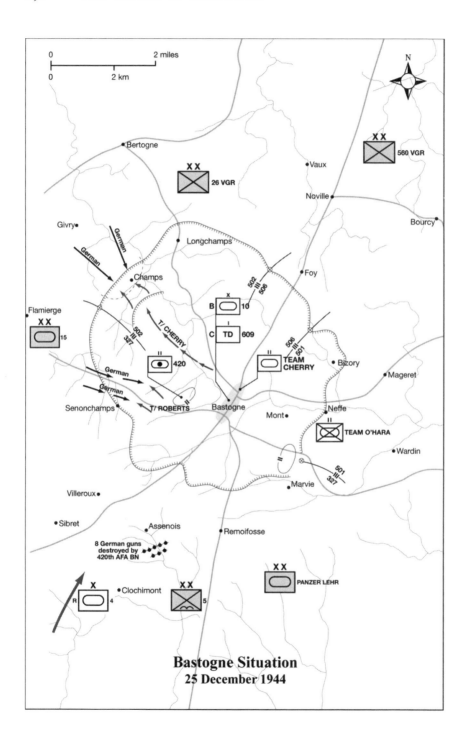

Bastogne Situation
25 December 1944

from wounds received in action on 24 December. Battalion very low on 105 ammunition, gas, and rations. Fired only 96 rounds all day. Heavy artillery and mortar fire on Battalion area. All personnel convinced of value of deep foxholes with overhead cover. Casualties: 1 officer died of wounds received in action.[181]

Battery B, 796th Antiaircraft Artillery Battalion, after action report:
25 December
Our battery was set up in a perimeter AA defense to Bastogne. We fired on some planes this night but our fire was ineffective because were only firing at sound. Our Orders were to fire on any plane that flew into the perimeter defense of the city.[182]

WALTER LEPINSKI, HEADQUARTERS COMPANY, 20TH ARMORED INFANTRY BATTALION

It was just another day; you never knew it was Christmas Day. It didn't seem like there was ever a Christmas there. I lost track of the days of the week.[183]

Moments before Team Cherry was scheduled to move out to Champs another threat had developed on the road to Mont. Team Ryerson moved out to counter the threat, which developed into an attempt to infiltrate German infantry through friendly lines with a flanking action on either side of the road. Ryerson's team had managed to disperse the infiltrators and by 1250 the German survivors had withdrawn westward toward Mande St. Etienne.

At 1145 a P-47 notified the headquarters in Bastogne that he had sighted what appeared to be eight enemy field guns just south of Assenois. The 420th AFA quickly noted the coordinates and with a few corrections relayed by the Thunderbolt pilot they were able to quickly destroy these guns. From this point onwards the ability of German artillery to inflict substantial damage was seriously diminished.

TECH SERGEANT THADDEUS KRASNOBORSKI, HEADQUARTERS, 420TH ARMORED FIELD ARTILLERY BATTALION

On Christmas, the battalion chaplain held mass on the hood of his peep. Every soldier not on duty at the time was there, such was the feeling of dread and the thought of impending death. Perhaps this Mass would shield us all from the advancing evil![184]

THOMAS HOLMES, INTELLIGENCE AND RECONNAISSANCE
PLATOON, 54TH ARMORED INFANTRY BATTALION

I woke up on Christmas morning. I was with a sergeant who had been with the machine-gun platoon; he had been injured slightly. He had crawled into a foxhole with me, it was a fairly good size one. He asked me "Hey do you have anything to eat?" and I said "I don't know, I haven't eaten in I don't know when." He started going through the little backpack we had that you would throw over your shoulders, I often kept my socks in there and other toiletries. He was looking around and he said "hey I've got something," and it was a tuna fish-sized can from a K-ration; it was a breakfast, one of those that I liked: bacon and eggs. So here are two guys in a foxhole on Christmas morning. We're looking at it—we couldn't light a fire, no smoke you can't do that—what were we going to do with this thing: it's half frozen. We held it between our legs, under our arms, anything we could do to cut the temperature of the thing down. We opened up and we split that bacon and eggs, in that little can, that little flat can, no crackers or anything. That was it.

Later on I went out to the road to talk to one the 101st guys and we were talking in the road, and all of the sudden there was a whoosh of air being displaced, and we both pushed away from it, and it was a large shell that had been fired down the center of the road. It was being fired the on road towards Marvie. I asked him, "My God, what was that?" He said, "I don't know but that was big stuff, whatever it was." I heard a crash but it was far removed from us. That was something that we never knew where it came from or if it was from a tank or not.[185]

Troop D, 90th Cavalry Reconnaissance Squadron (Mechanized)
after action report:

25 December

1ST PLATOON:
Remained in Bastogne except for elements with Captain Anderson in Champs

2ND PLATOON:
Remained in Bastogne except for elements with Captain Anderson in Champs

3RD PLATOON:
Remained in mobile reserve for Team O'Hara. Maintained outpost.

TROOP HEADQUARTERS:

At 0300 the town of Champs was attacked by a battalion of enemy infantry wearing white suits to blend with the snow. At 0830 the attack was quelled. We still held Champs. The TD attached with Capt. Anderson was destroyed but the Airborne Infantry inflicted several casualties and took numerous prisoners. At 0730 a new threat arose when enemy tanks were reported on the road to the rear, between Bastogne and Champs. Four TDs were sent from Champs to engage them and tanks from Team Cherry were sent from Bastogne. Seven enemy tanks were knocked out and Champs was still in our hands. The road between Champs and Bastogne remained open. From noon to the end of the day things were quiet at Champs with OP's reporting enemy movement and activity to our north and west.[186]

EARL VAN GORP, COMPANY D, 3RD TANK BATTALION

We didn't have a Christmas; we were surrounded at that time. We just had K-rations to eat. I missed my family, but I was glad to be alive for another day.[187]

MAJOR WILLIS D. CRITTENBERGER, HEADQUARTERS BATTERY, 420TH ARMORED FIELD ARTILLERY BATTALION

Before dawn the Germans had another coordinated attack towards the west side of town, the attack broke through the airborne lines. I was sleeping in a barn and the housing in that area had the animals hooked on next to the house. There was a cement floor so we put down fresh hay to sleep on. I woke up when I heard an attack coming and I told Stan Resor, who was my executive officer, to call our batteries and turn them to fire direct fire on these incoming Germans. I ran out to see what was happening in the headquarters area, just in time to see one of our perimeter defense posts burst in front of me, blowing over the machine gun, and four men running away, so I told them, "Come on men, help me put this machine gun back up." They came back and put it up. German infantry was coming and our howitzers were firing against their tanks. They only had four tanks, but we burned three of them and the fourth one surrendered later, and that was when one of the mess sergeants said, "Hey Major, come over." He made me Christmas dinner, two hotcakes and a half a cup of coffee. The hotcakes were made from the donut flour we had found earlier during the siege. [188]

Lieutenant John Brunson, 420th Armored Field Artillery Battalion, Silver Star citation:
During the period Dec. 23 to 25, 1944, Lieutenant Brunson, serving

as a forward artillery observer in the vicinity of Bastogne, Belgium, when the enemy launched a strong attack against an infantry company. Brunson skillfully directed artillery fire on the hostile force to within 100 yards of friendly troops, halting the enemy advance. During another attack by the enemy, when he lost radio communication with the supporting artillery unit, Lieutenant Brunson displayed extreme versatility by hastily manning a tank, and with an improvised crew, directed such effective fire that the enemy was decisively beaten off. The intrepid and courageous actions of Lieutenant Brunson under fire were largely responsible for the containing of the enemy to the outskirts of the town.[189]

ROBERT PARKER, COMPANY C, 21ST TANK BATTALION

President Roosevelt promised that everyone would have turkey for Christmas, and in Bastogne a jeep pulled up and put a frozen turkey on the front of our tank and we drove around with it on our tank from Christmas until January 12th. It never got warm but, he did keep his promise.[190]

Team O'Hara after action report:
December 25
Contact was maintained with the enemy by active patrolling. Mortar and assault gun fire on targets designated by patrols. Harassing artillery fire on all targets of opportunity.[191]

Team Cherry after action report:
December 25
Weather and visibility—Clear, Cold, Good
Bastogne bombed and strafed by enemy planes, number and type unknown at 0325 Hrs. AA Guns on all vehicles were manned and fired at planes. Team Hustead was alerted at 0820 Hrs. for movement. Team Ryerson moved from Bastogne at 0830 to positions held previous day. Team Ryerson occupied positions at 0920 Hrs. Team Hustead moved to position on road to Champs at 0940 Hrs. to repel enemy breakthrough at Champs. Both Teams were recalled to Bastogne at 1600 Hrs. and placed in mobile reserve. Team received artillery and mortar fire while occupying positions stated.[192]

CHAPTER TWELVE

TUESDAY 26 DECEMBER

Weather report for south Belgium, London
Meteorological Office, Tuesday 26 December, 1944:
*Clear skies expected all areas. Ground frost and mist
in the low lying areas clearing quickly. Winds from
the north at 15–35 km/h. Temperature: −25°C.*

This was going to prove to be a landmark day in the history of the
fight for Bastogne. In the wee small hours before dawn the Germans attempted yet another assault against Champs. At 0335 seven enemy tanks were observed by Troop D, 90th CRS, heading in the direction of the 502nd PIR lines. They were immediately met by the supporting tank destroyers and light tanks that managed to successfully beat them back. This was only a temporary respite because shortly after 0600 four Mark IVs succeeded in breaking through the infantry defenses at Hemroulle, whereupon they headed toward the artillery position of the 420th AFA. Thanks to decisive action that included direct fire from the artillerymen and the lightning swift maneuvers of the tank destroyers, the German intentions were foiled. By 0800 the original perimeter had been restored.

420th Armored Field Artillery Battalion after action report:
26 December
Long awaited supplies dropped by parachute by several flight of C-47's. Battalion picked up 1,050 rounds of 105 howitzer ammunition—no gas or rations. 10 gliders with gas and surgical team land. Battery "A" strafed—plane shot down. Two (2) men killed and one wounded by mortar fire. CCR of 4th Armored Division made first

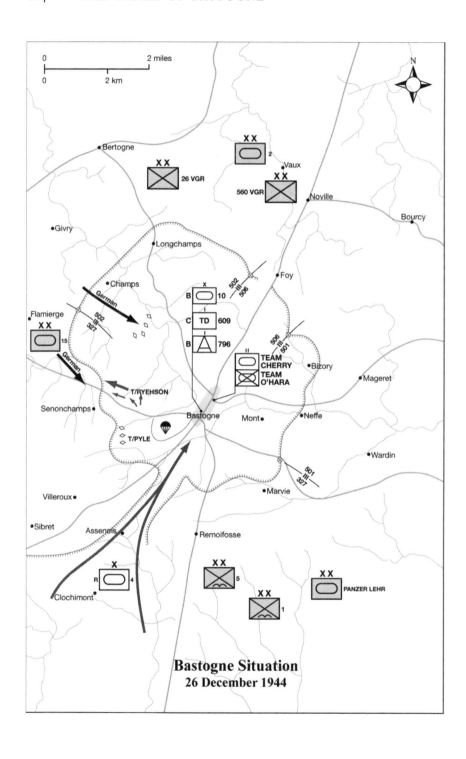

Bastogne Situation
26 December 1944

contact with Bastogne garrison about 1700 and then lost contact during night.[193]

Battery B, 796th Antiaircraft Artillery Battalion, after action report:
26 December
We were strafed by P-47s but we did not fire at them because we could not be sure that they were not friendly aircraft mistaking us for the enemy.[194]

Meanwhile yet another threat was materializing along the road to Mont at almost the exact spot that it had occurred the previous day. Team Ryerson of Lieutenant Colonel Cherry's reserve swiftly moved out of Bastogne to check the situation. At 1025 Ryerson's patrol encountered a substantial German force in the woods just five hundred yards north of Ilse la Hesses. Throughout the morning the team engaged the Germans by frontal assaults, until the remainder of Team Cherry arrived at 1637 to counterattack around Ryerson's right flank. By 1720 the enemy had been destroyed.

TECH SERGEANT THADDEUS KRASNOBORSKI, HEADQUARTERS, 420TH ARMORED FIELD ARTILLERY BATTALION

When the radio crackled and I heard the steady stream of profanity directed to the Krauts in front of their column I knew the 4th Armored was about to punch a hole in the *#~#!!4$ lousy Kraut bastards line. [195]

The medical team at the 101st Airborne HQ at the Heintz Barracks received an unexpected "present" when Dr. Sorrel flew into Bastogne in Piper Cub. He had a basic instrument kit and a few cans of ether with him when he landed. Due to a mistake in the decoding of a message sent out from Bastogne the doctor was only equipped to deal with sixty patients and not the six hundred that currently needed attention. When he saw the riding hall and the mass of patients needing surgery he was overwhelmed. Sorrell suggested attending to the gas infected extremities first. He said that more lives could be saved this way as opposed to spending too much time on stomach, chest and head wounds.

Troop D, 90th Cavalry Reconnaissance Squadron (Mechanized) after action report:

26 December

1ST PLATOON:
Remained in Bastogne except for elements with Captain Anderson in Champs

2ND PLATOON:
Remained in Bastogne except for elements with Captain Anderson in Champs

3RD PLATOON:
Remained in mobile reserve for Team O'Hara. Maintained outpost.

TROOP HEADQUARTERS:
At 0300 we were alerted for another counter attack. The 401st Glider unit on the left flank was attacked. The line held and the immediate alert was over. One armored car and two 1/4 tons were sent to the crossroad 700 yards to the rear of Champs. The patrol was driven out by heavy enemy artillery fire which was pinpointed on the crossroad. At 1300 an enemy communications patrol was captured in Champs and this ended the pin pointing of artillery fire.

At 1930 a peep with two German officers and driver entered Champs. Two were captured and the driver killed. At 2030 another peep was caught at the outpost. A German [officer], who was killed, had maps showing Champs to be clear of American troops. The remainder of the night was quiet with the OP's reporting movement to the north.[196]

In Bastogne even the scarred and battered ruins appeared to be at the point of total collapse as if they would shake off what little cement was holding their bricks together and simply collapse in a cloud of choking dust. To the observer it felt as if everything within the town's perimeter was dying a wretched and protracted death.

WALTER LEPINSKI, HEADQUARTERS COMPANY, 20TH ARMORED INFANTRY BATTALION
When the 4th Armored broke through I did not know that they were coming through and it just happened. [197]

LIEUTENANT COLONEL CREIGHTON W. ABRAMS JR., 4TH ARMORED DIVISION

Dawn of December 26, 1944, right after a cold Christmas, our unit was only three miles from Bastogne. I mounted my CO's personal tank for a very "special" mission! It had been decided that a special team, mainly consisting of C Company, 37th Tank Battalion, under temporary command of Capt William A. DWIGHT (S-3) would take a secondary road, leading from Clochimont thru Assenois to Bastogne, in order to break the siege of that town and to contact the surrounded American defenders. This kind of surprise attack was to take place in enemy-held territory ! Acting as point vehicle, I would lead with 'Cobra King' followed by another 7 tanks, half-tracks, and some other extra vehicles. My personal crew consisted of Pvt Hubert SMITH (driver)—Cpl Milton DICKERMAN (gunner)— Pvt Harold HAFNER (bow gunner)—Pvt James G. MURPHY (loader), and myself as commander, we were all battle veterans. We moved full speed, firing straight ahead, with the other tanks firing left and right. We weren't supposed to stop on the way either. As soon as we cleared the first little town, I called for artillery support (4 artillery battalions were available) on Assenois, that is, ahead of the convoy—our column entered the place still under friendly fire, such was our speed and progress! After clearing Assenois, we ran into more enemy resistance, and mopping up was required with help of our half-trackborne C Company, 53rd Armored Infantry Battalion. We then came across a large pillbox, which we at once destroyed. There certainly was a lot of confusion, since the Germans hadn't expected us to break thru via this secondary road, nevertheless enemy fire was considerable, and we lost 4 Shermans on the way.

As my tank cleared the following woods, we came upon an open field with colored canopies (from previous supply drops), I reckoned we were now approaching friendly lines. Our column subsequently slowed down, on the lookout for friendlies, and we seemed to recognize a number of foxholes with helmeted figures. Taking no chances, I called out to them, shouting to come out to us, indicating we were part of the 4th Armored Division ! After several calls, an officer emerged with a smile, and said; "I'm Lt. Webster, 326th Airborne Engineers, glad to see you guys!" It was 1650, December 26, the 4th Armored Division, had broken thru enemy lines, and reached its objective the siege of Bastogne was over . . . although the fighting wasn't yet.[198]

ELTURNIO "LUCKY" LOIACONO, COMPANY B, 54TH ARMORED INFANTRY BATTALION

The wounded in the school were evacuated from Bastogne and I was sent to England to recover. By the grace of God I had not lost my eye and later sight was only slightly impaired.[199]

Patton's 3rd Army had finally reached the perimeter of Bastogne and breached the German lines that had been managing to hold the city under siege for over a week. The 4th Armored Division had bravely run the gauntlet and battered a narrow, precarious corridor through the German lines and, despite ensuing strenuous German efforts to close it, the corridor remained open. The staunch defense of Bastogne had impeded the Fifth Panzer Army's drive to the west and Lt. Col. Creighton Abram's tanks broke through late in the afternoon of the 26th. Only twenty minutes later Lieutenant Colonel Abrams was shaking hands with General McAuliffe, who had driven out to the front line to welcome the relieving force. The 101st's greeting party, by McAuliffe's order, was well-dressed and clean-shaven, in an effort to display that they had everything under control.

SERGEANT WARREN SWANQUIST, HEADQUARTERS, 3RD TANK BATTALION

This jeep came down the alley with flags waving away like crazy, it was General Patton! He had all his guns, his pearl-handled pistols. [Patton's famed pistols were actually ivory-handled: "Only a pimp carries a pearl-handled pistol," he is reported as saying.] I was right next to him; I could've grabbed him I was so close. He was smiling, I rifle-saluted him and he hand-saluted me. He said something, but I cannot remember what it was. I think I took my first deep breath when the 4th Armored arrived. I was glad to see more people. I had figured I was dead.[200]

Accompanied by an aide, McAuliffe had driven a Willy's jeep out to see Patton's troops for himself. Captain William Dwight, the second soldier to arrive with his tank after 1st Lt. Charles P. Boggess, scrambled out, saluted, and asked, "How are you, General?"

"Gee, I am mighty glad to see you," said McAuliffe, happy to be reconnected with the outside world.

This marked the beginning of a new phase in the life of 10th Armored Division's Combat Command B. By the following day fresh armored units and other reinforcements would be pouring into the city. Hot on the heels of the 4th Armored division (known as the "Breakthrough" division) was the 6th Armored Division followed by elements of the 11th Armored Division. Finally the battered tankers of CCB with their bullet and shrapnel riddled vehicles were going to get some respite from the constant fighting they had endured throughout the previous eight days. It had been a bitter struggle that had tested the nerve of even the toughest American soldier. Nevertheless

CCB was proud to have played a pivotal role in keeping the German forces out of Bastogne for the duration of their engagement.

Profound respect and admiration had developed between the indomitable 101st Airborne and the 10th Armored divisions. The 101st were destined to progress forward with the Third Army and assisting in driving the enemy further from Bastogne.

RALPH K. MANLEY, 501ST PARACHUTE INFANTRY REGIMENT, 101ST AIRBORNE DIVISION

On the 26th of December, as I recall, the weather broke, and in came planes from the Allies to help us out. We were happy to see that. General McAuliffe sent a Christmas note to the troops in Bastogne. Here we were, far away from home and were called on to defend our country and give it the best we could. In the meantime, the Germans had dropped leaflets for us, leaflets saying this was our pass to a warm bed, and if we wanted to see our sweethearts again, and so on, the type of leaflets that were tried to encourage us to give up, and of course that was the perfect paper for us to use to relieve ourselves and what have you.

General McAuliffe sent the word "Nuts!" when asked to surrender; actually, it was much more than that, but that was the printable stuff. We kinda used some vulgar words at the time that we wouldn't use in the press or today. The "Nuts!" he said, from that, we were not about to give up, even though they encouraged us to (the Germans did). But it did block their advance on there, and that was the end of it for that part.

Many civilians were in their cellars, and a number of them had canned meat. This was before the days of freezers and that type of thing. They would cook meat and put it into jars and pour lard over it to preserve it. They shared this with us. When we were digging some of the foxholes around, some of our soldiers came across gardens that had some potatoes left and things like that, dark black potatoes that had been frozen. But it was something to eat, and one of us even killed a chicken that had about froze to death and ate the raw chicken in order to have something to eat. Of course we did not get a resupply of K rations, which were all we had in the paratroops. We didn't have the C or D rations . . . or the canned fruits from the local people who were scared to death. Many of the locals, of course, had gotten out, but others stayed there, and so they, too, were subjected to the bombing and shelling that we were.[201]

ROBERT PARKER, COMPANY C, 21ST TANK BATTALION

They came up when we were sort of road blocking and on the radio we heard, the company commander of that company of the 4th Armored Division, giving orders and he had a German accent. We heard him and we were hesitant about whether to say welcome them or shoot. After the breakthrough we sent out seven truckloads of German soldiers.[202]

Team O'Hara: after action report:

26 December

During the early morning hours artillery and counterbattery fires harassed the enemy. We were relieved by elements of the 501st Regiment and are constituted regimental reserve with headquarters at Bastogne, Belgium. Relief effected 1700.[203]

CHAPTER THIRTEEN

WEDNESDAY 27 DECEMBER

Weather report for south Belgium, London Meteorological Office, Wednesday 27 December, 1944: Heavy snow showers expected all areas. Winds from the north at 20–40 km/h. Temperature: −27°C.

During the night German bombers had managed to hit Bastogne twice but it hadn't prevented the U.S. Third Army from managing to expand its corridor to Bastogne, allowing American reinforcements to flock to the city. The road now opened from Assenois to Bastogne and military vehicles were moving along it bumper to bumper in both directions, and for the moment the Germans in this sector were apparently too demoralized by the speed and sharpness of the blow to react in any aggressive manner. Although the enemy troops around Assenois had been broken and scattered by the lightning thrust on the 26th, Third Army was still facing some strong opposition. As supply trucks and replacements for the 101st and 10th Armored divisions rolled through the shell-ravaged streets of Bastogne, a medical company arrived to move the casualties back to corps hospitals in the south. On December 27 a glider-borne surgical team arrived. This was a highly organized unit, and they worked as teams on the abdomen, chest, etc. It was their role to prepare as many casualties as possible for evacuation to the rear.

420th Armored Field Artillery Battalion after action report
27 December
Elements of the 4th Armored Division arrive in Bastogne at 1500 opening up supply route. Capt. McCloskey returned with S-4, MMO

[motor maintenance officer] and two truckloads of ammunition and first mail in 10 days. Lt. Cole, Liaison pilot received notification of promotion to 1st Lieutenant. Lt. Cole's plane shot down over enemy lines by AA fire; Lt. Cole bailed out—patrol unable to reach him. 6th Armored Division reported engaged West Southwest of Bastogne and 11 Armored Division report on the way. No casualties.[204]

Battery B, 796th Antiaircraft Artillery Battalion after action report:
27 December
About 2200 a Me110 flew towards the city and was engaged by Section 131. The plane was observed to burst into flames and crash south of the city.[205]

Fighting continued around the perimeter of Bastogne as more reinforcements arrived and more German divisions were thrown into the fray. The Führer Begleit (Escort) Brigade was ordered to stop their advance and head to Bastogne immediately. This particular order had come directly from Adolph Hitler himself who had been informed of Patton's breakthrough. Due to a lack of fuel the tanks of the Führer Begleit Brigade ground to a halt one after the other and most of them would never even reach Bastogne. The intention was to use the Brigade for the purpose of closing the gap in the encirclement around Bastogne by means of an attack in a southerly direction. To precipitate this they would need to protect their flanks. They discovered to their dismay that the 26th Volksgrenadier were no longer in a position to offer effective support because they had been severely weakened by the preceding battles and didn't have the capacity to field any serious armor at this stage in the battle. Further reconnaissance revealed that the high ground south of Chegnone would have to be captured and held for the attack conditions to remain favorable for the Axis forces. Gradually an air of desperation began to permeate the ranks of the attacking Germans and severely beginning to affect the moral of these troops.

ROBERT KINSER, COMBAT MEDIC, 3RD TANK BATTALION
On the 27th, the road was opened and they said we must take the wounded out. By then there was over two thousand wounded but still alive in Bastogne. I had an ambulance and went out with the first load, we had a convoy of over 100 ambulances. We could take men in each and we took them about 40 miles back and then transferred them to some of other ambulances and went back to Bastogne.[206]

Troop D, 90th Cavalry Reconnaissance Squadron (Mechanized) after action report:

27 December

1ST PLATOON:
Platoon leader and elements returned from Champs to Bastogne.

2ND PLATOON:
Elements returned to Bastogne with Capt. Anderson from mission at Champs.

3RD PLATOON:
Remained in mobile reserve for Team O'Hara. Maintained outpost.

TROOP HEADQUARTERS:
Mission accomplished Captain Anderson returned to Bastogne to reconstitute his Troop.[207]

Early on the morning of December 27 forty-some ambulances drove along the liberated corridor towards Bastogne. Around noon the ambulances returned from Bastogne loaded with a cargo full of wounded soldiers and civilians heading in the direction of Arlon. As reinforcements and food supplies entered the city, ambulances, trucks full of POWs, and civilians left. Despite the freezing cold, misty weather, and blizzard conditions around seventy ambulances transported almost a thousand wounded personnel away from Bastogne.

They convoy was accompanied by light tanks from Company D, 37th Tank Battalion. Throughout the course of the day 130 C-47s and 32 gliders flew resupply missions to Bastogne. German antiaircraft fire and Luftwaffe fighter aircraft managed to bring down 9 of the C-47s, but miraculously no gliders were hit that day.

————

The siege of Bastogne was a battle that deeply affected both the local civilians and the soldiers unlike any other before, but more importantly it forged bonds of lasting friendship between the two that have survived the generations. There are many reasons for this but the main one was the idea that "a problem shared is a problem halved." The shared adversity and the resulting sense of comradeship from the incredible hardship they all endured remains a most poignant aspect of the siege . . . even to this day.

Although many wounded soldiers were evacuated from Bastogne through

Patton's Third Army corridor there were still plenty of replacements to integrate into the American forces due to the ferocity of fighting that continued around the perimeter.

General Patton's relief of Bastogne has long since become one of the legendary feats of the Battle of the Bulge, but even when Third Army forces broke through to Bastogne he still harbored doubts about the eventual outcome of the battle. at one juncture he was heard to say, "We can still lose this war," because although he had effectively carved a path through German lines the fighting was still far from over. As early as 8 December he had asked his the Third Army chaplain to write a suitable prayer for the Third Army but what we have here is Patton's personal prayer to his maker, which gives us a better insight into the character and motives of the man.

GENERAL GEORGE PATTON'S PERSONAL PRAYER:

Lord, this is Patton speaking to you. The last fourteen days have been awful. Rain, snow, more rain, more snow . . . and I have begun to ask myself why not go to your headquarters. Which side are you on?

For three years, my chaplains have explained that this is a religious war. They have told me that this is a crusade, the only difference being that we move on tanks instead of horses. They have insisted that we destroy the German army and this atheist Hitler, so that freedom of religion can return to Europe.

Until now I followed them, the more so as you helped us without reserve. Blue sky and calm sea in Africa helped to make our unloading easy to eliminate Rommel. The capture of Sicily was relatively easy, and you gave us a perfect time for our armored push through France, the greatest military victory that you have granted me. You often gave me excellent counsel in my difficult decisions of command, and you dropped German units into my traps, which made their elimination relatively easy.

But now you seem to have changed horses. You seem to me to have given to Von Rundstedt the green light. My army is neither trained nor equipped for war in winter. And as you know, this weather is more appropriate for Eskimos than for Southern riders.

In fact, Lord, I have begun to think that I have offended you in some way. That suddenly you have lost your sympathy to our cause. That you are in complicity with this Von Rundstedt and his puppet.

You know, without my saying so, that our situation is desperate. Obviously, I tell my staff that everything is going as planned, but do I need to add that the 101st Airborne is opposing terrible forces in Bastogne, and that these continual storms make air supplies impossible? I sent good Hugh Gaffey, one of my able generals, with his 4th Armored Division, to this important Noeud road to help the encircled garrison, but he has more trouble with your rotten weather than with the Boches!

I do not like to complain unnecessarily, but my soldiers really suffered martyrdom from the Meuse to Echternach. Today I visited several hospitals, all full of cold people, while the wounded remain strewn across the fields, because we cannot bring them back to give them care. But that is not the worst of the situation. The poor visibility and the continual rains have completely paralyzed my air forces on the ground. My battle plan requires help from the fighter-bombers, and if my planes cannot fly, tell me how I can use them as air artillery?

This is not the only deplorable situation, but worse still, my reconnaissance aircraft have not taken to the air in fourteen days, and I do not have the slightest idea what is happening behind the German lines. Jesus, Lord, I fight a shadow! Without your cooperation on the weather, how can I lead effective attacks? All this probably appears irrational to you, but I have lost patience with your ministers who try to persuade me that this is one typical winter in the Ardennes, and that I must have confidence.

The devil with confidence and patience! You have to only choose which side you are on. You must come to my aid, so that I can liquidate the entire German army, and offer it like a birthday gift to the Baby Jesus. Lord, I have never been unreasonable. I do not ask the impossible of you. I do not even ask for a miracle, only four little days of beautiful weather.

Give me four clear days so my planes can fly, so my fighter-bombers can bomb the Germans (and punish them well), so my observation planes can pinpoint the targets for my splendid artillery. Give me four sunny days to dry this rotten mud, so my tanks can roll, so the ammunition and the rations can reach my starving and badly equipped infantrymen. I need these four days to send Von Rundstedt and his army of infidels to their valhalla.

I am sick of this useless butchery of young Americans, and in exchange for these four days of weather favorable to combat, I will provide you enough Boches to keep your accountants occupied with months of work.

So it is.[208]

On the day when the 4th Armored Division broke through a small group of civilians saw several hundred German soldiers moving up the road between Assenois and Bastogne. In an attempt to avoid the crossfire the civilians melted back into the woods. At around 1600 six M3 half-tracks arrived in Assenois. A lone enemy 88mm gun vainly attempted to stem the tide of American armor arriving in the village. The final obstacle to the 37th Tank Battalion's progress was a small pillbox on the road between Bastogne and Assenois. The lead tank carrying Lt. Charles Boggess emptied its shells at it and when they overpowered the German defenders of this pillbox they counted at least twenty dead German soldiers in the vicinity.

Major General Maxwell Taylor, 101st Airborne commander, had arrived back in Paris from the United States on the afternoon of 26 December. He initially asked to be parachuted into Bastogne, but this request was rebuffed by his superiors. So on 27 December he left for the front in a Willy's jeep driven by Sgt. Charles Kartus. Traversing the narrow corridor that was now open giving access to Bastogne they arrived there about four in the afternoon, some twenty-four hours after the 4th Armored Division breakthrough. Arriving at Heintz Barracks, General Taylor met acting 101st Commander, General McAuliffe, and inquired about the state of the Screaming Eagles: at that time the division still numbered 711 officers and 9,516 enlisted men.

CHAPTER FOURTEEN

THURSDAY 28 DECEMBER

Weather report for south Belgium, London
Meteorological Office, Thursday 28 December, 1944:
*Fog possibly clearing by late afternoon. More heavy
snow showers expected all areas. Winds from the north
at 20km/h increasing to 50 km/h by the end of the
day. Temperature: −20°C.*

Note: This chapter provides the cumulative reports commencing from 28 December up until the final reports were filed for each unit mentioned in the previous chapters. There was still a lot of fighting to do before the Germans could be subdued and forced into retreat, but for Combat Command B, 10th Armored Division, the battle was almost over.

Troop D, 90th Cavalry Reconnaissance Squadron (Mechanized) after action report:

28 DECEMBER–JANUARY 14
The first and second platoon and troop headquarters were in mobile reserve for Team Cherry.

JANUARY 4–JANUARY 14
The third platoon released from its duties with Team O'Hara and rejoined the Troop as part of mobile reserve for Team Cherry.[209]

420th Armored Field Artillery Battalion after action report:
28 December
Battalion mission changed from a direct support to reinforcing fires of 377th Parachute Field Artillery Battalion. Supply trains arrived

around 1800 with rations, mail, gas, and ammunition. Low flying planes reported over Bastogne. No casualties.[210]

Battery B, 796th Antiaircraft Artillery Battalion, after action report:
28 December
About 0030 when the city was being bombed, the entire battery opened fire and one plane was seen to break off from the formation leaving a trail of smoke and sparks. It was heard later that a plane had crashed but no witnesses have been found so that we cannot claim a destroyed plane.[211]

420th Armored Field Artillery Battalion after action report:
29 December
Battalion served "Christmas Dinner"—Turkey with all the trimmings. 168 Flying Fortresses overhead at one time around 1300. Our other liaison plane cracked up today during take-off due to icing on wings. Lt. Fowler, Ln Pilot, not injured. Enemy planes bombed area between 1900 and 2000 causing one casualty.[212]

420th Armored Field Artillery Battalion AA report
30 December
Enemy planes bomb area around 0400. Rest of day very quiet. No casualties.[213]

Although the 10th Armored Division was relieved by the 4th Armored Division on December 26, German bombing raids against Bastogne continued on with deadly results. At seven in the morning officers from Team Hustead in Lieutenant Colonel Cherry's command post were caught in a German bombing raid. Five officers were killed and the battalion's records were buried or destroyed. Warren Swanquist was standing in a doorway across the street and Earl Van Gorp was in the building next door to the CP that morning.

SERGEANT WARREN SWANQUIST,
HEADQUARTERS, 3RD TANK BATTALION
I was in an apartment across the street from Cherry's CP. I went down to the basement to eat something and when I came back up I was standing in the doorway and the bomb hit across [the street] and a hunk of shrapnel came along. I was

leaning against the doorjamb and that damn hunk of shrapnel went right over my shoulder and smashed into the doorway.[214]

EARL VAN GORP, COMPANY D, 3RD TANK BATTALION

I was staying in a building in Bastogne and there were five officers who were killed in a building right next to us that took a direct hit. The bomb didn't hurt us, but there was an awful concussion. We were in the cellar and you had to lift yourself up off the floor. The shockwave took my breath away. D Company comprised of about 106 people and only 24 escaped the Battle of the Bulge unwounded.

When the battle was over in the end, we had a celebration kind of deal in Bastogne, and McAuliffe spoke and he was on a platform. This took place after the 4th Armored had come through.[215]

420th Armored Field Artillery Battalion after action report:
31 December
Four inches of snow on ground. First contact with Rear Echelon in twelve days; Personnel Officer arrives to pay off troops. Generally quiet. Our Liaison Officer with CCB, 10th Armored Division, recalled and sent to 377th Parachute Field Artillery Battalion. 1 EM wounded.[216]

WILLIAM SIMONOFF, COMPANY B, 3RD TANK BATTALION

We did not really pay too much attention to street signs or where we were going until we got there. I never saw the city of Bastogne, I was on the outskirts. All the fighting I did was on narrow roads and the woods, only a house here and a house there. There were five tanks in my platoon. There was a constant change of crew and personnel because of casualties within my platoon. I remember my platoon lost three tanks but I sustained no injury and my crew members were wounded. I know that we were in the Longvilly-area for a time. Col. Cherry was running between there and the Bastogne area in a jeep. I never spoke to him. We were always in contact with artillery and without the artillery I would not have survived. The 101st were all around as our infantry support during that time. We did not have too many advances during that time. I did see a Tiger tank while fighting in the Ardennes. My gunner was able to disable a few German tanks by knocking off their tracks. On Christmas Day I slept in my tank. After the breakthrough, I left the Bastogne area in late December.[217]

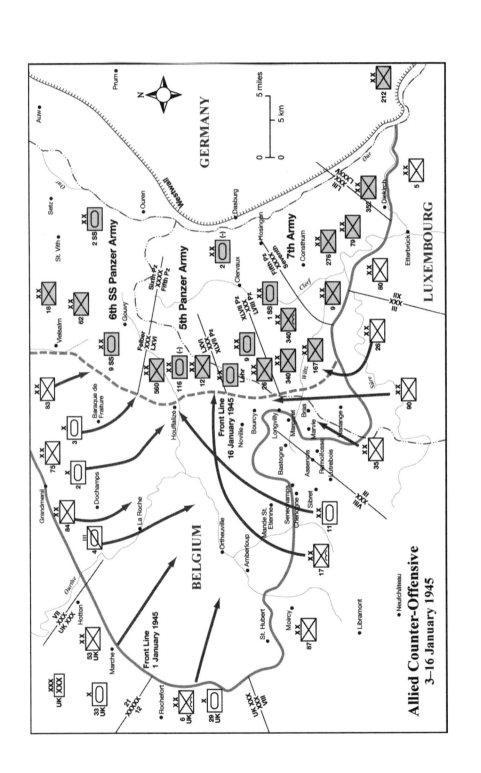

Allied Counter-Offensive
3–16 January 1945

CHAPTER FIFTEEN

THE FINAL CHAPTER

Weather report for south Belgium, London
Meteorological Office, Friday 15 December, 1944:
*Low lying mist and fog, ground frost, mild north
easterly wind. Temperature—5°C.*

Combat Command B of the 10th Armored Division had performed well and exceeded all expectations. They had cleared
most of the roads to the north while CCA and the 35th Division had battered
away against the German remnants that were clinging doggedly to the
Arlon-Bastogne highway in the south. The battle wasn't over yet but the
proverbial tide had turned and the U.S. Army was sweeping in, witnessing
the last dying gasps of a broken, dispirited enemy.

After the 4th Armored Division broke through to Bastogne on December 26th, the majority of the Combat Command B left Bastogne and traveled
to their original positions near Metz, France, where they had left some two
weeks earlier. But for select soldiers of Combat Command B the battle still
raged around the perimeter of Bastogne. Team O'Hara became the reserve
force for the 501st PIR from January 1 onward. On 3 January the 101st Airborne along with elements of Combat Command B began to drive the remaining pockets of German resistance from the Bastogne area.

LIEUTENANT COLONEL JAMES O'HARA,
54TH ARMORED INFANTRY BATTALION

*The 501st Parachute. Regt. jumped off at 12:00, 3 Jan. 45, and advanced to clear
out the woods north, northeast of Bizory. Attacking with two battalions abreast,
second on the right, third on the left, the first in reserve. Three medium tanks
from Team O'Hara were in direct support of each attacking battalion. The tanks*

operated under control of the infantry commanders. Mortar and assault gun platoons, Hq Co., 54th AIB, supported this attack by providing harassing fire on the road network and woods north of the regimental objective. The machine gun platoon of the 54th AIB, was given the task of protecting the positions of the mortar and assault guns. Troop D 90th Reconnaissance maintained liaison to the flanks and could if required reinforce the machine gun platoon. CC/B 6th Armored Division were allocated to the right flank of the attacking units to hold and provide support by fire from their positions, using the open, sloping terrain northeast of Bizory.

Jumping off as scheduled, the infantry supported by tanks moved forward with confidence and determination. Due to the density of the woods, tanks were channeled into winding, narrow trails that had been reconnoitered by the advancing foot elements. The mediums made reconnaissance by fire, using HE with delayed fuzes, well to the advance of the attacking echelons. The second battalion proceeded beyond the railroad tracks, which passed through the woods, from the southwest to the northeast, when they were pinned down by enemy machine gun fire. The leading right unit . . . located the source of the first and called for tank support. Moving forward into position, the tank commanded by Lt. Wicherd, engaged the target, at a range of 200 yards, firing one round of HE to silence it. Advancing slowly firing the supplementary weapons, Lt. Wicherd over ran machine gun nests. Protected by foot elements, the tanks in concealed position, supported by fire, the advance of the second battalion was furthered.

At 16:00, CC/B of the 6th Armored Division was taken by surprise, when attacked by an enemy column composed of armor and infantry. The left flank element of this unit made a hasty withdrawal to the southwest, leaving the right flank and rear of the 501st Parachute. Regt. exposed to the enemy. Pressing his opportunity, the enemy maintained pressure, and now located elements of the 501st Parachute Regt. who were entirely unaware of the new development. Up until that moment, they had been making excellent progress in the attack.

The regimental commander immediately evaluated this threat to his right flank and halted the attack, turned the right flank battalion, committed his reserve battalion on the right and prepared to defend his gains. The movement of the battalions to defensive positions was not accomplished without cost. Three medium tanks fell before the fire of the enemy 88's. An estimate of the situation showed a gap of 700 yards existed between the 501st Parachute. Regt. and the units of the 6th Armored Division that had held their position throughout the engagement.

Realizing the imminent danger to his men, the regimental commander, 501st Parachute Regt called upon Team O'Hara to provide immediate tank-infantry support. Baker Company and the remaining five tanks of C Company 21st Tank Battalion were moved into position on the reverse slope of the undefended gap. The tanks, upon moving into position, engaged approaching enemy armor and destroyed four Mark IV tanks. The visibility being poor American tanks fired one round of HE to bring them on target and then AP finished the job. The loss of the armor and the strength of the line they were trying to pierce discouraged the enemy causing them to withdraw. Taking advantage of the abatement all units consolidated their positions in preparation for enemy counter-attacks that never materialized. At 03:30 on the 4th Jan, Team O'Hara was withdrawn from the line and once again constituted the armored reserve for the 501st Parachute Regt.[218]

Stan Davis was part of the group of Company C tankers who supported the continued fight against the retreating German army. But Davis' small platoon faced a fervent enemy who fought to hold off any counterattacks by the remnants of Combat Command B and the 101st Airborne.

STAFF SERGEANT STANLEY E. DAVIS, COMPANY C, 21ST TANK BATTALION

We were still attached to the 101st and when they received offensive missions in the NE sector of the Bastogne suburbs, C Company went with them for their tank support. It was in this support mission that I had two tanks as a platoon sergeant. We were moving east in an open area with heavy woods on the north and south when my both tanks I commanded were knocked out by very accurate panzerfaust fire. They hit both tanks in the engine compartments at just about the same time causing dangerous fires inside which meant that most of our power equipment went back to hand controls.

We never did see any of the Germans, but we knew they had to be in the woods on our left. We were able to get some rounds off with the 50 Cal. AA gun mounted on the tank commanders turret ring, but with our tank on fire, and spreading rapidly, my primary thought at that time was to dismount as fast as possible. This is particularly critical for the tank commander to dismount as soon as possible as the gunner has to get out of the same hatch as the tank commander. The other three tank crew members have their own exit hatch. Both crews moved rapidly to get behind our burning tank so that the tank was between us and the enemy. Unfortunately the gunner in the other tank ran the wrong way into enemy lines and we later found out he was killed.

Our personal gun in the tank was the M3 submachine, better known as the "grease gun." When you were in the tank you laid it down someplace, but when your tank is on fire, getting out in your first and only thought. When the 9 of us assembled behind the burning tank, the only weapons we had were two hand grenades. We needed to get off the front lines as soon as possible so we headed into the woods to get back to our lines. A short distance into the woods we reached a good sized fox whole with a young healthy looking German infantryman in it. When he and I spotted each other all of us tankers stopped abruptly. Fortunately he did not appear to be armed. He probably figured we all had guns and raised his arms in surrender. At this point in time we have no idea where any Americans or Germans are and I figured if we take prisoner and we get captured before we can get back to our lines he could get us into trouble by what he might say. So we decided to let him stay where he was and we would get to some friendly forces as quick as we could.

So there are 9 tank crewmen in the middle of the combat zone, with no communications with anyone and no weapons except our two hand grenades. Everything we had for day to day living was burning up in our two tanks and we were heading away from the front line to find some friendly forces to get back to where we had started out two days ago. It was an unbelievably quiet area as we headed back to the area which, to the best of our knowledge, was the rear area.

The first thing we came to was a knocked out American tank on the road that I felt reasonably sure would take us back to where we came from. The next thing we came to was an immobilized American ambulance with dead Americans in it. A few more miles toward Bastogne we arrived at an active artillery battery with a small command post. They questioned me about what was going on up at the front and I showed them on their maps to the best of my knowledge where we had been and what happened. They were a 6th Armored division artillery unit and they treated us real good, they took us back to the Bastogne/Wiltz HQ building of Team O'Hara and gave us some K rations which we were very happy to get.[219]

———

12 JANUARY

While the members of Easy Company 506th PIR 101st Airborne were bogged down by German artillery in the Bois Jacques outside of Foy, on 12 January another group of 10th Armored Division tankers and 101st Airborne paratroopers were clearing out the woods east of Bastogne in the vicinity of Bizory. Once again, three tanks from Company C, 21st Tank Battalion, were sent out to help flush out the remaining German units.

ROBERT PARKER C COMPANY 21ST TANK BATTALION

We were no longer in Bastogne and we began the counterattack. There were air-borne and armored infantry with us, the platoon officer's tank was just in front of us when it got hit. Lt. Wishart got out of the turret, and he was cut down with machine gun fire. [220]

> *Second Lieutenant Sherwood D Wishart, Company C,*
> *21st Tank Battalion, Silver Star citation:*
> When his tank platoon suddenly encountered intense enemy artillery, mortar, and small arms, fire, Lieutenant Wishart, platoon leader, advanced in his tank, neutralizing several of the enemy positions and, when his own vehicle was set afire, he remained at his mounted machine gun covering the withdrawal of his crew until he was mortally wounded by enemy sniper fire. His supreme dedication to duty reflects great credit upon himself and the military forces of the United States. Entered the military service from Rensselaer, New York.[221]

AUTHORS' NOTE: The citation and Robert Parker's description of Wishart's death do not correspond. As a gunner Parker only had a sightline through his periscope and he may not have seen the sniper shot hit Wishart during the attack, especially with machine gun fire coming from all around.

According to the official report about the attack, the gunner from Wishart's tank Pvt. Frederick Salamon, survived the attack when he jumped out of the burning tank. Sadly, he was not found later on when Wishart's body was recovered.

LIEUTENANT RICHARD GILLIAND, COMPANY C, 21ST TANK BATTALION

They [Wishart's three tanks] left on the mission at about 1100 on 12 Jan 45. The Mission of the Platoon in which Pvt. Salamon was in had the mission of supporting a Bn. of the 101st Airborne Infantry in clearing out a woods 2 kilometers northwest of Mageret, Belgium. Small arms fire was holding up the advance of the airborne and this platoon of 3 tanks was called forward to assist in neutralizing this enemy strong point An enemy Tiger Royal mounting an 88 was in a concealed position about 25 yards behind the strong point and knocked the tank out set it afire that Salamon was in. [222]

ROBERT "NATE" BUSH, COMPANY C, 21ST TANK BATTALION

On the 12th of January 1945 I personally made a reconnaissance of the burnt tank that Pvt. Salamon was assigned. I located the body of Lt. Wishart, Sgt. Mann and PFC Schornack. I searched the area for Pvt. Salamon and I could not locate his body in the near vicinity. There was Germans in the area when I went to the tank and Pvt. Salamon could have been taken prisoner by the Germans. However, I have no idea as to his true whereabouts. [223]

The attack in the Bizory area just northwest of Mageret had taken a heavy toll on the tankers of 21st Tank Battalion. Thankfully Robert Parker survived the assault, but his tank was damaged.

ROBERT PARKER, COMPANY C, 21ST TANK BATTALION

During that same attack our tank was hit by artillery which forced us to go back for repairs since the tank would only move in reverse.

We picked Wishart's body up and a few others later on with litter bearers. I remember one wounded fella there, his last name was Kline. During our entire time in the service he was always bumming cigarettes and he liked Lucky Strike. Here he was lying on a stretcher with his whole chest full of blood and someone offered him a something other than a Lucky Strike and he turned it down. I never knew what happened to him.

[For Parker, not only did the tank need maintenance, but he became a victim of one of the deadliest epidemics in the Battle of the Bulge: frozen feet.]

The tank was taken back to maintenance to be fixed up. While at maintenance I showed my frozen feet to the officer there, and he sent me to the medics who put me on a stretcher, and I was sent to a hospital since my toes were bleeding. The inside walls of the tank were completely covered in ice during our time in Bastogne, your breath froze too. It was terrible because you had your feet on a cold steel floor. But we had everything in our tank and we slept in it. Because of my frozen feet, I spent the next two months at different hospitals and ended up in Paris for six months. [224]

Robert Parker's experience in the Bizory-area was not the last time that members of Combat Command B were killed during the waning days of the Battle of the Bulge. One of the busiest captains during the Battle of Bastogne was William Ryerson of Company C, 20th Armored Infantry Battalion. He was known as the "little Captain" to his men because he was not very tall, and he led many of the missions with Team Cherry during the first days of combat near Longvilly. Later on he was on call as part of Team Cherry's mobile reserve, and he led different patrol around Bastogne even after the 4th Armored Division broke through. On January 14, 1945, Captain Ryerson, along with soldiers of Company C, 20th AIB, and paratroopers of the Screaming Eagles, fought a pocket of Germans near the village of Bourcy, Belgium. During the battle a P-47 strafed the area and dropped a bomb near Captain Ryerson and his group of men.

S-1 Journal, 20th Armored Infantry Battalion:

14 January

Friendly planes overhead. Received word that one of our friendly planes dropped a bomb short and it landed on our lines, killing Capt. Ryerson and one enlisted man. It also wounded 16 others.[225]

RALPH CUSHING, COMPANY C, 20TH ARMORED INFANTRY BATTALION (IN A LETTER TO CAPTAIN RYERSON'S WIDOW AFTER THE WAR)

Capt. Ryerson was out with his men supporting the 101st Airborne Infantry when the air attack came. The Americans and Germans were only about fifty yards apart when the bombs began to fall. . . . I can honestly tell you that the Capt. did not suffer and I know in my own mind, he never knew what happened. . . . The Capt. and I used to do a lot of talking, sometimes to pass away time, others to keep each other awake and from what he told me, he died as he desired.[226]

Captain Ryerson was one of the last men in Combat Command B killed during the Battle of the Bulge as the 10th Armored Division withdrew from the area three days later.

CAPTAIN WILLIAM RYERSON, COMPANY C, 20TH ARMORED INFANTRY BATTALION

Born in Glens Falls, New York, on February 7, 1918, William F. Ryerson grew up in Garden City, Long Island, for most of his childhood. He graduated from Syracuse University in 1940. He was a member of the Reserve Officers' Training Corps at Syracuse as well as being a member of the Pershing Rifles drill team and Scabbard and Blade military fraternity. He received a master's degree in high school administration in 1941 from Syracuse, as well. On August 29, 1941, Ryerson was ordered to proceed to Pine Camp, New York for one year active duty with the Fourth Armored Division as a lieutenant. In June 1942 he was transferred to Fort Benning, Georgia, as one of the officers in a cadre which formed the 10th Armored Division. Ryerson fought with the 10th Armored Division throughout the Metz campaign into the Battle of the Bulge.

During the battle for Metz in November, 1944, Captain Ryerson was awarded the Bronze Star and the Silver Star:

Captain William F. Ryerson, Bronze Star citation:
For heroic achievement in connection with military operations against an enemy of the United States in France on 16 November 1944. Captain Ryerson, Commander of an Infantry Company, was placed in charge of an armored combat team with the mission of seizing the town Kirschnaumen, France. Upon reaching the edge of the town, further progress was impeded by an enemy road block and artillery shelling. Captain Ryerson, with complete disregard for his own safety, dismounted from the comparative safety of his half-track and went forward on foot under heavy sniper and mortar fire, reconnoitering for the column. When the column was again halted midway through the town by withering enemy fire, Captain Ryerson, undeterred by enemy action, calmly rallied his men and continued the advance. His exemplary performance, coolness, and display of courage inspired the men of his organization and reflect high credit upon himself as a leader of men and upon the military forces of the United States. Enter Military service from New York.[227]

Captain William F. Ryerson, Silver Star citation:
For gallantry in action in Germany on 29 November 1944. Captain Ryerson, commanding an Infantry Company, was given charge of a combat team whose mission was the taking and holding of Hilbringen, Germany and the destruction of the connecting bridge to Merzig, Germany. Upon reaching the objective, despite intense enemy fire from artillery and machine guns, Captain Ryerson moved into the town, and despite his being wounded by enemy fire, he continued to courageously lead his men until enemy was routed and the mission accomplished. Captain Ryerson's devotion to duty and gallant achievement, in spite of his wounds, reflect high credit upon himself and the military forces of the United States Entered the military service from New York.[228]

Patton may have forced a corridor through to Bastogne but now German divisions began to descend on it like flies around the muzzle of a snorting bull. The east side of the corridor deflected the repeated blows of an attack made by two Volksgrenadier divisions supported by elements of the 5th Infantry Division. Through the dense fog they stormed into Lutrebois just six kilometers south of Bastogne and only twelve hundred meters from the main highway. The confrontation that followed was the result of a carefully executed ambush orchestrated by six M4 Sherman tanks. Using the fog for cover they positioned themselves on the edge of the woods at Lutrebois. As German Mk V Panthers moved forward in twos and threes the Shermans opened enfilade fire that destroyed all the German tanks without sustaining a single loss to their own armor. The 35th Division supported by low flying P-47 Thunderbolts incapacitated fifty-five German tanks on that day.

The German offensive was grinding to a gasping halt as orders from OKW began to filter through to the German ranks to pull back behind the Siegfried line along the German border. Hitler was exasperated and bitterly disappointed by this defeat but in a rare moment of lucidity he decided to cut his losses and prepare for the final battle.

Germany attempted one more offensive in the Alsace region. Operation *Nordwind* was an abortive attempt to destroy a thinly held line of U.S. forces in the Vosges Mountains to the south. Eisenhower hurriedly brought in battered divisions that had fought in the Ardennes to strengthen the U.S. position. The offensive began on 1 January and had petered out by 25 January. This offensive effectively removed all Axis forces from France. Fighting continued in the Luxembourg area for another few weeks but the Battle of the Bulge and the battle for Bastogne were effectively over. Hitler's last gamble in the west had failed and now Germany was itself under siege as the Soviet armies drove toward Berlin from the east while the Western Allies continued their march into the country from the far side of the Rhine. On 17 January the10th Armored Division pulled out of Bastogne and headed to the Saar-Moselle triangle to continue their fight against the Third Reich.

JOHN "BOYD" ETTERS, 20TH ARMORED INFANTRY BATTALION (NEVER SENT V-MAIL WRITTEN IN PARIS JANUARY 1945)

Dear Kath, Lill, George and Bob,

It has been sometime since I have had a chance to write. Since my last letter I have experienced about the greatest days of my life. I saw things and did things that I never want to happen again. The clippings will tell you what happened. When I wrote my last letter I was in a rest area enjoying myself, when an emergency order was given to move out. The next thing I knew we were in Belgium. Nobody knew a thing about the situation. All we knew was that Germans had made a full scale counter attack, and we were to hold Bastogne and the area around the city at all cost. I was in the reconnaissance outfit that made first contact with the enemy, and they were really in full steam. They trapped us in a small town called Noville, it is in the clippings, and for a full day we held them off. The Krauts on one side of the road, we on the other. The following day the paratroopers came up and saved us from certain disaster, and me from spending Christmas in Germany or otherwise. With the aid of the paratroopers, we held on to that small town for another night and day, and then finally had to withdraw back into Bastogne five miles away. We got about three miles from Bastogne, when we were ambushed. It was a beautiful ambush, if I must say so, and what a fight we had to get back into the city. Words cannot describe what took place. Once again I wouldn't have given a nickel for my chances, but my luck still hung on, although it was during this action that ended my fighting career, even though I kept fighting until the siege was lifted. I caught the concussion of an artillery explosion in my eyes. I was lucky for the three fellows around me got it for good. We finally reached the city and the division set up a defense around the city. Our job then on was to go from side of our defense line to the other, where even enemy tanks would break through. For eight days we were surrounded. Eight Days of Hell. The enemy never ceased shelling the town and from Christmas Eve on, they bombed the city from the air three times nightly, which is a terrifying experience, when you have no protection what so ever. I'll never forget those days as long as I live. I saw everything up there. Tanks, infantry, paratroopers, gliders, air force all in action. I never saw so many enemy or enemy tanks in my life. They were everywhere, in front us, behind us, and sometimes practically on top of us. We also had a lot of close in fighting, and that is one thing I don't like. The Germans are tricky and their best troopers are in action now. Let's hope this is now the beginning of the end, although I have my doubts. The Krauts are really fighting up there. It is plenty rough. We sure were happy to see the 4th Armored break the siege. I am up for some sort of medal. Probably the bronze star, but at least it is something. The only bright spot of Bastogne was the fact that we had all the cognac, Champagne, wine, and brandy we wanted and we sure downed it and it didn't cost us a cent. You will all have to wait until I get back before I can really give you all a good description of what really took place up there. I just thank the Lord I am still around today. I am now writing this letter in the beautiful capital of France, Paris. Don't have to write until you get my new address.

Love,

Boyd

P.S. Have you received any money orders of mine? Probably the next time I hear from you all, it will a boy or girl for Lill.[229]

WILLIAM RICHARD BARRETT, BATTERY B, 420TH ARMORED FIELD ARTILLERY BATTALION

When we got orders to move out, there again normal procedure, we got lost and had to turn around and we ran into freezing rain and we ran into black ice. At the time my driver was sliding off the road, and I said Johnny creep ahead real slow and we will push you sideways. And we pushed that M7 sideways up the road so that we got back on the road. Also there was my Captain, who I did not see much during combat, and his driver, who the Captain had spoken up something terrible: his jeep and he run off the road into a ditch, all wheels up. Now a jeep, full set of chains, supposed to handle anything. I said, "Climb out and we'll push you back over." I told the driver to get it out of four-wheel drive and the four of us pushed the jeep back onto two wheels and the driver got it back moving.[230]

EPILOGUE

As the veterans of the 10th Armored Division gather for their annual meeting no one can fail to notice their dwindling numbers. Nevertheless the esprit de corps of these men is every bit as all-encompassing and cohesive as that of the illustrious 101st Airborne. More so in fact because the 10th Armored division were never venerated to any great extent for the sacrifices they made and the challenge that they ultimately met with exceptional courage and fortitude. The authors worked hard to get a memorial plaque placed for the 10th Armored Division and are glad we did. They deserve our profound respect and admiration for the task they performed during that bitterly cold winter all those years ago.

Today Bastogne is a busy little town that heaves with visitors at the weekends. The car park on the McAuliffe square quickly fills up and the cafés and snack bars in the vicinity do a lot business. One doesn't have to walk far to see the Stars and Stripes hanging outside the town hall (hotel de Ville) and various other establishments. In fact everywhere you look there are constant reminders to what occurred during that fateful winter of 44–45. The locals are relatively friendly but knowledge of English isn't universal, so it's always good to know a bit of French. I've always found it easy to make conversation in the local cafés and over the years I've got to know some charming characters there. There are a few decent hotels in the area but these book up really fast when there's anything happening in the town. Most of the visitors to Bastogne these days aren't there on any kind of nostalgic World War II pilgrimage, they're just there to do a bit of shopping, enjoy some tasty Ardennes specialties that they can wash down with a good glass of beer. It's also a popular destination for young people from surrounding villages to go for a night out. There aren't any night clubs there as such but the cafés stay open late and they're usually quite busy on the weekend. It's a small town with a current population of around fifteen thousand. You can walk from one end to the other at a decent pace in about fifteen minutes.

MARTIN KING, AUTHOR

Bastogne is one of my favorite towns in Europe. For the discerning war tourist there are enough monuments and memorabilia keep one occupied and it's well worth going off the beaten track to find these.

Personally I've always found it a great location to visit in the middle of winter. There's an unambiguous atmosphere of real history about the place when one walks around there in the early morning or late evening. You can just sense it. Something happened here. Knowing the history of course adds to this feeling but one doesn't have to be a historian to absorb the unique ambiance that pervades these streets and buildings. I recall looking at a house that was being renovated behind the main square just around the corner from Rue Docteur Chiwy. You could see the exposed black scorched bricks and timbers awaiting refurbishment or replacement just standing there like testaments to another time. Although many decades have passed since the siege there are still visible scars but most are now covered and concealed from view.

I've often sat outside cafés after a day of visiting battle sites chatting with visitors from the U.S. and occasionally an old man or woman will look across to my table when they hear us talking and utter the word "Americain" with a knowing, affectionate nod and a smile. Some of the town's elderly people still remember the days and long nights the Americans lived with them through that terrible struggle but they're in no hurry to talk about it and soon, like the U.S. Army soldiers who were there, they will all be gone.

MICHAEL COLLINS, AUTHOR

Through my many visits to Bastogne I believe that it is one of the most interesting places in Europe. On the surface it looks like any small city in Belgium with a nice town square, cafes, patisseries, and some great views of the countryside. But when you peel away the cosmopolitan cover it is full of history both visible and invisible. From building walls covered in bullet holes to the Sherman tank in McAuliffe Square, the physical damage from the battle is clearly visible. It is when you get out into the surrounding villages and see the rolling hills that the battle becomes more apparent. When I first visited Bastogne in 2006 I knew about the Battle of the Bulge, but I had no idea what it was like to be fighting in some of the worst conditions during World War II. The veterans' stories and the citations of the medals they earned opened my eyes to the sacrifices they made during Germany's last push of World War II.

The veterans who we recorded were ordinary people that just happened to be there at the time. Nothing special about that, but they were "special;" they know things that we'll never know; they saw things that we'll hopefully never see; and they all deserve to be remembered. Remember them, be proud of them, respect their deeds, and don't let the world forget. That's the least we owe them.

APPENDIX A: STATEMENT OF AMBASSADOR MADELEINE ALBRIGHT

On the Fiftieth Anniversary of the Battle of the
Bulge at Bastogne, Belgium, 16 December 1994.

Your Royal Highness, Mr. Prime Minister, Ministère, our own Ambassadors Blinken, Hunter and Eisenstat, Secretary of the Army West, Excellencies, Mr. Mayor, Ladies and Gentlemen and, above all, veterans of the Battle of the Bulge, Good Morning.

On behalf of all Americans, I am honored to convey to you the greetings and best wishes of the President of the United States. It is a privilege to participate in this day of proud memory and shared resolve.

I begin with a word of personal gratitude. For when Hitler invaded Czechoslovakia, my family sought and found refuge in England. Europe was our world and the war a battle for its survival. When we were not in the bomb shelter, we were glued to the radio. We wondered whether we would ever be able to return to our homes.

Through the darkness, we were sustained by the inspiring words of Roosevelt and Churchill, and by the courage of allied soldiers and résistance fighters. I was just a little girl, but in my heart, even then, I developed an abiding respect for those willing to fight for freedom, and I fell in love with Americans in uniform.

For the people of Belgium and Luxembourg and elsewhere in occupied Europe, this was a time of suffering, constant sorrow and quiet heroism. Between blitzkrieg and Normandy, five long years elapsed. Then, the struggle for Europe, and for mankind's soul, was finally and fully joined.

Fifty years ago, Hitler launched his last offensive. Striking where the lines were weakest, gambling on surprise, hoping poor weather would hamper the response, under the delusion that a victory would sever an unseverable

237

Western Alliance; the Nazis drove forward, at terrible cost, through the forests and fields of the Ardennes.

Here, the American Army faced, and met, its sternest test. Here, men marched and artillery roared through the fog, mud and night. U.S. Forces, undermanned, under-equipped, fought back, with help from the British and the brave people of the Ardennes.

For here, the world watched again as ordinary soldiers—not grand strategies or sophisticated weapons—determined the outcome of a war. Twenty-four German divisions assaulted. They were opposed fiercely by each and every one of the units whose colors are honored here today; opposed by the V Corps at Elsenborn Ridge, the 7th Armored Division at St. Vith, the "Damned Engineers" of the 291st at the Bridge over the Salm, and the 30th Infantry Division at Stoumont.

Despite bitter weather and relentless attack, the Americans would not yield. Finally, the 101st Airborne division and elements of the 9th and 10th Armored Divisions were encircled here at Bastogne.

This is when and where the tide of the battle turned. Asked to surrender, General Anthony McAuliffe said in one word what the world had been waiting to tell Hitler for Years, "NUTS." The German commander asker: "Should this be interpreted as a positive or a negative response?" The answer: "Negative, and it means go to hell."

With the clearing of the skies on December 23rd, came parachuted supplies to beleaguered Bastogne and air attacks on German armor. But the battle raged on until Patton's 4th Armored Division broke the encirclement. Then, the German attack stalled and retreat began. Although the war did not end here, the battle for Europe was truly won here. For the backbone of the Nazi military was broken and the allied victory became only a matter of time.

Later today, this historic event will be celebrated with parades and pageantry. But for the veterans of the Battle of the Ardennes, and for the Belgians who survived the war, spectacle will only reinforce private reflection, quiet pride, silent grief. None among us can recapture youth; noncan re-claim those who were taken from us too young. Seventy-six thousand Americans were killed, captured or imprisoned during the battles waged here; the number of civilians killed is not known.

If anniversaries are a time for recollection; they also are a time for re-dedication. You, the veterans of this conflict, may have felt you were fighting only for yourselves, for your buddies, for your unit, for your family. When the scourge of war is visited upon us, it is not countries that fought, it is people. The emotions of conflict are intensely personal.

But your skills, courage and sacrifice were enriched and ennobled by the cause for which you fought. Let us never forget why this war began, how this war was won or what this war was about. Let us not forget the lessons of this battle and this war.

Weakness in the face of aggression and evil invites more of both. The forces of freedom must remain strong and resolute. Victory depends not on the excisions of any single nation—however great—but on the will of proud-hearted peoples everywhere to ally themselves in defense of liberty.

History did not end here in these fabled woods; it did not end with the Nazi surrender or with the fall of the Berlin wall. Each generation is tested; each must choose; resistance or appeasement; tolerance or intolerance; the rule of law or no law at all.

The veterans of the Ardennes, and their compatriots from Iwo Jima to Inchon to the Persian Gulf, have bequeathed to us a legacy of principle backed by power. The guns here have long since fallen silent. German and Italy have become our allies. Now, even the elusive dream of an integrated and fully democratic Europe is within our grasp.

From those who fought here, living or dead, the torch of liberty has passed to our hands. Together, we must nurture and sustain it. Fascism must never again arise. Nationalism must receive its outlet in the celebration of culture and accomplishment, not aggression or persecution towards others. We know that freedom still has its enemies on this continent and elsewhere.

But as I look around here today, I know that it has vigorous and determined friends. And make no mistake, the Alliance between Europe and America that was forged here 50 years ago remains strong; like the friendship between the United States and Belgium, it will endure; it will flourish.

Let us, then, in the spirit of this occasion, affirm that although there is no glory inherent in war itself, there is dignity without measure in the memories we share here, the sacrifices we recall here, the prayers we offer here and the principles fought and died for here.

May our veterans be forever honored, for we can never fully thank them. May our honored dead rest in peace, for we will never forget them.

And we may ail prove worthy of freedom, which in their name and with God's help we now hold in sacred and solemn trust.

Thank you.[231]

APPENDIX B: COMMENDATIONS

As was written in the previous chapters, many 10th Armored Division soldiers received medals for different actions during the Battle of the Bulge. Members of two platoons from the 54th Armored Infantry Battalion were commended by the 101st Airborne Division for their actions with Team O'Hara:

> *Commendation*—The following named personnel of the Assault Gun Platoon, Headquarters Company, 54th Armored Infantry Battalion, are commended for meritorious service in action. From 18 December 1944 to 27 December 1944 in the vicinity of Marvie, Belgium, the platoon was set up in battery and was subjected constantly to heaby concentrations of enemy artillery and machine gun fire. When the enemy attacked with alrge forces of infantry and tanks, this platoon maintained its position with indomitable determination, fired over four hundred rounds of ammunition at enemy targets and completely repelled every enemy attempt to penetrate the position. Moving forward to high ground, the platoon functioned as light tanks and fired its guns into the enemy positions until delayed assistance arrived. The platoon then withdrew to its former position and continued to fire at the enemy with destructive effect. The actions of these men were in accordance with the highest standards of the military Service.[232]

First Lieutenant	Joseph K. Cook
Technical Sergeant	Joseph E. Van Pelt
Sergeant	George DeSimone
Sergeant	Norman H. Esch
Sergeant	John Najarian
Sergeant	Albert L. Belvitch

Commendation– The following named enlisted men of the Mortar Platoon, Headquarters Company, 54th Armored Infantry Battalion, are commended for meritorious service in action. When the enemy launched a very heavy attack on 18 December 1944 in the vicinity of Bastogne, Belgium, the platoon covered the withdrawal of other units despite very heavy enemy artillery fire. Assuming a new position exposed to continuous concentrations of enemy artillery and mortar fire, the platoon afforded unfailing support to infantry units in the area. Although its sector was subjected to three strong enemy attacks in two days, and enemy tank and machine gun fire continually harassed its position, the platoon remained on the front lines after all other units had withdrawn and coordinated its fire with friendly air support, driving the enemy from the area. While supporting infantry units and covering withdrawals, this platoon, subjected to enemy artillery, mortar, and automatic weapons fire, held its position and fired its missions with great affect. The indomitable spirit and technical proficiency of the platoon were in accordance with the highest standards of the military service.[233]

Staff Sergeant	Luther M. Duffield
Staff Sergeant	Benny Keylor
Staff Sergeant	Albert H. Hansen
Corporal	Edward J. Cranisky
Corporal	Louis J. Daniels
Corporal	Athony Giorgeri
Corporal	Irvin R. Kluth
Corporal	Thomas P. Quinn
Corporal	Clive A. Taylor
Technician Fifth Grade	Curtis W. Gibson
Technician Fifth Grade	Jesse J. Switek
Technician Fifth Grade	William W. Elgin
Technician Fifth Grade	Wilbur b. Hawkins
Private First Class	Orval D. Smithart
Private First Class	John Fletcher Jr.
Private First Class	Philip Kimmelblatt
Private First Class	Frank A. Lawrence
Private First Class	Joseph E. L. Gionet
Private First Class	Perry F. Bird

Private First Class	Frank Sokol
Private First Class	Murrell O. Godwin
Private First Class	Russell O. Olson
Private First Class	Lloyd W. Palmer

Combat Command B, 10th Armored Division, was also commended for their gallant stand at Bastogne and was awarded the Distinguished Unit Citation on 25 May 1945 in a parade and cemerony at the Olympic Ski Stadium in Garmisch Partenkirchen, Germany. The citation was given to the follwing units of CCB for their part in the epic defense of Bastogne, Belgium, during the Ardennes Breakthrough December, 1944: Headquarters and Headquarters Company, Combat Command "B"; 3rd Tank Battalion (less Company C); 20th Armored Infantry Battalion (less Company A); 54th Armored Infantry Battalion (less Companies A and C); 420th Armored Field Artillery Battalion; Troop D, 90th Cavalry Sqaudron (Mechanized); Company C, 609th Tank Destroyer Battalion (less 1st Platoon, with 2nd Platoon, Reconnaissance Company, attached); Battery B, 796th Antiaircraft Artillery Battalion; Company C, 55th Armored Engineer Battalion; Company C, 21st Tank Battalion; and Collecting Section, Company B, 80th Armored Medical Battalion.

The citation read as follows:

These units distinguished themselves in combat against powerful and aggressive enemy forces composed of elements of eight German divisions during the period from 18 to 27 December 1944 by extraordinary heroism and gallantry in defense of the key communications center of Bastogne, Belgium. Essential to a large-scale breakthrough into Belgium and northern Luxembourg, the enemy attempted to seize Bastogne by attacking constantly and savagely with the best of his armor and infantry. Without benefit of prepared defenses, facing almost overwhelming odds and with very limited and fast-dwindling supplies, these units maintained a high combat morale and an impenetrable defense despite extremely heavy bombing, intense artillery fire, and constant attacks from infantry and armor on all sides of their completely cut-off and encircled positions. This masterful and grimly determined defense denied the enemy even momentary success in an operation for which he paid dearly in men, materiel, and eventually morale. The outstanding courage, resourcefulness, and undaunted determination of this gallant force are in keeping with the highest traditions of the service.[234]

By order of the SECRETARY OF WAR:

/s/ G. C. Marshall

Chief of Staff

APPENDIX C: U.S. ARMY ORGANIZATION IN WORLD WAR II

STAFF

Division level or above/below division level:
G-1/S-1 Personnel
G-2/S-2 Intelligence
G-3/S-3 Operations
G-4/S-4 Supply
G-5 Civil Affairs

STRUCTURE

Army Group: between 250 and 600 thousand soldiers commanded by a four-star general: two or more armies.

Army: between 60 and 120 thousand soldiers commanded by a three-star lieutenant general: two or more corps.

Corps: between 30 and 60 thousand soldiers. Two or more divisions commanded by a senior level two-star major general.

Division: 14 thousand soldiers (about 12 thousand for airborne divisions) commanded by a two-star major general: three regiments.

Regiment: 3,500 soldiers commanded by a colonel: three battalions.

Battalion (squadron for cavalry): 900 soldiers commanded by a lieutenant colonel: four companies.

Company (troop for cavalry and battery for artillery): 190 soldiers commanded by a captain: four platoons.

Platoon: 40 soldiers commanded by a lieutenant: three squads

Squad: 12 soldiers commanded by a sergeant.

APPENDIX D: U.S. ARMY UNITS THAT WERE IN AND AROUND BASTOGNE, 16–26 DECEMBER

Total American strength defending Bastogne during the siege: 1,019 officers and 14,167 noncommissioned officers and enlisted men

101ST AIRBORNE DIVISON (ARRIVED 18 DECEMBER):

Commanding General: Maj. Gen. Maxwell D. Taylor (arrived in Bastogne 27 December)

Acting Division Commander: Brig. Gen. Anthony C. McAuliffe

Assistant Division Commander: Brig. Gen. Gerald J. Higgins

Staff Officers:

    G-1, and Acting Chief of Staff: Lt. Col. Ned D. Moore

    G-2: Lt. Col. Paul A. Danahy

    G-3: Lt. Col. H. W. O. Kinnard

    G-4 Lt. Col. Carl W. Kohls

    Surgeon (chief division medical officer): Lt. Col. David Gold

    Civil Affairs Officer: Capt. Robert S. Smith

Division Artillery Commander: Col. Thomas L. Sherburne Jr.

501st Parachute Infantry Regiment: Commanding Officer: Lt. Col. Julian J. Ewell

    1st Battalion (Companies A, B, C and Hq.): Commanding Officer: Major Raymond V. Bottomly Jr.

    2nd Battalion (Companies D, E, F and Hq.): Commanding Officer: Major Sammie N. Homan

    3rd Battalion (Companies G, H, I and Hq.): Commanding Officer: Lt. Col. George A. Griswold

502nd Parachute Infantry Regiment: Commanding Officer: Lt. Col. Steve A. Chappuis

1st Battalion (Companies A, B, C and Hq.): Commanding
Officer: Major John D. Hanlon

2nd Battalion (Companies D, E, F and Hq.): Commanding
Officer: Lt. Col. Thomas H. Sudiffe

3rd Battalion (Companies G, H, I and Hq.): Commanding
Officer: Lt. Col. John P. Stopka

506th Parachute Infantry Regiment: Commanding Officer: Col.
Robert F. Sink

1st Battalion (Companies A, B, C and Hq.): Commanding
Officer: Lt. Col. James L. LaPrade

2nd Battalion (Companies D, E, F and Hq.): Commanding
Officer: Lt. Col. Robert L. Strayer

3rd Battalion (Companies G, H, I and Hq.): Commanding
Officer: Major Gus M. Heilman

327th Glider Infantry Regiment: Commanding Officer: Col. Joseph
H. Harper

1st Battalion (Companies A, B, C and Hq.): Commanding
Officer: Lt. Col. Hartford F. Salee

2nd Battalion (Companies E, F, G and Hq.): Commanding
Officer: Lt. Col. Roy L. Inman

3rd Battalion (Companies A, B, C and Hq.): Commanding
Officer: Lt, Col. Ray C. Allen

321st Glider Field Artillery Battalion: Commanding Officer: Lt. Col.
Edward L. Carmichael

907th Glider Field Artillery Battalion: Commanding Officer: Lt. Col.
Clarence F. Nelson

377th Parachute Field Artillery Battalion: Commanding Officer: Lt.
Col. Harry W. Elkins

463rd Parachute Field Artillery Battalion: Commanding Officer: Lt.
Col. John T. Cooper Jr.

81st Airborne Antiaircraft Battalion: Commanding Officer: Lt. Col.
X. B. Cox Jr.

326th Airborne Engineer Battalion: Commanding Officer: Lt. Col.
Hugh A. Mozley

426th Airborne Quartermaster Company: Commanding Officer:
Capt. George W. Horn

101st Airborne Signal Company: Commanding Officer: Capt.
William J. Johnson

801st Airborne Ordnance Maintenance Company: Commanding
Officer: Capt. John L. Patterson
326th Airborne Medical Company: Commanding Officer: Major
William E. Barfield

ATTACHED UNITS:
Combat Command B, 10th Armored Division (arrived 18 December,
eight hours before 101st AirborneDivision)
7015th Tank Destroyer Battalion
755th Field Artillery Battalion
Company C, 9th Armored Engineer Battalion
969th Field Artillery Battalion (Colored)
Note: In the segregated army of World War II African American units
were designated "Colored." Typically, all or most officers were
white while all enlisted men were African American.
333rd Field Artillery Battalion (Colored)
37th Tank Battalion, Combat Command R, 4th Armored Division

COMPOSITION AND COMMAND OF MAJOR ATTACHED UNITS:
Combat Command B, 10th Armored Division: Commanding Officer:
Col. William L. Roberts: This unit operated autonomously in
conjunction with the 101st Airborne Division until 21
December, when it was placed under the command to the 101st
Airborne Division. Combat Command B was divided for tactical
purposes into four main parts: the units held directly under the
commander, and Teams Cherry, Desobry, and O'Hara. The
following elements of Combat Command B were directly under
the command of Colonel Roberts:
Headquarters and Headquarters Company
3rd Tank Battalion (less Company C)
Company C, 21st Tank Battalion
54th Armored Infantry Battalion (less Companies A and C)
20th Armored Infantry Battalion (less Company C)
Company C, 609th Tank Destroyer Battalion (less platoons with
teams)
Company C, 55th Armored Engineer Battalion (less platoons
with teams)
420th Armored Field Artillery Battalion: Commanding Officer:

Lt. Col. Barry D. Browne

Battery B, 796th Antiaircraft Artillery Battalion

Troop D, 90th Cavalry Reconnaissance Squadron (less platoons
with teams)

Team Cherry: Commanding Officer: Lt. Col. Henry T. Cherry
(also commanding officer of 3rd Tank Battalion)

> 3rd Tank Battalion (less Company B and 2nd Platoon,
> Company D)
>
> Company A: Lt. Edward P. Hyduke
>
> Company C, 20th Armored Infantry Battalion: Capt.
> Willis F. Ryerson; Lt. Earl B. Gilligan
>
> 3rd Platoon, Company C, 55th Armored Engineer
> Battalion
>
> One Platoon, Company C, 609th Tank Destroyer
> Battalion
>
> 2nd Platoon, Troop D, 90th Cavalry Reconnaissance
> Squadron

Team Desobry: Commanding Officer: Major William R.
Desobry (also commanding officer, 20th Armored Infantry
Battalion). Major Charles L. Hustead assumed command
after Major Desobry was wounded.

> 20th Armored Infantry Battalion (less Companies A
> and C)
>
> Headquarters Company: Capt. Gordon Geiger; Lt.
> Eugene Todd
>
> Company B: Capt. Omar M. Billett
>
> Company B, 3rd Tank Battalion
>
> One Platoon, Company C, 609th Tank Destroyer
> Battalion
>
> One Platoon (Light Tanks), Company D, 3rd Tank
> Battalion
>
> One Platoon, Company C, 55th Armored Engineer
> Battalion
>
> One Platoon, Company C, 609th Tank Destroyer
> Battalion
>
> One Platoon, Troop D, 90th Cavalry Reconnaissance
> Squadron

Team O'Hara: Commanding Officer: Lt. Col. James

> O'Hara (also commanding officer of 54th Armored Infantry Battalion)
> 54th Armored Infantry Battalion (less Companies A and C)
> Company B: Lt. John D. Devereaux
> Company C, 21st Tank Battalion
> One Platoon, Company C, 55th Armored Engineer Battalion
> One Platoon, Company D (Light Tanks), 3rd Tank Battalion Lt. Sherwood D. Wishart
> One Platoon, Troop D, 90th Cavalry Reconnaissance Squadron
> Force Charlie 16: Lt. Richard C. Gilliland

705th Tank Destroyer Battalion: Commanding Officer: Lt. Col. Clifford D. Templeton. This unit operated independently in conjunction with the 101st Airborne Division until 21 December when it was attached to the 101st and came under its command.

Ninth Air Force (members of liaison group attached to 101st Airborne Division during Bastogne operation: Capt. James E. Parker; Lt. Gorden O. Rothwell; Sgt. Frank B. Hotard)

Team SNAFU: This was a composite unit assembled from remnants of other units, mainly from the 28th Division and the 9th Armored Division's CCR, that had been heavily engaged on 16 December in the opening attacks of the German offensive. Initially designated as a reserve they were effective in plugging gaps on the Bastogne perimeter.

APPENDIX E: 10TH ARMORED DIVISION

The mixture of insignia and distinctive colors of several arms incorporated in the Armored Force symbolize integrity and esprit. It is an interlocked ornament, found in Nordic monuments, composed of three torques: red for artillery; blue for infantry; and yellow for cavalry. The symbols represent the characteristics of armored divisions: the tank track, mobility and armor protection; the cannon, fire power; and the red bolt of lightning, shock action.

COMMAND AND STAFF

COMMANDING GENERAL
22 Sep 44   Maj. Gen. William H. H. Morris, Jr.

ARTILLERY COMMANDER
22 Sep 44   Col. Bernard F. Luebbermann
13 Apr 45   Col. Edward H. Metzger

CHIEF OF STAFF
22 Sep 44   Col. Basil G. Thayer
25 Feb 45   Lt. Col. Joseph A. McChristian
8 May 45   Col. Richard Steinbach

ASSISTANT CHIEF OF STAFF G-1
22 Sep 44   Lt. Col. John F. Laudig

ASSISTANT CHIEF OF STAFF G-2
22 Sep 44   Lt. Col. William E. Eckles

ASSISTANT CHIEF OF STAFF G-3
22 Sep 44   Maj. John W. Sheffield
3 Dec 44   Lt. Col. Joseph A. McChristian

25 Feb 45   Lt. Col. John W. Sheffield
8 May 45   Lt. Col. Joseph A. McChristian

ASSISTANT CHIEF OF STAFF G-4
22 Sep 44   Lt. Col. Clark Webber

ASSISTANT CHIEF OF STAFF G-5
3 Oct 44   Maj. John M. Gregory
10 Jan 45   Capt. Leigh S. Plummer

ADJUTANT GENERAL
22 Sep 44   Lt. Col. Francis J. Malloh

COMMANDING OFFICER, COMBAT COMMAND A
22 Sep 44   Brig. Gen. Kenneth G. Althaus
15 Dec 44   Brig. Gen. Edwin W. Piburn
25 Apr 45   Col. Thomas M. Brinkley
3 May 45   Col. Basil G. Thayer

COMMANDING OFFICER, COMBAT COMMAND B
22 Sep 44   Col. William L. Roberts
5 Nov 44   Brig. Gen. Edwin W. Piburn
16 Dec 45   Col. William L. Roberts
18 Mar 45   Col. Basil G. Thayer
3 May 45   Col. Thomas M. Brinkley

COMMANDING OFFICER, RESERVE COMMAND
22 Sep 44   Col. Julian E. Raymond
6 Nov 44   Col. Wade C. Gatchell

STATISTICS

CHRONOLOGY
Activated   15 July 1942
Arrived ETO   23 September 1944
Arrived Continent
(D+109)   23 September 1944
Entered Combat   1944
Days in Combat   124

CAMPAIGNS
Ardennes
Rhineland
Central Europe

INDIVIDUAL AWARDS

Distinguished Service Cross	19
Legion of Merit	12
Silver Star	217
Soldiers Medal	23
Bronze Star	1,400
Air Medal	13
Distinguished Flying Cross	2

PRISONERS OF WAR TAKEN   43,208

COMPOSITION

Headquarters Company
Combat Command A
Combat Command B
Reserve Command
3rd Tank Battalion
11th Tank Battalion
21st Tank Battalion
20th Armored Infantry Battalion
54th Armored Infantry Battalion
61st Armored Infantry Battalion
90th Cavalry Reconnaissance Squadron (Mechanized)
55th Armored Engineer Battalion
150th Armored Signal Company
10th Armored Division Artillery
419th Armored Field Artillery Battalion
420th Armored Field Artillery Battalion
423rd Armored Field Artillery Battalion
10th Armored Division Trains
132nd Ordnance Maintenance Battalion
80th Armored Medical Battalion
Military Police Platoon
Band

ENDNOTES

CHAPTER 1
1. Interview with author September 27, 2012
2. Interview with author, November 6, 2012
3. Army, United States, *Terrify and Destroy: The Story of the 10th Armored Division* (Germany: Desfossés-néogravure,1945)
4. Interview with author January 17, 2012
5. *The Night Before Christmas,* John "Jack" Prior.
6. Interview with the author. Numerous dates.
7. Krasnoborski, Thad J., *The 420th at War* (unpublished booklet, 2004) 79–80. T.J. Krasnoborski provided the booklet to co-author Collins and it was compiled from different members of the 420th Field Artillery Battalion.
8. Interview with author.
9. National Archives, College Park, MD, 101st Airborne Division, General Order 1.
10. National Archives, College Park, MD, 101st Airborne Division, General Order 1.
11. Tiger Tales
12. Tiger Tales Spring 1985.
13. National Archives, College Park, MD, 101st Airborne Division, General Order 3.
14. Interview with author.
15. National Archives, College Park, MD, 10th Armored Division, General Order
16. Interview with author, November 25, 2012
17. Burge, Phil Unpublished memoir.

CHAPTER 2
18. Compiled by Krasnoborski, Thad J. *The 420th at War* (unpublished booklet, 2004) 73–4.
19. Unpublished letter to the author.
20. Unpublished interview, Carlisle Barracks.
21. Collins, Michael and King, Martin, *Voices of the Bulge* (Minnesota: Zenith Press, 2011)
22. Interview with author February 9, 2008.
23. Interview with author, February 14, 2009
24. Interview with author, September 26, 2009.
25. National Archives, College Park, MD, After Action Reports, 3rd Tank Battalion.

CHAPTER 3

26. National Archives, College Park, MD, After Action Reports, 420th Armored Field Artillery Battalion.
27. Interview with author, August 11, 2012
28. Unpublished history of the 796th Armored Anti-Aircraft Artillery Battalion
29. Unpublished interview, Carlisle Barracks
30. Nichols, Donald Unpublished memoir
31. Interview with author, April 21, 2012
32. Interview with author September 27, 2012
33. Interview with author April 30, 2010
34. Davis, Stanley Unpublished memoir
35. Compiled by Krasnoborski, Thad J. *The 420th at War* (unpublished booklet, 2004) 74.
36. Interview with author February 16, 2012
37. National Archives, College Park, MD, After Action Reports, 3rd Tank Battalion.
38. National Archives, College Park, MD, After Action Reports, 54th Armored Infantry Battalion.
39. Letter sent to author, July 9, 2012

CHAPTER 4

40. National Archives, College Park, MD, After Action Reports, 420th Armored Field Artillery Battalion.
41. After Action Report, 796th Armored Anti-Aircraft Artillery Battalion
42. Compiled by Krasnoborski, Thad J. *The 420th at War* (unpublished booklet, 2004) 74–5.
43. Interview with author January 17, 2012
44. Interview with author April 30, 2010
45. Nichols, Donald, Unpublished memoir
46. Interview with author September 27, 2012
47. Interview with author, November 6, 2012
48. Interview with author, August 11, 2012
49. Interview with author, April 21, 2012
50. Interview with author September 26, 2009
51. Burge, Philip, Unpublished memoirs
52. Davis, Stanley Unpublished memoir
53. Interview with author, February 14, 2009
54. Interview with author February 16, 2012
55. Unpublished interview, Carlisle Barracks
56. Kinser, Robert Unpublished letters and diary entries
57. National Archives, College Park, MD, History, Team O'Hara.
58. Collins, Michael and King, Martin, *Voices of the Bulge* (Minnesota: Zenith Press, 2011)
59. National Archives, College Park, MD, After Action Report, 90th Cavalry Reconnaissance Squadron (Mechz), Co. D.

60. National Archives, College Park, MD, 101st Airborne Division, General Order 3
61. National Archives, College Park, MD, After Action Reports, 3rd Tank Battalion.

CHAPTER 5
62. Interview with author September 27, 2012
63. National Archives, College Park, MD, 101st Airborne Division, General Order 1
64. National Archives, College Park, MD, 101st Airborne Division, General Order 20
65. National Archives, College Park, MD 10th Armored Division General Order 30
66. Interview with author, November 6, 2012
67. Interview with author, August 11, 2012
68. National Archives, College Park, MD, 101st Airborne Division, General Order 3.
69. National Archives, College Park, MD, 101st Airborne Division General Order 4.
70. Interview with author January 17, 2012
71. Burge, Philip, Unpublished memoirs
72. Interview with author April 30, 2010
73. National Archives, College Park, MD, After Action Reports, 420th Armored Field Artillery Battalion.
74. Interview with author, April 21, 2012
75. After Action Report, 796th Armored Anti-Aircraft Artillery Battalion
76. National Archives, College Park, MD, After Action Report, 90th Cavalry Reconnaissance Squadron Co. D.
77. National Archives, College Park, MD, 10th Armored Division General Order 50
78. Marshall, SLA. *Bastogne: The First Eight Days*
79. National Archives, College Park, MD, 101st Airborne Division General Order 5
80. Davis, Stanley Unpublished memoir
81. Compiled by Krasnoborski, Thad J. *The 420th at War* (unpublished booklet, 2004)
82. Nichols, Donald Unpublished memoir
83. Compiled by Krasnoborski, Thad J. *The 420th at War* (unpublished booklet, 2004) 75–6.
84. Interview with author, February 14, 2009
85. Unpublished interview, Carlisle Barracks
86. Stone, William, Unpublished memoir
87. National Archives, College Park, MD, 101st Airborne Division General Order 1
88. Kinser, Robert Unpublished letters and diary entries
89. Interview with author February 16, 2012
90. Unpublished interview, Carlisle Barracks
91. Letter to the author.
92. National Archives, College Park, MD After Action Reports, Team O'Hara
93. National Archives, College Park, MD, After Action Report, 54th Armored Infantry Battalion.
94. National Archives, College Park, MD, After Action Reports, 3rd Tank Battalion.
95. National Archives, College Park, MD, After Action Reports, 3rd Tank Battalion.

CHAPTER 6

96. Armor at Bastogne. Armored School, May, 1949, 39–40.
97. Interview with author September 27, 2012
98. Interview with author, February 14, 2009
99. National Archives, College Park, MD, After Action Reports, 420th Armored Field Artillery Battalion.
100. Interview with author, August 11, 2012
101. Armor at Bastogne. Armored School, May, 1949, 40–41.
102. National Archives, College Park, MD, 101st Airborne Division, General Order 5
103. Interview with author, November 6, 2012
104. National Archives, College Park, MD, 10th Armored Division General Orders
105. Unpublished history of the 796th Armored Anti-Aircraft Artillery Battalion
106. Stone, William, Unpublished memoir
107. National Archives, College Park, MD, 10th Armored Division General Order 206
108. National Archives, College Park, MD, 101st Airborne Division General Order 20
109. Interview with author, April 21, 2012
110. Compiled by Krasnoborski, Thad J. *The 420th at War* (unpublished booklet, 2004) 76–7.
111. National Archives, College Park, MD, After Action Report, 90th Cavalry Reconnaissance Squadron Co. D.
112. Compiled by Krasnoborski, Thad J. *The 420th at War* (unpublished booklet, 2004) 76–7.
113. National Archives, College Park, MD, History, Team O'Hara
114. Davis, Stanley Unpublished memoir
115. National Archives, College Park, MD After Action Reports, Team O'Hara
116. National Archives, College Park, MD, After Action Reports, 3rd Tank Battalion.

CHAPTER 7

117. National Archives, College Park, MD, After Action Report, 90th Cavalry Reconnaissance Squadron Co. D.
118. Interview with author, November 15, 2012
119. National Archives, College Park, MD, After Action Reports, 420th Armored Field Artillery Battalion.
120. *Tiger Tales*
121. Compiled by Krasnoborski, Thad J. *The 420th at War* (unpublished booklet, 2004)
122. Interview with author February 16, 2012
123. Interview with author, November 6, 2012
124. Unpublished history of the 796th Armored Anti-Aircraft Artillery Battalion
125. Interview with author, August 11, 2012
126. National Archives, College Park, MD, After Action Reports, 54th Armored Infantry Battalion.
127. National Archives, College Park, MD, After Action Reports, 3rd Tank Battalion.

CHAPTER 8

128. National Archives, College Park, MD, After Action Reports, 420th Armored Field Artillery Battalion.
129. Unpublished history of the 796th Armored Anti-Aircraft Artillery Battalion
130. National Archives, College Park, MD, After Action Report, 90th Cavalry Reconnaissance Squadron Co. D.
131. Henry Kinnard interview, *Tigers on the Loose.*
132. Interview with author, November 6, 2012
133. *Tiger Tales*
134. National Archives, College Park, MD, After Action Reports, 54th Armored Infantry Battalion.
135. National Archives, College Park, MD, After Action Reports, 3rd Tank Battalion.

CHAPTER 9

136. National Archives, College Park, MD, After Action Reports, 420th Armored Field Artillery Battalion.
137. After Action Report, 796th Armored Anti-Aircraft Artillery Battalion
138. Interview with author, April 21, 2012
139. Interview with author September 27, 2012
140. Interview with author January 17, 2012
141. Interview with author, November 6, 2012
142. Loiacono, Elturnio "Lucky" Unpublished Memoir
143. National Archives, College Park, MD, 101st Airborne Division, General Order 37.
144. Interview with author, February 14, 2009
145. Interview with author February 16, 2012
146. Davis, Stanley Unpublished memoir
147. National Archives, College Park, MD, 101st Airborne Division, General Order 48
148. Nichols, Donald Unpublished memoir
149. National Archives, College Park, MD, History, Team O'Hara
150. National Archives, College Park, MD, 101st Airborne Division, General Order 108.
151. National Archives, College Park, MD, After Action Report, 90th Cavalry Reconnaissance Squadron Co. D.
152. National Archives, College Park, MD, History, Team O'Hara
153. Interview with author April 30, 2010
154. Compiled by Krasnoborski, Thad J. *The 420th at War* (unpublished booklet, 2004)
155. Kinser, Robert Unpublished letters and diary entries
156. Nichols, Donald Unpublished memoir
157. National Archives, College Park, MD, After Action Reports, 54th Armored Infantry Battalion.
158. National Archives, College Park, MD, After Action Reports, 3rd Tank Battalion.

CHAPTER 10

159. Interview with author, February 14, 2009

160. National Archives, College Park, MD, After Action Reports, 420th Armored Field Artillery Battalion.
161. National Archives, College Park, MD, 10th Armored Division General Order 41
162. Interview with author April 30, 2010
163. Interview with author November 26, 2012
164. National Archives, College Park, MD, 101st Airborne Division General Order 6
165. After Action Report, 796th Armored Anti-Aircraft Artillery Battalion
166. National Archives, College Park, MD 10th Armored Division General Order 13
167. Loiacono, Elturnio "Lucky" Unpublished Memoir
168. National Archives, College Park, MD, 10th Armored Division General Order 175
169. National Archives, College Park, MD, After Action Report, 90th Cavalry Reconnaissance Squadron Co. D.
170. National Archives, College Park, MD, 101st Airborne Division, General Order 3
171. Interview with author August 24, 2008
172. Davis, Stanley Unpublished memoir
173. Kinser, Robert Unpublished letters and diary entries
174. Nichols, Donald Unpublished memoir
175. National Archives, College Park, MD, 10th Armored Division General Order 112
176. Interview with author September 27, 2012
177. Waters, George, Unpublished Letter
178. Interview with author, April 21, 2012
179. National Archives, College Park, MD, After Action Reports, 54th Armored Infantry Battalion.
180. National Archives, College Park, MD, After Action Reports, 3rd Tank Battalion.

CHAPTER 11
181. National Archives, College Park, MD, After Action Reports, 420th Armored Field Artillery Battalion.
182. After Action Report, 796th Armored Anti-Aircraft Artillery Battalion
183. Interview with author September 27, 2012
184. Compiled by Krasnoborski, Thad J. *The 420th at War* (unpublished booklet, 2004)
185. Interview with author, November 6, 2012
186. National Archives, College Park, MD, After Action Report, 90th Cavalry Reconnaissance Squadron Co. D.
187. Interview with author January 17, 2012
188. Interview with author, February 14, 2009
189. National Archives, College Park, MD, 10th Armored Division General Order 16
190. Interview with author February 16, 2012
191. National Archives, College Park, MD, After Action Reports, 54th Armored Infantry Battalion.
192. National Archives, College Park, MD, After Action Reports, 3rd Tank Battalion.

CHAPTER 12
193. National Archives, College Park, MD, After Action Reports, 420th Armored Field Artillery Battalion.
194. After Action Report, 796th Armored Anti-Aircraft Artillery Battalion
195. Compiled by Krasnoborski, Thad J. *The 420th at War* (unpublished booklet, 2004)
196. National Archives, College Park, MD, After Action Report, 90th Cavalry Reconnaissance Squadron Co. D.
197. Interview with author September 27, 2012
198. http://users.skynet.be/jeeper/page135.html
199. Loiacono, Elturnio "Lucky" Unpublished Memoir
200. Interview with author, April 21, 2012
201. Collins, Michael and King, Martin, *Voices of the Bulge* (Minnesota: Zenith Press, 2011)
202. Interview with author February 16, 2012
203. National Archives, College Park, MD, After Action Reports, 54th Armored Infantry Battalion.

CHAPTER 13
204. National Archives, College Park, MD, After Action Reports, 420th Armored Field Artillery Battalion.
205. After Action Report, 796th Armored Anti-Aircraft Artillery Battalion
206. Kinser, Robert Unpublished letters and diary entries
207. National Archives, College Park, MD, After Action Report, 90th Cavalry Reconnaissance Squadron Co. D.
208. O'Neill, Msgr. James H., Review of the News, October 6, 1971

CHAPTER 14
209. National Archives, College Park, MD, After Action Report, 90th Cavalry Reconnaissance Squadron Co. D.
210. National Archives, College Park, MD, After Action Reports, 420th Armored Field Artillery Battalion.
211. After Action Report, 796th Armored Anti-Aircraft Artillery Battalion
212. National Archives, College Park, MD, After Action Reports, 420th Armored Field Artillery Battalion.
213. National Archives, College Park, MD, After Action Reports, 420th Armored Field Artillery Battalion.
214. Interview with author, April 21, 2012
215. Interview with author January 17, 2012
216. National Archives, College Park, MD, After Action Reports, 420th Armored Field Artillery Battalion.
217. Interview with author, November 25, 2012

CHAPTER 15
218. National Archives, College Park, MD After Action Reports, Team O'Hara

219. Davis, Stanley Unpublished memoir
220. Interview with author February 16, 2012
221. National Archives, College Park, MD 10th Armored Division General Order 109
222. Witness Statement in regards to Wishart's death IDPF
223. Witness Statement in regards to Wishart's death IDPF
224. Interview with author February 16, 2012
225. National Archives, College Park, MD S-1 Journal 20th Inf. January 14, 1945.
226. Letter to Captain Ryerson's widow, July 28, 1945.
227. National Archives, College Park, MD 10th Armored Division General Order 38
228. National Archives, College Park, MD 10th Armored Division General Order 35
229. Unpublished V-Mail Carlisle Barracks
230. Interview with author, April 30, 2010

APPENDIX A
231. http://belgium-usa-2-brothers.skynetblogs.be/archive/2011/11/27/ambassador-madeleine-albright-statement-50th-anniversary-ba.html

APPENDIX B
232. National Archives, College Park, MD, 101st Airborne Division, General Order 37.
233. National Archives, College Park, MD, 101st Airborne Division, General Order 37.
234. National Archives, College Park, MD, History 10th Armored Division.

INDEX